Advance Praise

This powerful study shows how the debates and struggles involved in banning alcohol in India blended imperial ideas of the civilising mission, nationalist efforts to modernise Indian morality and the ongoing efforts of the Indian state to balance the tax benefits of the alcohol market against the ethical aspirations of its leaders. This book makes a distinctive contribution to the comparative social history of cultural hegemony and its capillary somatics.

Arjun Appadurai, New York University

Can sobriety co-exist with democracy? *Sober State* builds a new history of state-building and politics in India, by following the emergence of alcohol prohibition both as policy and an ideal over the twentieth century. Drawing from rich archives ranging from statistics to songs, *Sober State* is generative in rethinking relationships between state and society, the colonial and the postcolonial, elites and subalterns, the province and the nation, authoritarianism and democracy.

Rohit De, Yale University

In this beautifully written and deeply textured book, Darinee Alagirisamy unravels the complex forces that predicate the compelling and at times flagrantly contradictory history of prohibition in southern India. Prohibition as an upright political cause was attached to emerging nationalist ideologies, while also reflecting prejudices and moral values that were not just anti-Western but also upper caste, paternalist, and proto-feminist all at once. While the colonial state sought to balance its interest in revenue with its continuing desire to assert moral supremacy, contests over prohibition led to conflicting policy outcomes and longstanding political ambivalence. After independence, as prohibition was written into the Indian constitution, even this level of legal codification could not resolve the multiple narratives that made any single or lasting policy response to this critical moral crusade impossible.

Nicholas B. Dirks, University of California, Berkeley

A pioneering, archivally rich, and theoretically deft account of the discourse of prohibition in colonial India. The author brings together a cast of players including social reformers arguing for temperance and purity, colonial authorities intent on an inelastic source of revenue and, of course, the Mahatma himself combining moral self-righteousness and naivety about drinking cultures. Alagirisamy has an eye for historical detail as much as quirky anecdote; a riveting read.

Dilip M. Menon, University of Witwatersrand

Sober State

What happens when a democratic state, still in the process of formation, commits to banning a substance, especially one as controversial as alcohol? This book traces the origins and evolution of alcohol prohibition in India, drawing on extensive archival research and rich vernacular sources to explain its surprising resilience over time. Since its inception, prohibition has served both as an ideal and a tool of state power, a dual role that has worked to shape its shifting trajectories. Each phase of enforcement has served to reaffirm prohibition's founding logic, thereby further embedding it in the machinery of governance, even as it has constrained its future implementation. Foregrounding intersections with caste and gender, the book illuminates how diverse social responses have made prohibition a deeply contested – *sobering* – yet enduring project. While prohibition may be a thing of the past in the West, history helps to keep it alive in India.

Darinee Alagirisamy is a historian and Senior Lecturer in the South Asian Studies Programme at the National University of Singapore, where she is also Deputy Head of Department. She specialises in the history of social movements and the state in colonial and postcolonial India, with the history of the Indian diaspora in Southeast Asia being a secondary area of interest. She has been a Gates Cambridge scholar and held the Holland Rose Studentship. Her research has been published in *Modern Asian Studies* and *The Indian Economic and Social History Review*.

METAMORPHOSES OF THE POLITICAL: MULTIDISCIPLINARY APPROACHES

The Series is a publishing collaboration of Cambridge University Press with The M. S. Merian–R. Tagore International Centre of Advanced Studies 'Metamorphoses of the Political' (ICAS:MP). It publishes new books that both expand and de-centre current perspectives on politics and the 'political' in the contemporary world. It examines, from a wide array of disciplinary and methodological approaches, how the 'political' has been conceptualized, articulated and transformed in specific arenas of contestation during the 'long twentieth century'. Though primarily located in India and the Global South, the Series seeks to interrogate and contribute to wider debates about global processes and politics. It is in this sense that the Series is imagined as one that is regionally focused but globally engaged, providing a context for interrogations of universalized theories of self, society and politics.

Series Editors:
- Prathama Banerjee, *Centre for the Study of Developing Societies, Delhi*
- Antje Linkenbach, *University of Erfurt, Germany*
- Samita Sen, *University of Cambridge, Cambridge*
- Indra Sengupta, *German Historical Institute London, London*
- Sanjay Srivastava, *SOAS, University of London, London*

Coordinating Editor:
- Debjani Mazumder, *M. S. Merian–R. Tagore International Centre of Advanced Studies 'Metamorphoses of the Political', Delhi*

Advisory Board:
- Martin Fuchs, *University of Erfurt, Germany*
- Jörg Gengnagel, *University of Würzburg, Germany*
- Christina von Hodenberg, *German Historical Institute London, London*
- Shail Mayaram, formerly at *Centre for the Study of Developing Societies, Delhi*
- Awadhendra Sharan, *Centre for the Study of Developing Societies, Delhi*
- Ravi Vasudevan, formerly at *Centre for the Study of Developing Societies, Delhi*

ICAS:MP is an Indo-German research collaboration of six Indian and German institutions funded by the German Federal Ministry of Education and Research (BMBF). It combines the benefits of an open, interdisciplinary forum for intellectual exchange with the advantages of a cutting-edge research centre. Located in New Delhi, ICAS:MP critically intervenes in global debates in the social sciences and humanities.

The research on which this work is based was funded by the German Federal Ministry of Education and Research (BMBF) through the M. S. Merian–R. Tagore International Centre of Advanced Studies and its initiative 'Metamorphoses of the Political: Comparative Perspectives on the Long Twentieth Century' (ICAS:MP).

Books in the Series:
- *Shifting Landscapes: Education and Urban Transformations in India*
  Edited by Geetha B. Nambissan, Nandini Manjrekar, Shivali Tukdeo, and Indra Sengupta
- *Elusive Democracy: Dalit Politics, Elections, and the Dilemmas of Representation*
  Michael A. Collins
- *Women and Colonial Law: A Feminist Social History, 2nd Edition*
  Janaki Nair
- *Through the India–China Border: Kalimpong in the Himalayas*
  Prem Poddar and Lisa Lindkvist Zhang
- *Claiming the People's Past: Populist Politics of History in the Twenty-First Century*
  Edited by Berber Bevernage, Eline Mestdagh, Walderez Ramalho, and Marie Gabrielle Verbergt
- *Evacuee Cinema: Bombay and Lahore in Partition Transit, 1940–1960*
  Salma Siddique
- *Women, Gender and Religious Nationalism*
  Edited by Amrita Basu and Tanika Sarkar
- *Streets in Motion: The Making of Infrastructure, Property, and Political Culture in Twentieth-century Calcutta*
  Ritajyoti Bandyopadhyay
- *Rule of the Commoner: DMK and Formations of the Political in Tamil Nadu, 1949–1967*
  Rajan Kurai Krishnan, Ravindran Sriramachandran, and V. M. S. Subagunarajan
- *Saffron Republic: Hindu Nationalism and State Power in India*
  Edited by Thomas Blom Hansen and Srirupa Roy
- *Properties of Rent: Community, Capital and Politics in Globalising Delhi*
  Sushmita Pati
- *The Secret Life of AnOther Indian Nationalism: Transitions from the Pax Britannica to the Pax Americana*
  Shail Mayaram
- *Debt, Trust and Reputation: Extra-legal Finance in Northern India*
  Sebastian Schwecke

Sober State

Origins of Alcohol Prohibition in India

Darinee Alagirisamy

Shaftesbury Road, Cambridge CB2 8EA, United Kingdom

One Liberty Plaza, 20th Floor, New York, NY 10006, USA

477 Williamstown Road, Port Melbourne, VIC 3207, Australia

314–321, 3rd Floor, Plot 3, Splendor Forum, Jasola District Centre, New Delhi – 110025, India

103 Penang Road, #05–06/07, Visioncrest Commercial, Singapore 238467

Cambridge University Press is part of Cambridge University Press & Assessment,
a department of the University of Cambridge.

We share the University's mission to contribute to society through the pursuit of
education, learning and research at the highest international levels of excellence.

www.cambridge.org
Information on this title: www.cambridge.org/9781009683166

First published 2026

A catalogue record for this publication is available from the British Library

A Cataloging-in-Publication data record for this book is available from the Library of Congress

ISBN 978-1-009-68316-6 Hardback
ISBN 978-1-009-68315-9 Paperback

*To my mother, Jayanthi Balakrishan,
and to my partner, Prashant Pandey*

With deepest gratitude

Contents

Figures

Acknowledgements

This book is the outcome of numerous conversations over the years and there are many who have journeyed with me through it all. I would like to begin by recording my deepest gratitude to the late David Washbrook, whose wit and humour I drew much from as I researched a topic that redefined my horizons as a scholar. David brought a certain mirth to his engagement with my work that was matched only perhaps by the depth of his erudition. I am also immensely grateful to the late Christopher Bayly. Besides his towering intellect, I remember his warmth and generosity especially fondly from my time at the University of Cambridge. The questions Chris raised during our last meeting germinated into important lines of inquiry years later. I should like to think that David and Chris would have been happy to see this book in print.

I owe a debt of gratitude to colleagues and scholars whose support for *Sober State* has enabled it to become what it is today. Dilip Menon and Faisal Devji were among the first beyond my immediate community whose enthusiasm for the project convinced me of the value of pursuing it. I would especially like to thank Dilip for his incisive feedback during a recent book workshop, which helped immensely in revising the manuscript for publication. I owe much to the brilliant Aditya Balasubramanian for his meticulous reading of various chapters over the years. Sunil Amrith's kind support and encouragement for this and other research projects is testimony to his generosity as a scholar. I have also drawn much from Loh Kah Seng and Edgar Liao, friends and colleagues who have enthusiastically engaged me in discussions on various aspects of the book. I am grateful to A. R. Venkatachalapathy for his suggestion that I look at the archives of Roja Muthiah Library, Chennai, which availed rare source materials. I would also like to thank Arnab Chakraborty and Aditya Ramesh, fellow scholars I met at the Tamil Nadu State Archives, Chennai, who quickly became friends, for their helpful tips on navigating the archival collections. Samita Sen, Susan Bayly, Rosalind (Polly) O'Hanlon, David Arnold, Anand Yang, Sumathi Ramaswamy, Rupa Viswanath, Crispin Bates and S. Anandhi have all supported *Sober State* in different ways through the many iterations it has taken over the years.

I would like to thank the Bill and Melinda Gates Foundation for the Gates Cambridge Scholarship, which made it possible for me to commence my graduate studies at the University of Cambridge. I am grateful to Joya Chatterjee, who always made the time to engage with young scholars on their research. Shailaja Fennell's suggestions on the resources available for the study of prohibition's political economy led to many surprising discoveries. Tim Harper pointed me in the direction of archival material that redefined the direction of my research. As thesis committee members, Polly and Sujit Sivasundaram offered several helpful suggestions that helped me pin down the idea for this book. My thanks also to Barbara Roe and Kevin Greenbank from the Centre of South Asian Studies, University of Cambridge, for their patience and readiness to locate reference materials from the library's vast collections. Friends at the university have been a great source of support and inspiration during my years there and well beyond. I am grateful to Shakthi Manickavasagam, Devyani Gupta, Saumya Saxena and Liberty Bunce for their cherished company.

The multi-archival research for this book was conducted in archives and libraries in London, Chennai and New Delhi. I would like to thank the librarians at the British Library, London, especially for their help with accessing the extensive collections of the India Office Records. My thanks also to the deputy commissioner of the Tamil Nadu State Archives and the chief librarians, whose support greatly expedited my research there. I am also grateful to the chief librarian of Chennai's Connemara Public Library, Varadarajan, who pointed me in the direction of relevant sources. My sincere appreciation also to the staff of Periyar Thidal Library, Chennai, for referring me to specific *Kudi Arasu* editions, which proved valuable. I am grateful to the staff of the Nehru Memorial Museum and Library, New Delhi, and the National Archives of India, New Delhi, for their help with last-minute research requests.

From the University of Hong Kong, I would like to thank David Pomfret for providing me with an opportunity to experience first-hand the rigours of university teaching. Thank you also to Frank Dikötter, whose encouragement and feedback spurred me to keep writing during a very busy time in my life. Robert Peckham invited me to attend several workshops on the history of medicine, which helped shape the critical lens through which I subsequently reflected on much of my research findings. I would like to thank Alastair McClure and

Devika Shankar for the warmth of their friendship as fellow South Asianists in Hong Kong.

From the National University of Singapore (NUS), I would like to thank colleagues and friends from the Faculty of Arts and Social Sciences. Thank you to the Faculty of Arts and Social Sciences' Research Division for the FASS Book Strategising Grant, which was of great help to me during the revision process. My deepest gratitude particularly to Gyanesh Kudaisya, Medha Kudaisya and Malcolm Murfett, mentors and former teachers. Though not at NUS anymore, Malcolm has supported my research plans and projects for many years now. I have had the greatest pleasure of working with Gyanesh and Medha as colleagues for the past five years. Words cannot adequately convey my gratitude to Gyanesh, who has long been a great source of inspiration.

My thanks also to the head of department from the South Asian Studies Programme at NUS, Rajesh Rai, and department colleagues Ronojoy Sen, Sneha Annavarapu, Rajshree Jetly, Bhoomika Joshi, Vani Murali, and Vithya Subramaniam. I would like to express my heartfelt gratitude to also Faizah Zakaria, who holds a joint appointment with the departments of Southeast Asian Studies and Malay Studies. Faizah's feedback on manuscript drafts helped greatly in the final rounds of revision. From the Department of History, I would like to thank Timothy Barnard and Jack Chia for the many wonderful conversations over the years.

From Cambridge University Press, I would like to thank Qudsiya Ahmed, Anwesha Rana, Saniya Puri, Aniruddha De, and the entire editorial team for their readiness to help with various aspects of the publication process. I would also like to thank Debjani Mazumdar, Coordination Editor at the M. S. Merian–R. Tagore International Centre of Advanced Studies 'Metamorphoses of the Political', Delhi, for the enthusiasm with which she approached this project. I would especially like to thank the peer reviewers, whose careful and considered critique of the book's arguments helped immensely in revising it for publication.

I would also like to thank my friends and family who inspire me in so many ways. I credit my father, Alagiry, with showing me through his life's example the value of embracing unconventionality. Thank you to parents-in-law, Jamuna Prasad and Shobha Pandey, for their encouragement through the years. My aunt and uncle Jacintha Balakrishnan and R. Balakrishnan have been the best godparents one could wish for, celebrating my successes as theirs and sharing my burdens so they never got too great to bear. I would like to also thank uncles and aunts Anand, Bharathi, Shyam Sundar and Bhamini, who have been so generous with their time and energy during my stay in India. My thanks also to my children, Riti, Rohan and Riyan, who have had to endure all the demands research has made on my time with them. Thank you for being so patient and forgiving through it all. Thank you to my friends Ekaterina Dynina, Yong En En, Tan Weiming, Chong Yue En, Uma Mageswari and Faizun Marziyah for the warmth of your friendship over the years.

Finally, my greatest thanks to my two pillars of strength. My mother Jayanthi Balakrishnan's life is a life of struggles and sacrifices, a life by which I measure greatness in my own. I credit my partner, Prashant Pandey, with sustaining my interest in this project all these years. It makes a world of difference to have an ally who never lets one forget how the journey began in the first place.

To all these people I owe an enormous debt of gratitude. Any faults in this book are, of course, my own.

Abbreviations

AIADMK	All-India Anna Dravida Munnetra Kazhagam
AICC	All India Congress Committee
AITA	Anglo-Indian Temperance Association
APCC	Andhra Provincial Congress Committee
BJP	Bharatiya Janata Party
DMK	Dravida Munnetra Kazhagam
E & O	Economic and Overseas Department
IMFL	Indian-made foreign liquor
IOR	India Office Records, London
KPCC	Kerala Provincial Congress Committee
ICTA	Indian Christian Temperance Association
L/PJ	Political and Judicial Department
NAI	National Archives of India, New Delhi
NML	Nehru Memorial Library, New Delhi
NNPR	Native Newspaper Reports
NPCC	Nagaland Pradesh Congress Committee
P & J	Public and Judicial Department Records
PLI	Prohibition League of India
PTL	Periyar Thidal Library, Chennai
RML	Roja Muthiah Library, Chennai
TASMAC	Tamil Nadu State Marketing Corporation
TDP	Telugu Desam Party

TNA	Tamil Nadu Archives, Chennai
TNCC	Tamil Nadu Congress Committee
TNTM	Tamil Nadu Toddy Movement
UBG	United Breweries Group

Note on Translation

Unless otherwise specified, all the translations that have been provided in this book are by the author, who has consulted *Kriyaavin tarkala tamil akaraati* (Kriya Contemporary Tamil Dictionary) (Chennai, 1992) for this purpose. Most of the translations are from Tamil to English, except in a handful of cases where words of Hindi or Sanskrit origin (for example, *swadeshi*) have been used. All the translations have been provided either in the main text or in the notes, except where longer works have been referenced.

Introduction
Setting the Stage

Sober State

Locating Prohibition's Origins in Colonial India

India is the only country in the world to have prohibition[1] written into its national constitution as an ideal. Article 47 of the Constitution of India establishes that 'the state shall undertake rules to bring about prohibition of the consumption, except for medicinal purposes, of intoxicating drinks and of drugs which are injurious to health'.[2] Although the state is obligated to implement the policy, there is no compulsion to do so within a stipulated time frame, which makes it a Directive Principle of State Policy – an ideal. As much a national ideal as an instrument of state power, prohibition's fate has been entwined with the rise and fall of state governments since the country's independence.

Prohibition has also spawned its own political economy in India, with a broad spectrum of political parties professing commitment – though usually short-lived – to its enforcement. The specific circumstances of its introduction have varied across the country, as have the policy's trajectories and outcomes. Local cultures, economic circumstances and the demands of state governance have directly contributed to these differences. Besides Gujarat, which has enforced prohibition since 1947 despite a series of hooch-related tragedies and other controversies, Bihar, Mizoram and Nagaland are all 'dry' states at the time of this book's writing. Alcohol is all but banned in the union territory of Lakshadweep, although prohibition has been greatly contested in recent years. The association between prohibition and M. K. Gandhi has been the strongest in Gujarat, whereas evangelical Christianity paved the way for the policy's introduction in Nagaland. Tamil Nadu, Andhra Pradesh, Kerala, Manipur and Haryana have all tried prohibition on for size at various times since independence, only to suspend it as better suited for implementation at an unspecified time in the distant future. Crippling fiscal deficits and a strong liquor lobby heralded prohibition's termination in Andhra Pradesh and Kerala respectively.

Although the Constitution of India has enabled all kinds of negotiations relating to prohibition following the achievement of independence, the policy has a much longer history in the subcontinent.[3] The story of prohibition's introduction in the United States of America perhaps comes closest as a point of comparison to that in India. Prohibition activism reached a fever pitch in both countries in the interwar period as the Eighteenth Amendment to the Constitution of the United States paved the way for the dry law's introduction there in 1920. The policy operated through the workings of American federalism in a manner comparable to how it intersected with provincial politics in India. In America, as in India, politicians 'harnessed moral aspirations to politics and partisan strategies' to acquire and maintain political relevance through the policy.[4] Prohibition's introduction necessitated and brought forth an expanded police force, laws and administrative functions, all of which significantly strengthened the long arm of the state in both countries. In America, these mechanisms and institutions continued to influence the liberal state's functioning long after prohibition ended. The Indian nationalist leadership that presided over prohibition's introduction deliberately referenced the American example in expressing optimism and hope in the policy: Mother India would succeed where Uncle Sam had failed.

This is where the similarities end. After an ill-fated thirteen years, prohibition came to a spectacular end in the country where the policy had enabled the meteoric rise of personalities like Al Capone. Its termination marked a watershed moment in American history as the only time a constitutional amendment was repealed. Whereas the policy's termination was effected through the ballot box in America, the prohibition ideal is kept alive through democratic processes in contemporary India. The experience and memory of colonialism have been pivotal in shaping it as a democratic policy intervention, a key distinguishing feature of Indian prohibition. Notwithstanding India's exceptional tryst with the policy, a history of prohibition's origins in the subcontinent – which stands in counterpoint to much of what we know about prohibition's global history – has yet to be written. Instead, the story of banning alcohol in America, and elsewhere in the West, has shaped extant understandings of prohibition's intersections with democracy.

While the story of prohibition in India is exceptional owing to the policy's entanglements with democratic government, it overlaps in important ways with alcohol studies in the Global South, which show that the impact of colonial governance on local drinking cultures was often quite profound. In many parts of the world, the introduction of new administrative frameworks and bureaucracies transformed existing social meanings attached to drinking, in turn engendering new ways of representing and governing the colonised. In the Americas, alcohol policy supported the construct of the original 'drunk Injun' and allowed the state to justify the relocation of indigenous peoples to reserves far removed from European society in moral as well as medical terms, thus facilitating white settler expansionism. Likewise, the French in colonial Vietnam established a monopoly over distilled liquor production and distribution that they subsequently used to consolidate power over Vietnamese society.[5]

However, the story of alcohol in the Global South is not just a story of policy impositions. In fact, it is not a singular story at all, but rather encompasses *stories* in the plural. Richly peopled, diverse and complex in their trajectories, histories of the West African *akpetshie* and the Latin American *chicha* display the intricate networks of circulation that indigenous liquors carved in their respective cultural milieus – networks that often confounded European colonial administrators.[6] Similar to toddy and arrack in India, these liquors put down deep roots in the local economy and society that colonial policymaking could not easily dislodge. As they were interwoven with local lives and livelihoods, supporting complex systems of meaning in the process, local drinking cultures frequently eluded and frustrated official attempts at control.

Alcohol also factored into more direct and deliberate forms of resistance with the rise of anti-colonial nationalist movements in the British Empire. Akin to the situation in India, the temperance movement in early-twentieth-century Ceylon, present-day Sri Lanka, developed where political resistance to British rule met and intersected with religious revivalism. The Buddhist *nayaka*s, or chief monks, were at the vanguard of anti-alcohol agitation to achieve two related goals: overthrowing British rule and consolidating their own political position. The movements they helmed, like the Sura Virodhi Vyaparaya campaign, achieved their objective of bringing about a severe dent in alcohol revenues for the colonial state. Yet, as intense as it was in the colonial period, the Sri Lankan anti-alcohol movement did not survive the transition into the postcolonial context as it failed to develop national political momentum.[7] Unlike the situation in India, the Sri Lankan temperance movement failed to make inroads into the workings of the state. In this book,

I argue that prohibition was crucial to both the dismantling of the colonial state and the installation of the postcolonial state in India. The overarching contestation for the state that prohibition was simultaneously part of, and in turn fuelled, had far-reaching implications for the very nature of Indian prohibition.

The colonial roots of contemporary policy measures targeting addiction are discernible in other case studies from India itself. Although the legal cultivation of opium for exclusively medicinal and scientific purposes is restricted to only three states today – Madhya Pradesh, Rajasthan and Uttar Pradesh – the drug had been an important source of revenue for the Mughals and Rajputs alike. The East India Company in the Bengal Presidency subsequently developed it into an imperial monopoly. As part of that province, Assam witnessed one of the most sustained movements against opium seen anywhere in the subcontinent, inflected as it was by caste and gender dynamics. Women and upper-caste communities were opposed to opium-smoking and, to a lesser extent, opium-eating, their efforts focused on banning opioid use amongst the Assamese hill tribes. Amidst serious opposition from various quarters of society arising from opium's medicinal and cultural importance, not to mention its economic utility as a cash crop, the Indian National Congress–coalition government attempted to ban the drug in 1939, thus setting a crucial precedent for the Assam Opium Prohibition Act of 1947.[8]

Cannabis presents a similar story. Better known by its street names, weed or marijuana, it is the poster drug for legalisation efforts aimed at narcotics in many parts of the world today. Cannabis, too, surfaces a layered history of state–society interactions in the context of empire. Efforts to regulate the drug in India directly affected the push for its regulation in the United Kingdom in the late 1920s.[9] In India itself, the drug was banned only in 1985 with the passing of the Narcotic Drugs and Psychotropic Substances Act, with important exceptions like that made for *bhang*.

As contested as it was, the prohibition of narcotic drugs in India – first within the auspices of the Indian nationalist movement and subsequently by the independent Indian state – has never been quite as polarising as the alcohol question. In many parts of India, alcohol continues to influence notions of conviviality, cultural and religious traditions, and livelihoods to a much greater degree than drugs. Moreover, alcohol – particularly country liquor – has been so widely accessible relative to narcotics that alcohol legislation has often set the momentum for subsequent policymaking on drugs. Debates relating to prohibition in India continue to revolve around the costs and benefits of banning alcohol in contemporary India, much as they did in the colonial era when the Madras Prohibition Act of 1937 was introduced.

'Like Swallowing a Ripe Plantain'

The Madras Prohibition Act of 1937 became law at a time when British India was divided into several provinces and hundreds of princely states. The provinces were directly administered by the British Raj, albeit with Indian collaboration, while Indian rulers governed the princely states under a system of indirect colonial rule. The Congress had just formed governments in most of the provinces it had contested in the elections earlier that year. From previously opposing the colonial government, the nationalist organisation now found itself having to think and act like the government, that too in the company of an especially bristly British governor. The Madras Congress ministry introduced prohibition as its first major programme of national social reform in the space it was allowed by the colonial government in just four districts of the Madras Presidency: Salem, Chittoor, Cuddapah and North Arcot. The chief minister of the province, C. Rajagopalachari, declared that the people would embrace the policy with 'the ease of swallowing a ripe plantain'.[10]

It was a strange thing to say. Far from being a ripe plantain, prohibition proved to be a tough pill to swallow. While other provinces emulated the example that Madras had set and followed suit with the policy's introduction, crippling fiscal deficits, soaring unemployment rates, embarrassing problems of enforcement and stiff political resistance all tested its implementation in the southern province. Prohibition crime wrought serious practical limitations on the space within which state power could operate. The prohibition manual, issued to police officers, set out that 'illicit distillers could be caught by quizzing intoxicated persons and disgruntled addicts to whom sales had been refused'.[11] The state clearly remembered its lessons from the past; it just could not stop their recurrence.

The signs, however, had been there all along. Prohibition had had a long incubation period between 1886 and 1937. As the policy took shape over this period, limited experiments had already provided a worrying preview of the difficulties that lay ahead. In response to liquor shop closures in the mid-1920s, thirty labourers had appealed to the government to reopen the toddy shop near their workplace. 'To those of us who are fishermen and have to work on the sea,' their petition read, 'toddy is the only indispensable drink before starting and after returning from work. No other intoxicating drinks will suit us.'[12]

Similarly, businessmen from 'the toddy-tapping castes' asserted their hereditary right to draw a livelihood from country liquor – a right they expected the state to uphold. A few months before prohibition's introduction, toddy shop renters had turned to colonial officials for assurance that the impending change in government policy due to the Congress Party, 'a party dead against all these shops, assuming power', would not affect their rights as vendors.[13] As diverse segments of society interacted with both the idea of the policy and the measures it informed, their responses left an indelible imprint on Indian prohibition itself as the latter developed. The nationalists made difficult compromises that often undermined their idealised view of 'good' governance in order to dispense effective governance.

The colonial government suspended prohibition in 1943. Instead of spelling the policy's demise, however, the processes that informed its conceptualisation, the formative experience of its implementation and its suspension together sowed the seeds for its reintroduction as soon as the Congress returned to power. In fact, the Constituent Assembly debates on prohibition, which brought forth Article 47 of the Indian Constitution, drew extensively on the then recent experience of the Madras Prohibition Act. A similar pattern would replay in subsequent decades, with each policy suspension simultaneously paving the way for future attempts to make prohibition work and restricting the policy's scope in crucial ways.

There are several possible approaches to this history, each with its opportunities and limitations. We could trace prohibition's social history as a history of the people with the politics left in, spiralling out from women's mobilisation or the demands made by labouring groups.[14] An economic history of prohibition would heed its fiscal and commercial implications by studying policy impacts like unemployment or alternative sources of taxation. Studying the policy's contours as a history rooted in the Global South would prompt a rethinking of how the American Volstead Act, 1919, acted as a model for the Madras Prohibition Act, but also how the laws differed significantly in their respective trajectories. Although these themes feature in the following chapters, my focus in this book is the policy's place in the workings of the state, where they converge. *Sober State* examines the politics of the policy – politics here broadly construed as the field of interactions wherein the motivations and actions of political actors and parties met diverse social responses to produce prohibition as a negotiated settlement.

The Colonial State, Congress Nationalism and Prohibitioning

So, what of *Sober State*? Is it a history of the state or of its people? The answer is that it is necessarily a history of both. Specifically, it is a history of the ways in which they interacted in the late colonial period to produce prohibition as simultaneously a policy and an ideal. By tracing the genealogy of a policy from the colonial era into the postcolonial period, I present here as much a history of the Indian state as it gradually took shape as of prohibition as an expression of its power. Incorporating methodological interventions that foreground the role of caste, class and gender in mediating state power, I develop the conceptual framework of *prohibitioning* to show that each iteration of the policy informed its subsequent iterations. I do not use the suffix '-ing' here to simply indicate an ongoing action. Instead, I see 'prohibitioning' as a concept and process spanning the colonial and postcolonial periods, wherein each phase of prohibition's development contained within it the impetus for the next. Relatedly, I examine how debates that crystallised in a province of British India came to have national significance.

But how does prohibition, which implies a top-down exercise of state power, align with democratic aspirations and modes of government? Any discussion of Indian prohibition must necessarily grapple with this question, for while the policy took shape within the patently undemocratic context of empire, it was introduced within an emerging framework of democratic politics. In fact, prohibition was introduced as the very expression of democracy in India. This curious situation presents us with the issue of moral politics, wherein a family-based code of moral values – paternalism – informs state intervention in society.[15] As others have argued, preoccupations with morality left an indelible imprint on both political discourses and public policy in the subcontinent.[16] Moral politics has historically also been at the heart of prohibition, more so in India than anywhere else in the world, owing to its intersections with state formation. Colonialism had produced a 'rational state' and 'disciplinary society' in India, which in turn brought forth the search for moral-modern solutions to problems hindering governance.[17] Intemperance was one such problem.

Viewed through a Foucauldian lens, prohibition is a biopolitical project, wherein the political processes, structures and ethics informing it operate within an overarching power–knowledge nexus of 'governmentality', a concept combining government and rationality.[18] Colonial and nationalist alcohol policy sought to co-opt individuals in governing their own bodies and drinking behaviours. In doing so, colonial and nationalist governments alike claimed the mantle of good government. At the same time, however, prohibition as an exercise of sovereign state power became necessary precisely because liberal governmentality kept falling short of producing the normative outcome: sober subjects.

I reference Michel Foucault here not to map his theorisations onto our discussion of Indian prohibition, but rather for the insights they surface on the exercise of state power, which are discernible in the policy's features. While Foucault based his analysis on his observations of Western societies, subsequent scholarship has illuminated the possibilities of thinking with governmentality to understand processes of state formation in India, shaped as it was by the peculiar historical experience of colonialism. Here, Partha Chatterjee's discussion of governmentality as a function of the exercise of colonial power and the range of social responses it engendered is helpful in framing our study of Indian prohibition's origins and characteristics.[19]

Prohibition emerged as a response to colonial alcohol policy over the long and staggered experience of imperial governance between the late nineteenth and mid-twentieth centuries. I show that alcohol policy, the product of colonial knowledge production to begin with, consequently stretched to accommodate such diverse concerns as health, morality and revenue maximisation. The state's stance on alcohol developed in tandem with a transition from a reliance on coercive, sovereign forms of power to liberal governmentality as its modus operandi. I demonstrate that both forms of power remained firmly imprinted on alcohol policy. In fact, the 'varying strategic combinations' of the two tactics of power gave rise to an 'abnormal political rationality', of which colonial alcohol policy developed as a manifestation.[20]

The years 1886 and 1937 are especially pertinent as they mark, respectively, the colonial government's introduction of the Madras Abkari Act and the nationalist government's introduction of the Madras Prohibition Act. Policymaking was greatly complicated by the fact that the colonial state itself was not a monolithic entity over this period. Far from it, it was a significantly weakened state whose control over society was tenuous at best by the 1920s, a time that – not coincidentally – also saw the intensification of prohibition politics. As the alcohol policy of a 'limited' Raj came to reflect the oft-contradictory aims that produced it, segments of Indian society criticised it as insincere, inadequate and, ultimately, ineffective. I show that the colonial state's approach to alcohol contributed to the emergence and development of prohibition in two ways: it simultaneously became the blueprint for the Congress's alcohol policy and set the political momentum for prohibition to emerge as the moral-modern policy stance of the Indian state.

Significant shifts that took place within the field of operation of colonial power between the Madras Abkari Act and the Madras Prohibition Act became crucial exercises in statecraft for the nationalists. Prohibition as a nationalist demand emerged as a cumulative development of these shifts, catalysed by the particular constellation of political and social circumstances in the interwar period. At the same time, the processes, apparatuses and institutions that had been put in place by the colonial state provided opportunities for a broad cross-section of Indian society to weigh in on what India's alcohol policy should be.

Notwithstanding these entanglements, however, prohibition figures in the extant literature as a movement – one that developed in association with global temperance networks and local anti-alcohol movements to eventually coalesce with Congress mass mobilisation in opposition to the colonial state.[21] Instead, I argue that the idea of prohibition, the politics it spawned and the actual experience of the policy's implementation in the late colonial context were all part of broader processes that brought forth the emergence of the Indian state. Prohibition became a crucial site for the Congress to critique the colonial state and advance an alternative vision of state intervention – an improved, if not actually new, governmentality – in the prickly area of social reform. In fact, prohibition was not only the first real test of governance for the nationalist leadership; it also became a site where the nationalist state was imagined, negotiated and forged in the process. Prohibition originated as an abnormal political rationality in this context owing to two overarching paradoxes that framed its emergence.

The prohibition demand was a product of the Congress's ideations of the state, which it saw as being both a central moral force and the primary source of modernity. In formulating its vision of the Indian state and what it should be, the Congress leadership derived from and detested the autocratic colonial state, whilst seeking to outdo it, including in its alcohol policy. This is the first paradox framing prohibition. Defeating the Raj necessitated a modern state propped up by modern policies.[22] Prohibition fit the bill perfectly as an exercise in modern statecraft that was at that time fast gaining global currency. Wielded by the nationalist leadership, it supported the assertion of India's cultural–spiritual superiority over the materially advanced West. The nationalists turned inward to their upper-caste cultural norms and values in rationalising prohibition, which the policy's ethos reflected.

A policy that did not yet exist needed to be imagined for a nation that did not yet exist, by a state that was still in the process of emerging. Relatedly, the prerequisite for the functioning of a modern state – a 'modern' society – did not yet exist in colonial India. This was the second paradox influencing prohibition's development. Prohibition was conceptualised and implemented in a context wherein the nationalist leadership was attempting to discipline society into modern citizenship, while preparing it for policies like prohibition. Representing society as it was and transforming it to become modern and 'ethical' injected another layer of complexity into policymaking.[23] In fact, the Congress was attempting to discipline people into becoming the modern society that it claimed to represent through prohibition, beginning in the late colonial period.

The Congress insisted that prohibition would be introduced, and not imposed, as it was what the people really wanted. Its claim of being the nation's representatives in a context of anti-colonial competition meant that prohibition's democratic credentials needed to be proved. I demonstrate that the nationalist leadership sought out support from different parts of the population, attempting to create widespread moral pressure for the policy across constituencies in the process. Besides the largely upper-caste Indian middle classes, a segment of the Indian underclasses also readily answered the call for prohibition.

It might be tempting to think of Indian prohibition as a case of state-sponsored Sanskritisation, although, as others have pointed out, the concept flattens and homogenises non-elite actions to motivations that ultimately enthrone the logic of caste – 'a game of snakes and ladders where the board never changes'.[24] Instead, non-elite groups interacted with the idea and reality of prohibition through responses that fell along a broad spectrum as they struck bargains with the state based on practicalities. While prohibition certainly involved processes that enshrined upper-caste norms as national norms, it also managed to capture the imagination and support of many among the Indian underclasses.

Globally, women have been at the forefront of movements for prohibition, so much so that they have become the policy's public face.[25] As guardians of the home defending the Indian home against an avaricious Raj, women's mobilisation as prohibition activists particularly imbued the policy with moral force. Their spectacular shows of mass mobilisation constituted attempts as much to build a broad consensus on prohibition as to demonstrate that such a consensus had already been reached. A subset of civil society activism, women's anti-alcohol campaigning helped to bring together the 'institutional logic of democratic forms and the logic of popular mobilisation'.[26] The key role that women played in evolving a national culture of prohibition helped to raise it above the realm of politics to enshrine it instead as the state's sacred, patriotic mission.

I show that by focusing on building consensus for prohibition, the Congress sought to generate a semblance of consent for the policy – and by extension – the state it promised to usher in. Arguably the most influential concepts to come out of Antonio Gramsci's *Prison Notebooks*, 'passive revolution' and 'cultural hegemony' together point to how the ruling class in society maintains power.[27] Specifically, they suggest that the ensuing processes are reformist rather than actually revolutionary, allowing for subtle and gradual changes that neutralise potential opposition without a social upheaval. The ruling classes are aided in this endeavour by the widespread dissemination of hegemonic ideology throughout society, which enables them to maintain and consolidate their control through the generation of consent, rather than coercion. As Chatterjee has argued, the transition to Indian independence can be seen as a passive revolution in that it left key colonial institutions and the hegemony of the dominant social classes largely untouched.[28]

As a policy that was forged within the constraints imposed by the late colonial state, and that subsequently developed within the 'parallel governmentality' of the Congress government, I argue that prohibition was inherently conservative to begin with.[29] It could not become too radical in its scope as that would have lost the Congress the support of influential social groups that had too much to lose themselves if the policy was implemented to its full extent. Prohibition thus became part of the process wherein the middle classes, and the groups allied with them, laid claim to the authority and apparatuses of the colonial state to engineer a modern society, crucially, without effecting an actual revolution. It did not matter that the envisioned consensus could not be perfectly or fully achieved at that time. The processes involved in building it demonstrated the legitimacy of the Congress government's credentials as good government. Nevertheless, consensus-building meant that prohibition was pulled and stretched in different directions as diverse constituencies engaged with it. At the same time, the widespread dissemination of a spectacular national culture of prohibition enshrined it as an ideal that could keep being revived even if the policy itself were to fail in the short run. Indeed, scholars would subsequently read the enduring culture of prohibition as proof of its popular mandate.[30]

Subaltern Society, Political Society and Prohibition

Indian prohibition embodied the paradoxes that produced it in several ways. Neither a wholly authoritarian imposition nor a democratic intervention on behalf of the people, it contained elements of both. As an exercise in consensus-building, prohibition reflected the attendant hopes and promises, frictions and fractures, tensions and compromises that had produced it. The nationalist state necessarily had to become 'sober' – measured – in its approach to prohibition in the face of the diverse responses that it encountered. Consequently, the policy bore – indeed, has borne – the imprint of this pragmatism.

Although prohibition as a policy stance suggests a distinct top-down orientation, it is defined precisely by the responses it translates to on the ground. In global histories of prohibition, bootlegging, smuggling and the creation of a thriving underground liquor economy often figure as proof of the policy's failure.[31] Opposition to prohibition took several forms in the Madras Presidency. Under the leadership of E. V. Ramasamy, popularly known as Periyar, the Self-Respect movement resisted prohibition as a Brahminical imposition on Dalit rights. Liquor businesses criticised the state for its highhanded denial of their right to a livelihood. Catholics condemned what they saw as the Congress government's deliberate attack on religious rights.

Beyond the realm of organised protest to prohibition, I show that subaltern drinking cultures also forced changes in what prohibition became. Elaborating on Foucauldian conceptions of power, the Subaltern Studies Collective posited the argument of the subaltern domain as an autonomous domain that neither originated from elite politics nor depended upon it.[32] While subaltern politics – and drinking cultures – may not have originated from elite politics, the politics of prohibition shows that they were certainly affected by it, with significant repercussions for both the groups involved and subsequent policymaking. After all, while alcohol policy transformed an activity that had 'nothing whatsoever to do with the commission of a crime' into what the state subsequently punished as illicit distillation in South Gujarat, the negotiations that it thus brought forth among tribals over the *daru* and toddy industries reveal for us the power of the people in throwing a wrench into the workings of the state.[33] Equally, the question of whether the subaltern could actually speak – or, more accurately, drink and not die – becomes particularly relevant for prohibition.[34] The policy has historically left drinkers, particularly from the underclasses of society, with little choice but to turn to any available, often lethal, source of intoxication.

Indeed, the problem of illicit hooch – distilled liquor that is frequently also adulterated – has been among prohibition's unintended, but widely anticipated, effects necessitating state intervention. The state has not only had to intervene to mitigate the worst effects of the fallout, it has also often done so in the Indian context to uphold prohibition's relevance to society. I argue that while prohibition thus certainly elicited responses that challenged the state's writ, in doing so, it also provided the impetus for the next round of negotiations on what it ought to be instead. Prohibition's failings became proof precisely of the people's inability to govern themselves. Simultaneously, it became justification that the state would need to be further strengthened. Each iteration of prohibition thus constrained and overdetermined its subsequent articulation and implementation, with far-reaching repercussions. I demonstrate that prohibition's development within the state shows that 'resistance' does not exist separately from the exercise of power but is, rather, constitutive of it.

Several key methodological interventions in recent years have explored the relationship between government policy on the one hand and caste, class and gender, on the other. Whether in terms of the 'caste–state nexus' that developed in response to 'the Pariah problem', the state's ultimately futile attempts to phase out 'the Hijra problem', or the constraints that caste and class presented for the production of colonial urban space, they collectively show us that state power has been inflected by pragmatism and adaptation.[35] Like them, I position the state as a human community whose power derives from, and is therefore constrained by, society. However, by studying prohibition simultaneously from the inside-out and the outside-in, I show that the range of responses that it elicited from diverse segments of society shaped its further development by being continuously absorbed and fed back into the workings of the state. The question to ask then, I argue, is not whether the state was all-powerful or whether certain communities had more political purchase than others – they did – but, rather, how prohibition was mutually constituted as a result of ongoing interactions between the state and various constituencies.

A key contribution this book brings to conversations on state power in India is the long-term perspective it adopts in examining processes of state formation over the colonial and postcolonial contexts. In prohibition, we see how a policy of social reform that was conceived in the context of colonialism navigated – indeed, *could* navigate – the transition to independence. I show that the manner in which this happened again had tremendous implications for the nature of the policy after 1947. As the postcolonial state continued to 'lead' society into the future through policymaking, policies like prohibition came to reflect the tensions that produced them. Through a discussion of Chatterjee's much-debated concept of 'political society', I argue that the state was forced to become progressively more conservative – sober – in its approach to the policy, as various groups granted, withheld or negotiated consent for prohibition.[36] Prohibition thus continued to develop in the postcolonial context as a surprisingly versatile and resilient policy stance that could accommodate a range of demands, interpretations and contexts.

Prohibition: From Province to Nation through the State

Whereas previous works on prohibition have examined the policy's emergence as an outcrop of developments at the all-India level, I demonstrate that the province was prohibition's laboratory. It was here that prohibition was conceptualised and implemented, resisted and negotiated. Prohibition's emergence and development in the Presidency of Fort St George became entwined with the workings of the state, so much so that it spilled over to influence the policy's origins elsewhere in the country. Moreover, as the states of the Indian republic were carved out of the provinces, the experience of prohibition in the late colonial period directly affected the policy's postcolonial development as well. The state in *Sober State* thus signifies the exercise of power at two levels: the state as a territorially bounded sovereign polity and as a constituent part of the Indian republic.

The negotiations that prohibition prompted at various levels are thrown into especially sharp relief in the Presidency of Fort St George, which led the country in introducing prohibition. The province, officially known after 1937 as the Madras Presidency, encompassed all of the Telugu districts that today make up Andhra Pradesh, most of the Tamil districts comprising contemporary Tamil Nadu and parts of what are now Karnataka, Kerala, Odisha and Telangana. In the West, it included the districts of South Canara and Malabar; in the Deccan were Cuddapah, Kurnool, Anantpur and Bellary; Ganjam, Vizagapatam and Godavari lay in the northeast of the province. With the end of the Mysore Wars, the Presidency of Fort St George emerged as an important site for the exercise of state power. The region's cultural particularities informed distinct forms of colonial knowledge production and, hence, social responses to state power that departed in crucial ways from trends and patterns elsewhere in British India (Figure I.1).

More crucially, prohibition originated as an especially contested policy as it became politicised in the province where alcohol sales and taxation were particularly important to the workings of the local economy. Liquor excise contributed more to colonial coffers in Madras than in any other province, supplying 21.7 per cent of its total revenue in 1922 and a staggering 31 per cent by 1930.[37] I demonstrate that, far from being just a stage for elite programmes or non-elite agencies to play out on, the province conditioned the particular sociopolitical dynamics that prohibition developed in response to. Specifically, the particular caste–state nexus that presented in the province is especially relevant in informing understandings of prohibition's emergence and subsequent development. Madras boasted numerous toddy-tapping castes, vibrant drinking cultures and robust liquor industries, all of which affected the tenor of prohibition debates and determined the contours of the policy's implementation subsequently.

The rise of the non-Brahmin movement also meant that subalternity informed engagements with the colonial state that were frequently driven by shifting relationships of, and engagements with, power.[38] The dynamics that presented between caste and class, converging at some points and diverging at others, was of crucial importance in determining prohibition's career in the colonial period and beyond. The centrality of the Tamil districts in Indian prohibition history cannot be discussed without referencing C. Rajagopalachari's personal dedication to the policy. Rajaji, as the Tamil Brahmin Congress leader was often called, wore many hats. As the secretary of the All-India Prohibition Committee and, subsequently, the chief minister

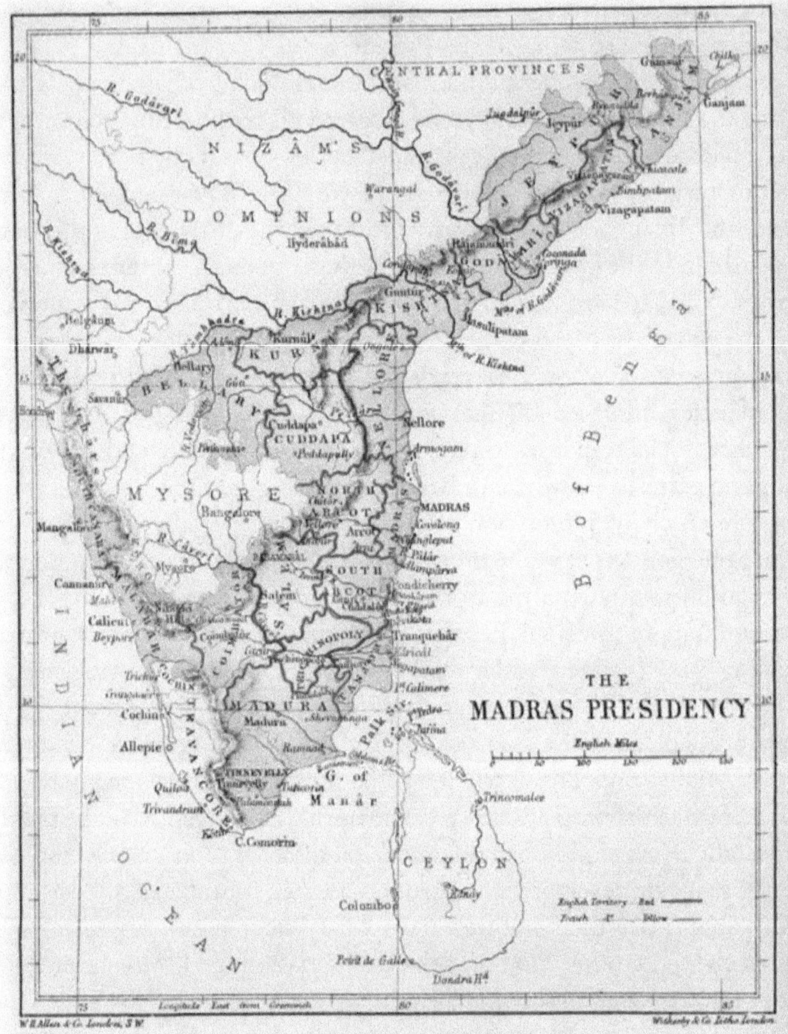

Figure I.1   Map of 'Madras Presidency'

Source: G. U. Pope, *Text-book of Indian History: Geographical Notes, Genealogical Tables, Examination Questions* (London: W. H. Allen & Co., 1880), vii, 574.

of the Madras Presidency, Rajaji did not only play a pivotal role in introducing prohibition in Madras; he also led efforts for the nationwide introduction of the policy. Prohibition's launch by a Brahmin premier in a province where politics had come to be defined by the non-Brahmin movement again shaped the policy's trajectories in far-reaching ways.

The sources for the study of prohibition's introduction presented in this book are as diverse as the people whose politics it brings together. The road to prohibition and its subsequent crystallisation as a policy measure brought into the equation the politics of liquor merchants and grog shop picketers, women from different social classes, labourers and their overseers, Catholic churchgoers, and Hindu social reformers. Letters exchanged between the India Office in London and British governors in India shed light on secret agreements that took place between political elites. Petitions by labourers, often haphazardly inserted into revenue records, inadvertently open a rare window into subaltern lives, livelihoods and demands. The All-India Congress Committee papers present us with perspectives on not just the priorities and prerogatives of leaders like Rajaji, Jawaharlal Nehru and Gandhi but also hint at the many disagreements that emerged over prohibition policy. Tamil newspapers, magazines, films and folk songs not only yield key insights into the dialogues that prohibition opened up in civil society but also throw light on the vernacularisation of prohibition culture. Read against the grain, these sources illuminate a history of prohibition's introduction that is as expansive as it is granular.

Chapter Outline

The Madras Prohibition Act was a legal document that outlined what was permissible and what was not under the terms of the policy. It became the Madras Congress ministry's codification of its alcohol policy in 1937. The Act was propped up, however, by processes that sought 'a new constitutive relationship between the people and their state'.[39] There are thus two aspects to prohibition's origins in the subcontinent: the policy itself and the intellectual, cultural and political undercurrents that informed it. Of course, the first is more easily addressed than the second, although the two combined confer upon prohibition the qualities of simultaneously being a policy and transcending the realm of politics as an ideal. The following chapters show how prohibition was as much a site of consensus-building as its outcome, in the process becoming foundational to the very formation of the Indian state.

Chapter 1 discusses the diverse concerns that shaped the colonial state's approach to alcohol drinking over the long period of colonial rule in the province of backyard breweries. The result was not just the Madras Abkari Act of 1886 but also the emergence of administrative categories that transformed drinking cultures and elicited dynamic engagements between government and society. The conflicting aims contained within colonial alcohol policy and the inconsistencies that they gave rise to influenced the nationalist leadership's resolve of the necessity of an absolute stance against alcohol.

Chapter 2 examines the political shifts that took place between the Madras Abkari Act of 1886 and the Madras Prohibition Act of 1937, shifts that proved pivotal for prohibition's emergence in relation to the nationalist state. Inasmuch as the Congress's establishment was the most important development, it was by no means the only one. Instead, I show that prohibition became integral to the gradual formation of the nationalist state over this incubation period. The ongoing processes of debate, dialogue and consensus-building that occurred within the province on the one hand and between the province and at the all-India level on the other brought about prohibition's crystallisation as the nationalist organisation's flagship social reform programme.

Chapter 3 studies the roots of civil society prohibition activism and examines its points of convergence with Congress nationalism through the development of a distinctive prohibition culture. Caste and gender became pivotal to this prohibition culture, which had the effect of perpetuating prohibition as a resilient ideal, and not just a policy. The development of prohibition culture in the interwar period intersected with the Congress's spectacular boycott campaigns to intensify and catalyse the movement for prohibition.

Chapter 4 traces subaltern engagements with colonial alcohol policy as consumers of alcohol between 1920 and 1937. The colonial state's liquor legislation for the working classes, while pivoting on concerns like labour welfare or productivity, often had little to do with what labouring segments of the population themselves wanted. Subaltern engagements with colonial alcohol policy tested existing legal frameworks and institutions at times, thus playing a pivotal role in informing the state's subsequent policy stance. This becomes especially evident when we consider the partial prohibitions that the state experimented with in the 1920s.

Chapter 5 examines the three-way tango that played out between the colonial government, Congress leadership and liquor businesses amidst the troubles of the turbulent 1920s and 1930s. As the liquor industries were not all created equally to begin with, they differed in their ability to withstand the storms brought forth by the Non-Cooperation and Civil Disobedience movements. Moreover, the internal diversity of this motley group prevented the emergence of a unified anti-prohibition lobby. The colonial state's approach to liquor businesses influenced the approach of the nationalist state in this area too, as the Congress's *neera* campaign would show.

Chapter 6 discusses the Madras Prohibition Act's actual enforcement, focusing on the challenges that the policy surfaced in the four districts of the Madras Presidency, until its suspension in 1943. Controversies brewed in spite of the Congress's consensus-building efforts, which in turn forced several substantial amendments in the policy. Whilst some compromises were made publicly, many others took place behind closed doors. The chapter discusses the Act's pivotal role in bridging ideas and pragmatic considerations, focusing on the policy's fallout for the next round of prohibitioning that it thereby necessitated.

Chapter 7 focuses on prohibition's impact on, and implications for, the postcolonial state. It demonstrates how prohibitioning continued apace in the postcolonial context, beginning with the framing of the national constitution. As the chapter shows, the Madras Prohibition Act formed the basis of several assumptions and presuppositions that shaped the Constituent Assembly debates on the policy, with far-reaching ripple effects that render prohibition an ongoing story of consensus-building in various parts of the country.

The conclusion summarises the book's arguments and distils the importance of prohibition's origin story in India.

To this story we shall now turn.

Notes

1. This book uses the convention of 'prohibition' in lower case to signify its nature as a negotiated and, hence, decentred policy. Whereas Prohibition in the American context signifies the distinct historical juncture that the policy is associated with, prohibition in the Indian context has been evolving with time. We see that it is inherently decentred from this aspect of its development too.

2. Article 47, Constitution of India. See, for instance, https://lddashboard. legislative.gov.in/sites/default/files/COI...pdf (accessed on 13 April 2023). Several Muslim-majority countries also prohibit alcohol consumption, although India is unique in its constitutional commitment to prohibition.

3. Rohit De, *A People's Constitution: The Everyday Life of Law in the Indian Republic* (Princeton: Princeton University Press, 2018), p. 22.

4. Lisa M. F. Andersen, *The Politics of Prohibition: American Governance and the Prohibition Party, 1869–1933* (Cambridge: Cambridge University Press, 2013), p. 3. The minority political party referenced here is the Prohibition Party, which Andersen argues utilised ideology applied to politics and partisan strategies to become relevant in a two-party structure dominated by the Republicans and Democrats. See also Lisa McGirr, *The War on Alcohol: Prohibition and the Rise of the American State* (New York: Norton & Company, 2015).

5. I refer here to several works that have traced the impact of colonial alcohol policies. See Ann Jefferson and Paul Lokken, *Daily Life in Colonial Latin America* (New York: Bloomsbury, 2011); Matthew D. O'Hara, Andrew B. Fischer, *Imperial Subjects: Race and Identity in Colonial Latin America* (Durham: Duke University Press, 2009); Brenda J. Bowser and Justin Jennings, *Drink, Power, and Society in the Andes* (Florida: University of Florida Press, 2009), pp. 88–92. Gilberto Quintero, 'Making the Indian: Colonial Knowledge, Alcohol and Native Americans', *American Indian Culture and Research Journal* 25, no. 4 (2001), pp. 57–71. See also Gerard Sasges, *Imperial Intoxication: Alcohol and the Making of Colonial Indochina* (Honolulu: University of Hawaii Press, 2017), pp. 3–10.

6. See, for instance, Emmanuel Kwaku Akyeampong, *Drink, Power, and Cultural Change: A Social History of Alcohol in Ghana, c. 1800 to Recent Times* (London: Pearson, 1996), for a discussion of *akpeteshie* in colonial Ghana. Akyeampong shows us that *akpeteshie* sustained an intricate social hierarchy in the Gold Coast which gave the British-backed foreign liquor economy a run for its money. See also Gretchen Pierce and Áurea Toxqui, *Alcohol in Latin America: A Social and Cultural History* (Arizona: University of Arizona Press, 2014), for perspectives on the place of *cachaça* and *aguardiente* in the colonial economy.

7. Mark Frost, '"Wider Opportunities": Religious Revival, Nationalist Awakening and the Global Dimension in Colombo, 1870–1920', *Modern Asian Studies* 36, no. 4 (2002), pp. 937–967.

8. Kawal Deep Kour, *A History of Intoxication: Opium in Assam, 1800–1959* (London: Taylor & Francis, 2019), pp. 200–203.

9. James H. Mills, *Cannabis Britannica: Empire, Trade, and Prohibition, 1800–1928* (Oxford: Oxford University Press, 2003), pp. 209–211. See also James H. Mills, *Cannabis Nation: Control and Consumption in Britain, 1928-2008* (Oxford: Oxford University Press, 2013), pp. 53–57.

10. *The Hindu*, 4 October 1939. Rajagopalachari's speech on the occasion of prohibition's extension to North Arcot was quoted in *The Hindu*.

11. G.O. No. 1394, Home Department, 13 March 1939, *Prohibition Police Manual*, pp. 58–62, Tamil Nadu Archives, Chennai (TNA).

12. G.O. No. 1290, Revenue Department (Mis.), 15 August 1925, p. 18, TNA. Revenue Department officials translated the petition from the Tamil language, in which it was written.

13. G.O. No. 861, Revenue Department (Mis., Confl.), 30 March 1938, TNA.

14. George Macaulay Trevelyan, *English Social History: A Survey of Six Centuries, Chaucer to Queen Victoria* (London: Longman, 1944), p. 1. I refer to Trevelyan's critique of reductive approaches to social history 'as the history of a people with the politics left out'.

15. George Lakoff, *Moral Politics* (Chicago: Chicago University Press, 1996).

16. See, for instance, Faisal Devji, 'Morality in the Shadow of Politics', *Modern Intellectual History* 7, no. 2 (2010), pp. 373–390. See also Ranjita Chakraborty, 'Managing Public Morality: The Politics of Public Policy in India', *Indian Journal of Political Science* 70, no. 4 (2009), pp. 1099–1108; and Deana Heath, *Purifying Empire: Obscenity and the Politics of Moral Regulation in Britain, India and Australia* (Cambridge: Cambridge University Press, 2010), pp. 24–29.

17. For a discussion of Max Weber's 'rational state', see Max Weber, 'Politics as a Vocation (1919)', in *Max Weber's Complete Writings on Academic and Political Vocations*, ed. John Dreijmanis (London: Algora Publishing, 2008). See also Michel Crozier, *The Bureaucratic Phenomenon* (Chicago: University of Chicago Press, 1964); and Paul Breiner, *Max Weber and Democratic Politics* (Ithaca: Cornell University Press, 1996). For a discussion of Michel Foucault's 'disciplinary society', see Michel Foucault, *Discipline and Punish: The Birth of the Prison*, trans. Alan Sheridan (New York: Vintage Books, 1995); and John O'Neill, 'The Disciplinary Society: From Weber to Foucault', *British Journal of Sociology* 37, no. 1 (1986), pp. 42–60.

18. Michel Foucault, 'Governmentality', in *The Foucault Effect: Studies in Governmentality*, ed. Graham Burchell, Colin Gordon and Peter Miller (Chicago: Chicago University Press, 1991), pp. 88–104. See also Nikolas Rose and Peter Miller, 'Political Power beyond the State: Problematics of Government', *British Journal of Sociology* 43, no. 2 (1992), pp. 173–205.

19. Partha Chatterjee, *Nationalist Thought and the Colonial World: A Derivative Discourse* (Minneapolis: Minnesota University Press, 1993), pp. 25–28. See also Partha Chatterjee, *Lineages of Political Society: Studies in Postcolonial Democracy* (New York: Columbia University Press, 2011).

20. Partha Chatterjee, 'Governmentality in the East', in *South Asian Governmentalities: Michel Foucault and the Question of Postcolonial Orderings*, ed. Stephen Legg and Deana Heath, pp. 37–57, especially p. 37 (Cambridge: Cambridge University Press, 2018). See also David Scott, 'Colonial Governmentality', *Social Text* 43 (1995), pp. 191–220; and Nivedita Menon, 'Foucault and Indian Scholarship: History, Governmentality, Modernity' (2009), http://kafila.org/2009/06/07/and-arent-obc-women-women-loudthinking-on-the-womens-reservation-bill (accessed on 21 May 2024). I refer also to Christopher Alan Bayly, 'Returning the British to South Asian History: The Limits of Colonial Hegemony', *South Asia: Journal of South Asian Studies* 17, no. 2 (1994), pp. 1–25; Radhika Singh, 'Colonial Law and Infrastructural Power: Reconstructing Community, Locating the Female Subject', *Studies in History* 19, no. 1 (2003), pp. 87–126; and Sumit Guha, 'The Politics of Enumeration and Identification in India, c. 1600-1900', *Comparative Studies in Society and History* 45, no. 1 (2003), pp. 148–167.

21. Historians have shown that the global temperance movement converged with anti-colonialism as key nationalist figures, foremost among them Gandhi, transposed their personal views, philosophies and ethics onto the national movement. For an overview of alcohol's role in Congress mass mobilisation, see Bipan Chandra, Mridula Mukherjee, Aditya Mukherjee, Sucheta Mahajan and K. N. Panikkar, *India's Struggle for Independence, 1857–1947* (New Delhi: Orient Longman, 1992); and Rajnarayan Chandavarkar, *Imperial Power and Popular Politics: Class, Resistance and the State in India, c. 1850–1950* (Cambridge: Cambridge University Press, 1998). See Robert Eric Colvard, 'Drunkards Beware!': Prohibition and Nationalist Politics in the 1930s', in *A History of Alcohol and Drugs in Modern South Asia: Intoxicating Affairs*, ed. Harald Fischer-Tiné and Jana Tschurenev, pp. 173–195 (London: Routledge, 2013); and David M. Fahey and Padma Manian, 'Poverty and Purification: The Politics of Gandhi's Campaign for Prohibition', *The Historian* 67, no. 3 (2005), pp. 489–506, for a discussion of Gandhi's individual role in transposing his personal moral code onto the politics of anti-alcoholism.

22. See Sudipta Kaviraj, 'On the Enchantment of the State: Indian Thought on the Role of the State in the Narrative of Modernity', *European Journal of Sociology / Archives Européennes de Sociologie* 46, no. 2 (2005), pp. 263–296; and Sudipta Kaviraj, *The Imaginary Institution of India: Politics and Ideas* (New York: Columbia University Press, 2010), p. 12. I refer to the arguments presented by Kaviraj and Chatterjee here. Kaviraj argues that

the enchantment of the state brought about a tremendous transformation in that institution – from an institution that was traditionally seen as necessarily limited and somewhat detached to becoming a central force in India's intellectual life. Chatterjee had previously argued that the nationalist leadership's articulation of modernity had been directly shaped by the experience of colonialism. See Chatterjee, *Nationalist Thought and the Colonial World*, pp. 37–42; and Partha Chatterjee, *The Nation and Its Fragments* (Princeton : Princeton University Press, 1993), pp. 35–40, 135–138.

23. Rachel Sturman, *The Government of Social Life in Colonial India: Liberalism, Religious Law, and Women's Rights* (Cambridge: Cambridge University Press, 2012), pp. 8–10.

24. M. N. Srinivas, *Religion and Society among the Coorgs of South India* (Bombay and Calcutta: Asia Publishing House, 1952), pp. 98–100. Srinivas, a sociologist, described Sanskritisation as a process wherein 'lower'-caste groups imitate and incorporate 'upper'-caste customs, rituals, ideology and ways of life to achieve upward social mobility. For a critique of Sanskritisation, see, David Hardiman, *The Coming of the Devi: Adivasi Assertion in Western India* (Delhi: Oxford University Press, 1987), p. 160.

25. See, for instance, Ian Tyrell, *Woman's World/Woman's Empire: The Woman's Christian Temperance Union in International Perspective, 1880–1930* (Chapel Hill: University of North Carolina Press, 2014). For perspectives on women's emancipation and temperance in post-independence India, see Marie-Louise Larsson, *'When Women Unite!' The Making of the Anti-Liquor Movement in Andhra Pradesh, India* (Stockholm: Stockholm University Press, 2006).

26. Kaviraj, *The Imaginary Institution of India*, p. 32.

27. Antonio Gramsci, *Selections from the Prison Notebooks*, ed. and trans. Quentin Hoare and Geoffrey Nowell Smith (New York: International Publishers, 1971).

28. Chatterjee, *Nationalist Thought and the Colonial World*, p. 50.

29. William F. Kuracina, *The State and Governance in India: The Congress Ideal* (London and New York: Routledge, 2010), pp. 17, 28–30. I refer to Kuracina's argument that the Congress was inherently pragmatic as a state builder, opting to institute a parallel government – and, hence, governmentality – within the federal structure of the late colonial state.

30. Chandra, Mukherjee, Mukherjee, Mahajan and Panikkar, *India's Struggle for Independence*, p. 269. I refer to Chandra's argument that

prohibition was legitimised by 'the popular tradition of regarding abstinence as a virtue and as a symbol of respectability'.

31. See, for instance, Honorée Fanonne Jeffers and David E. Kyvig, *Repealing National Prohibition* (Chicago: Chicago University Press, 1979); Andersen, *The Politics of Prohibition*, pp. 137–145; Eric Burns, *The Spirits of America: A Social History of Alcohol* (Philadelphia: Temple University Press, 2004); and Mark Beyer, *Temperance and Prohibition: The Movement to Pass Anti-Liquor Laws in America* (New York: Rosen, 2006).

32. Ranajit Guha, 'On Some Aspects of the Historiography of Colonial India', in *Subaltern Studies I: Writings on South Asian History and Society*, ed. Ranajit Guha, pp. 37–43 (Delhi: Oxford University Press, 1988). See also Brent L. Pickett, 'Foucault and the Politics of Resistance', *Polity* 28, no. 4 (1996), pp. 445–466.

33. David Hardiman, 'From Custom to Crime: The Politics of Drinking in South Gujarat', in *Subaltern Studies IV*, ed. Ranajit Guha, pp. 165–228 (Delhi and Oxford: Oxford University Press, 1985.)

34. Gayatri Chakravorty Spivak, 'Can the Subaltern Speak?' in *Marxism and the Interpretation of Culture*, ed. Cary Nelson and Lawrence Grossberg, pp. 271–313 (Illinois: University of Illinois Press, 1988).

35. See, respectively, Rupa Viswanath, *The Pariah Problem: Caste, Religion, and the Social in Modern India* (New York: Columbia University Press, 2014), pp. 5–6; Jessica Hinchy, *Governing Gender and Sexuality in Colonial India: The Hijra, c. 1850–1900* (Cambridge: Cambridge University Press, 2019), pp. 195–197; Juned Shaikh, *Outcaste Bombay: City Making and the Politics of the Poor* (Washington, DC: University of Washington Press, 2021), p. 5; and Anand A. Yang, *The Limited Raj: Agrarian Relations in Colonial India, Saran District, 1793–1920* (California: University of California Press, 2023), pp. 8–12.

36. See Partha Chatterjee, *The Politics of the Governed: Reflections on Popular Politics in Most of the World* (New York: Columbia University Press, 2004), pp. 64–66. See also Chatterjee, *Lineages of Political Society*, pp. 87–90.

37. C. J. Baker and D. A. Washbrook, *South India: Political Institutions and Political Change, 1880–1940* (Delhi: Macmillan, 1975), p. 104.

38. David Ludden, *Reading Subaltern Studies: Critical History, Contested Meaning and the Globalisation of South Asia* (London: Anthem Press, 2002), p. 113.

39. Kaviraj, *The Imaginary Institution of India*, p. 12.

1

The Madras Abkari Act of 1886

Caste, Country Liquor and Company Raj

The year was 1710. The wardens of a European cemetery in Madras wrote to East India Company officials complaining about the nuisance they had to put up with owing to the coconut trees on the property. This was a peculiar complaint; we do not normally imagine coconut trees when we think about sources of public nuisance. The crux of the matter at hand was that the gates had to be kept open all the time so that a certain country liquor could be drawn and sold. Variously described as the homegrown beer or palm wine of the Madras Presidency, the miscreant in question was toddy, the word deriving from the Hindi *tari*. In this imperial account, the cemetery was rendered noisier than all the punch houses in Madras put together as basket makers, scavengers, buffalo keepers 'and other Parriars (Paraiyars)' converged there at night to drink toddy, whereupon inebriated 'beggars and other vagabonds' even proceeded to lie down in freshly dug graves.[1] Company officials wrote to the governor recommending replanting the trees elsewhere to relieve the European community of their troubles. The offending coconut trees were promptly removed.

As Company officials increasingly found themselves thrust into the role of a governing body in the Presidency of Fort St George, they found themselves having to develop a coherent response to the issue of alcohol, which eventually became the precursor to the colonial state's alcohol policy. Observations of local drinking cultures that a broad cross-section of European society had contributed became the basis of their response, which evidenced a growing reliance on strategies constituting governmentality over time. Churchwardens and missionaries, merchants, travellers, soldiers and sailors were all involved in shaping three overarching imperial understandings of country liquor and its place in Indian society. The first was that country liquor was ubiquitous and deeply embedded in local ways of life. The second was that it was synonymous with the people who were associated with it, thereby becoming distilled untouchability. The third was the notion that Europeans were drinking country liquor to their ruination. Over time, these understandings acquired the force of truth as they became reified through constant repetition and reproduction. By influencing the Company's policies, they eventually also shaped the Raj's policy of maintaining a strict segregation between alcohol industries. Country liquor needed to be kept in its place, far removed from white society, which remained the ideological and practical basis for subsequent prohibitioning as well.

To begin with, European accounts of toddy and arrack emphasised the ease with which these varieties of country liquor – the most common in southern India – could be procured. Derived from 'almost any palm with no more skill than is required to cut an incision or dress a spathe, and no more apparatus than a knife and a pot', toddy invited numerous observations about how easy it was to make. A particularly influential account whose reverberations would be felt through several future writings appeared in a passage in James Forbes's *Oriental Memoirs* in the early nineteenth century. 'A small incision being made' in the coconut tree, it set out, 'there oozes in gentle drops a cool pleasant liquor called *tarce* or toddy, the palm wine of the poets. This, when first drawn, is cool and salutary, but when fermented and distilled, produces an intoxicating spirit.'[2]

In the process of explaining the toddy-making process, such accounts simultaneously fed into Orientalist imaginings of Indian culture and reinforced the country liquor's place in the *country*: in the local ecology, economy and cultures. All it took to make 'the palm wine of the poets' was the fresh sap of the coconut or palmyra tree, which just had to be collected in a pot and left to ferment, a process that took little to no time at all owing to the tropical climate found everywhere in the province. The economist Gilbert Slater would thus write that 'every coconut palm was a potential toddy brewery'.[3]

European accounts of country liquor routinely emphasised its ubiquity, thereby conferring a degree of normalcy and permanence to its place in Indian society. A fascinating firsthand account of toddy's social life comes from the travel memoirs of the Englishwoman Julia Charlotte Maitland as she was travelling by palanquin through rural south India in the early nineteenth century. Noticing that the palanquin had been set down in the middle of the night, the travel party surveyed its surroundings, only to find itself in a coconut grove. With more than a hint of amusement, Maitland remarked that all the bearers were either 'employed in stealing toddy' or were drunk as a result.[4] Decades later, medical workers in Kurnool raised the alarm that toddy-soaked Muharram celebrations were triggering cholera outbreaks. As scholars have noted, drinking among Muslims was part of the cultural landscape of the Deccan in this period, although Muslims generally eschew alcoholic drinking out of deference to Quranic injunctions. Returning to the medical workers in Kurnool, they reported that the toddy drawers collected as much toddy as they could before the festival ended and sold it at an exorbitant price to the 'thousands' of drinkers who drank freely of this 'decomposing liquid'.[5] Coarse curry prepared from animal entrails and half-rotten mangoes purportedly complemented the merriment.

Colonial officials reported cholera outbreaks near arrack distilleries with increasing frequency over the nineteenth century. Arrack – the word commonly attributed to the Arabic *arraga*, meaning 'to sweat' – was often obtained by 'cooking' toddy. Distilling jaggery, molasses and other forms of sugar also yielded the spirit. Copper pots and other rudimentary stills were routinely used to produce *puttay* arrack, also called *pariah* arrack. This liquor was characterised by the sheer diversity of the ingredients found in it, a list that included different types of tree bark. Indeed, the word *puttay* literally derives from the Tamil word for bark. Before the nineteenth century, Batavia supplied most of the arrack considered superior to *puttay* arrack in the Madras Presidency, owing to the lucrative contracts that Company officials had forced with sugar producers in that settlement.[6] Besides the distilleries that the Company subsequently established, Ceylon also supplied arrack. The imported varieties were generally priced higher than their locally produced counterparts.

In 1715, *A New Voyage to the East Indies* by a 'Captain William Symson' set out that numerous white soldiers had lost their lives due to excessive intake of the country liquor with which, 'once inflamed' they became 'so restless that no place [was] cool enough'.[7] The liquor in question was arrack. A hundred years later, a traveller in Madras would recall that 'many Hindoos, who reject Arrack, drink toddy till they are scarcely able to walk'.[8] In its early stages of fermentation, toddy was considered benign in most Western accounts. In fact, European observers also rationalised its place in Indian society by interpreting it from a biblical frame of reference. According to one such account, if one were to go by the Bible's definition of wine, 'toddy in India meant only a tipsifying spirit drank by our Lord [*sic*]!'[9] Such observations would influence the discriminatory approach that colonial alcohol policy would subsequently adopt towards toddy, arrack and foreign liquor. Indeed, a hierarchy between country liquor varieties gradually took shape in European narratives. Toddy was accepted as the least of the three evils and one that was peculiarly suited to the Indian constitution, while arrack was targeted as a liquor to be regulated. Foreign liquor stood a class apart, earmarked as it was for European society.

Europeans associated country liquor with lowly caste status in India. They saw it as being synonymous with untouchability. Fr Jean Venant Bouchet, a Portuguese Jesuit missionary, lived in seventeenth-century Pondicherry. He ironically warned missionaries to avoid mingling too much with fellow Europeans. 'The Indians, except the Untouchables', Bouchet wrote, 'hate drunkenness.'[10] Bouchet was concerned that too close an association would impede Christianity's progress in the country as the locals regarded Europeans as inveterate alcoholics. John Fryer, a Company surgeon, had similarly alluded to the relationship between country liquor and untouchability when he reported that the savage natives could be seen 'singing and roaring all night long, all drunk with toddy'.[11] 'The Out-Caste has no hopes,' wrote the French Catholic missionary, Abbe Dubois. 'No sooner does a beast die, be the disease what it may,' he explained, 'than a crowd of these hungry beings surround the carrion ... drunkenness follows to crown their shame and woe.'[12] Dubois's account of late-eighteenth- and early-nineteenth-century India was particularly influential as it was considered the definitive European work on Indian culture.

From the second half of the eighteenth century, the Company established revenue farms to exploit the trade in toddy, arrack, and hemp drugs. Under the system, the exclusive right to manufacture and vend toddy and arrack in a given district was auctioned off to persons called contractors for a fixed number of years. It was common practice for contractors to sublet the right to smaller merchants as well. Producing toddy in one's own home was prohibited, except in a few exempted hill districts where Company officials deemed it essential to allow tribal communities the right to tap and consume limited amounts of the alcohol.

Revenue farming did two things. First, it opened up opportunities for Indian merchants to rise to positions of wealth and influence as suppliers of liquor rations to company troops. Once the tax farmer had paid his dues to the state, he invariably sought to maximise his revenue by selling as much liquor as possible, contributing to soaring consumption rates. This translated to a tremendous and sustained increase in profits for the Company. Over the last few decades of the eighteenth century, country liquor in the province yielded revenue that gradually increased from 7,000 rupees to 15,000 rupees to 70,000 rupees by 1801.[13] Relatedly, it created a laissez-faire system with no checks and balances on the quality of the liquor produced. Profit maximisation was the only imperative, notwithstanding the Company's stated commitment to regulating consumption.

Due to the production side of the equation, caste and country liquor also went hand in hand in European observations. As easy as toddy was to produce once the sap was obtained, scaling the towering palm and coconut trees to collect it in the first place was no mean task. The numerous specialist toddy-tapping castes in the Madras Presidency carried out this work. Aside from the Tamil districts' Shanars/Nadars, there were the Idigas, Gramanis, Gamallas and Segidis of the Telugu districts; the Ezhavas, Tiyyas and Chogans in the Keralan districts; and the Kannadiga Billavas, Halepaikas, and Idigas. There were important caste-based spillovers and crossovers in the production of country liquor. Besides their primary occupation of scaling trees to lower toddy, the Shanars of the Tamil districts conducted a large-scale trade in arrack by selling it to distillers as well.

Writing about the Shanars, a Wesleyan Methodist missionary account observed that individuals from the community had to remain at least thirty-six paces away from Brahmins, announcing their arrival loudly to warn the latter about the looming 'threat' of pollution.[14] The stigma attached to toddy tapping had partly influenced the mass conversion of Shanars to Christianity, although notably not as 'passive objects of missionary outreach but on their own spiritual and material terms'.[15] In various parts of Tinnevelly, the district that saw the most spectacular mass conversions, the Shanars looked to Christianity as much to escape caste-based discrimination as to seek protection against exploitation by upper-caste Vellalar landlords looking to secure a cheap and pliant labour force. A British account described the Shanars as 'a hard-working, industrious people', although the district gazetteer for North Arcot was far less charitable. The latter described the Idigas and Shanars alike as 'equally a drunken, dissipated, and impoverished class'.[16]

Alongside the growing awareness of country liquor and its intersections with caste and the growth of the auction system of revenue farming, there gradually emerged a concern that 'the country' was invading the European body. Before the Suez Canal was opened, thus significantly reducing the time and expenses involved in importing fine European liqueurs to India, many – particularly among the lower classes of white society – had been left with little real choice but to consume toddy and arrack. Tavern keepers had been free to sell 'any kind of Wine, Beere, Rum or other European liquors; Punch, Arrack or other Indian liquors'.[17] The relative affordability of country liquor varieties rendered them attractive alternatives to imported liquor. The rise of hybrid liquor varieties involving the addition of country liquor thus produced 'a colonial third culture', as the culture of the metropole interacted with the cultures of the colonised.[18]

The sensitivity of Company officials not 'to be seen to drink too much before Indian servants' directly intersected with the caste associations of country liquor, as the servants in question were often drawn from lower-caste communities.[19] Indeed, as much as segments of European society recognised the importance of avoiding country liquor, they found to their dismay that they could not prevent country liquor from encroaching into white spaces. Regulating drinking became important among the white underclasses, particularly in spaces of European power like the cantonment, where the show of white masculine superiority especially mattered.[20] The racialised hierarchies that thus emerged around alcoholic drinking were fostered, in the first place, on the basis that untouchability threatened the myth of British invincibility.

The term 'pariah arrack' had gained currency from the late seventeenth century onwards with subsequent European writings remarking that it could denote 'an inferior spirit, or an adulterated compound'.[21] European consumption of arrack, mixed with punch or cold water, caused such alarming levels of drunkenness in young soldiers and officers in 1670 that the then governor of Madras framed a set of rules punishing the habit with heavy fines and time in the stocks. In mid-seventeenth-century Madras, the underclasses of European society had considered 'a curious concoction of toddy, porter and brown sugar known as "country beer" to be very refreshing'.[22] In 1835, British magazines in the subcontinent bemoaned that the European traveller in India had little choice but to imbibe the crassest of country liquors. Only 'the commonest pariah arrack' could be obtained relatively cheaply at four *fanam*s per bottle in Sadras. In contrast, even toddy had to be imported from Madras at the exorbitant price of half a rupee per quart bottle.[23]

Anxieties stemming from European overindulgence of country liquor soon gave rise to governmentality as a tactic of power. From a previous position of taverns being free to sell any liquor, controls were introduced to ensure that country liquor was kept at bay. Individuals could only be served half a pint of arrack in taverns. The cantonment was also gradually distanced from the native bazaar in order to distance troops from its temptations, particularly indigenously produced liquor. The earliest demonstrations of governmentality, through efforts that sought to regulate the quantity and type of alcohol consumed, were thus directed not at Indians but at Europeans. The danger that caste posed to carefully nurtured imperial hierarchies was directly responsible for motivating legislation like Regulation VII of 1832 in Madras, which aimed at preventing the excessive use of spirituous and fermented liquors among European soldiers. Increasingly, the Company Raj alternated between using liberal and sovereign forms of governmentality to regulate drinking among Europeans.

At the same time, nascent understandings of tropical medicine, filtered through observations of mortality rates in the presidency armies, produced another set of 'truths' about different varieties of liquor and the health of European and Indian bodies in the tropics. Men from the military and medical establishments were primarily responsible for propagating this set of views. The importance of rationing alcohol in the army had been established in principle in the eighteenth century. Each soldier received two drams of daily allowance of alcohol – with a dram being a fifth of a pint of spirit. The first spirit to be rationed was arrack, before being replaced by rum, owing to pragmatic considerations. Arrack was, after all, cheaper than rum. Moreover, since keeping this country liquor out of the cantonment proved nearly impossible, measures had to be evolved to regulate its consumption in other ways. Arrack subsequently spawned numerous observations about the effects of different types of alcohol on Indian, as opposed to European, bodies.

By the mid-nineteenth century, the Presidency of Fort St George presented observers with a curious paradox: the mortality rates of white soldiers were the lowest of all the presidency armies, while the mortality rates of Indian troops were, conversely, the highest. Observers attributed the low mortality rates of European troops to the Madras army's preference for porter and relatively low consumption of spirit, 'what they [did] consume being arrack'.[24] In contrast, the high mortality rates of Indian troops in the province were attributed to its dominant composition of Muslims and low-ranking castes who, 'unrestrained by caste', apparently ate and drank like Europeans.[25] According to this discourse, the European body – being stronger – could withstand the effects of alcohol, while the low-caste Indian body – being weaker – could not. In the hierarchy of alcohol varieties that thus emerged, arrack fared worse than toddy for the general Indian population, although it was still more 'wholesome' than the rum the Bengal army received or the spirits the Bombay troops got.

Even given these considerations, however, it was beer, and not arrack, that the troops eventually received as liquor rations in the barracks, where temperance canteens were also subsequently set up. Colonel William Henry Sykes's recommendation that 'if fermented liquors must be provided for the soldier in India', then that liquor should be beer 'substituted for distilled spirit', had been reproduced in several other reports that had followed, thus paving the way for the policy change.[26] Emerging ideas of addiction hinged on the pivotal distinction that was raised between fermented alcohols and distilled spirits, which was itself part of medical discourses that were circulating with increasing frequency in Europe in this period. Collectively, these measures upheld the superiority of fermented alcohol over its distilled counterparts and relatedly of beer over arrack, with significant repercussions for colonial alcohol policy – and hence prohibitioning – subsequently.

The British Raj and Liquor Excise

As 'historically constituted complexes of knowledge/power', the observations of missionaries, medical workers, merchants and military men all had a significant bearing on colonial governmentality.[27] Specifically, they informed the development of alcohol policy. Direct Crown rule brought forth a hybrid state, the Raj subsuming elements of an empire and a sovereign state.[28] In this context, governmentality enabled the colonial state to expand its moral claim over sovereign power. The events of 1857 had shown that brute force had brutal limits and would need to be moderated. Colonial officials subsequently asserted that the government's legitimacy should be judged by the good governance that it alone could provide. However, this claim foremost served the needs of the state's territorial and administrative expansionism. Imperial finances were severely stretched in the decades following the Indian rebellion. Revenues had to pay for an army that defended British security interests, both within the subcontinent and beyond. The overheads of administration, which now included extensive transport and communications networks, exerted a growing strain on the treasury. The Raj had to find new sources of income and increase its efficiency in exploiting existing avenues, as land could no longer be taxed as comfortably as it once was.[29] A growing emphasis on liberal governmentality thus became evident in the state's approach to several aspects relating to governance, although it did not hesitate to assert its sovereign power when immediate interests were at stake. The tensions contained within this hybrid form of state power became firmly imprinted on alcohol policy.

Michel Foucault saw governmentality as the production of specific 'regimes of truth' that enable the 'ordering' of target populations.[30] In this framework, the governed do not just accept governance; they regulate their actions and behaviours to enable self-governance. With direct rule, European observations of Indian drinking cultures were systematically mined to become regimes of truth that were hinged to the service of the state. Moreover, the rationalisation of alcohol excise was pursued as a function of the rationalisation of provincial administration. The colonial government endeavoured to improve the flow of information from the peripheries to the center, motivated primarily by facilitating tax collection. The steps taken in this direction included the establishment of district-level excise advisory councils that gathered detailed information about local drinking cultures and public grievances arising from alcohol policy. The state thus equipped itself with the data that it would need to raise taxes and undertake new administrative tasks with improved efficiency.

Nicholas Dirks termed the colonial state an 'ethnographic state', which exercised power and asserted legitimacy through the immense amount of data it collected, sorted, studied and reproduced.[31] Of course, much of this data was grossly in excess of the practical uses to which it was put. At any rate, as the primary object of colonial knowledge production, caste was applied to the state's evident interest in rationalising drinking cultures. Through annual censuses, legal records, district gazettes and meticulous ethnographic surveys, government officials drew linkages between hereditary occupations and religious observances. Censuses noted, for instance, that the Idiga caste 'especially adored pots containing toddy' in their religious rituals.[32] Encyclopaedic entries noted that 'the palm cultivators and toddy makers' in the province numbered more than one and a half million of the population by the end of the nineteenth century, while district gazettes set out that the Shanars occupied a caste rank below that of 'robber castes' like the Kallars.[33]

While colonialism certainly did not invent caste, colonial enumeration and classification did bring about the reification of existing social identities.[34] Just as the Nadars resisted the official use of the caste name Shanar to claim Kshatriya descent instead, the communities involved in producing country liquor exploited the state's knowledge grids for their own ends.[35] In late-nineteenth-century Tinnevelly, Shanar converts to Roman Catholicism petitioned the government against the Maravars. They referenced the Maravars' apparent proclivity towards violence in their petition, prompting the Raj to include a community that had traditionally been feted for its martial prowess in the Criminal Tribes Act, 1871, instead. Segments of European society resisted the move on the basis that the colonial government was representing 'aggressive low caste Christians as martyrs to Hindu bigotry'.[36] Similarly, when excise officials passed an order prohibiting toddy tapping without permits in the Nilgiris in 1876, the Kurumba Adivasis petitioned against it stating that 'their gods were very displeased at no longer receiving offerings of strong drink … and were in consequence bringing down all manner of misfortunes'.[37] Public dissatisfaction was so strong that it prompted the Bill's withdrawal that very year. Policymaking met its limits when it ran into complaints of interference with local customs and traditions, which the government took very seriously after 1857.

Indeed, official accounts of country liquor frequently referenced the notion that toddy and arrack consumption had ancient roots and routes of circulation. An administrative report described toddy as an 'absolute necessity of life' and any attempt by the state to intervene in its production as 'an innovation on ancient custom'.[38] Another report noted that 'there has always been much drunkenness in India in connection with religious observances' and that 'the lower castes had, from time immemorial, been addicted to drink'.[39] In his address to the British parliament in 1895, the then prime minister, William Gladstone, rationalised the state's emerging alcohol policy in India thus:

> Our Revenue from Excise is derived from two principal sources: toddy and arrack. Toddy, the milder and comparatively innocent drink, is the immemorial beverage of the agricultural classes, while Arrack, which is far stronger and more harmful, is chiefly consumed by the industrial laborer … Our increased revenue from toddy is almost wholly the result of improved management, while that from arrack is due to both improved management and increased consumption.[40]

Drinking in India was thus made synonymous with country liquor, just as country liquor was yoked to Indian cultures, traditions and customs. These associations served two purposes for the state. First, they reinforced the notion that the British were not responsible for introducing drinking to the subcontinent. Emphasising that country liquor was steeped in Indian traditions, customs and culture allowed the authorities to attribute intemperance entirely to Indians. Second, subsequent state intervention in regulating drinking – governmentality – could be legitimised as proceeding from an informed understanding of local ways of life. The state thus attempted to counter the critique that its sins of omission and commission had been responsible for the growing problem of intemperance in the subcontinent.

Perhaps unsurprisingly, it was Christian missionary organisations that launched this critique, that too with great gusto. The English were the first rulers, accused a missionary account, to make alcohol an article of government revenue.[41] Likewise, the Baptist Missionary Society set out that 'not only the low caste people but people of all castes and creeds' had taken to drinking. They attributed the situation to the 'extra facilities' to obtain liquor that the government had provided 'for revenue purposes'.[42] Alongside the insistence that drinking had always existed in Indian society, British parliamentary debates on intemperance in the empire routinely referenced the missionaries' concerns. The view that colonial alcohol policy – or, rather, the lack of a coherent policy – had been responsible for intemperance thus started to circulate in the metropole and colonies alike. From the mid-nineteenth century onwards, these developments came to have a significant bearing on official thinking. Alcohol policy, which had up until then been largely focused on revenue maximisation, now had to incorporate regulatory measures more substantially owing to growing pressure for good governance. Consequently, governmentality proceeded apace under the familiar organising principle of reform, now cloaked in a new garb of modernity.

State centralisation brought forth a new system to manage arrack production with the introduction of the contract distillery system in the 1870s. Unlike the previous system, which left the manufacturing process, choice of still and the use of ingredients entirely to the discretion of the highest bidder, the contract distillery system limited licit arrack production to large distilleries. Quality was regulated because only leftover molasses from sugar factories and jaggery derived from palmyra and date toddy could now be used to manufacture arrack. Licensed vendors were authorised to sell the arrack from the distilleries to shopkeepers at stipulated strengths and prices that were determined between standardised maximum and minimum levels. Owing to this intervention, the right to manufacture alcohol and the right to vend alcohol were effectively separated. Just as the modern state was rationalised through modern apparatuses, frameworks and processes, the Raj claimed that 'modern scientific distilleries' enabled it to provide 'liquor of good quality' to even 'remote localities at reasonable prices'.[43]

Moreover, a further administrative separation occurred in 1875, this time between toddy and arrack. Motivated by concerns that the previous system was concentrating too much power in the hands of successful bidders who could monopolise both toddy and arrack production, toddy farming was separated from the right to sell arrack. By this point, there were four classes of toddy shops, each supplied by a fixed number of coconut trees. The contractors of the most superior classes of toddy shops paid the highest rents to the government. An additional tree-tax system was introduced within the toddy farming system so that each tree that was used in the production process was taxed according to its expected output. An account set out the unprecedented level of bureaucratic intervention that this measure brought about thus:

> Every morning and evening, when the Sanar goes to draw the toddy, a servant or someone connected to the owner or contractor for the trees usually accompanies him with a chatty (small pot), into which is emptied the toddy from the property (larger collection pot). When all the trees have been visited and the toddy measured, it is carried away to the bazaar rented by the contractor from the Government at a fixed price.[44]

The state resisted pressure from missionaries and Indian elites alike to raise the price of country liquor, claiming that such a move would induce people to turn to more harmful sources of intoxication like opium, hemp and denatured spirits. Instead, it gradually increased the duty payable on toddy and arrack and reduced the number of both licences and shops where they could be sold.

The reforms of the 1870s directly influenced the reforms of the next decade, which in turn set the tone and overall direction of colonial alcohol policy until prohibition's introduction in 1937. The colonial government passed the Bombay Abkari (Excise) Act in 1878, thus effectively formalising its monopoly over the right to manufacture and sell intoxicating liquors. The Act sought to 'regulate consumption' and 'secure a good quality of liquor', although both aims were still subordinated to the chief aim of revenue maximisation.[45] Policy outcomes soon made this apparent. By the mid-1880s, the market was flooded with low-quality adulterated drinks as sellers tried to maximise profit to cope with skyrocketing liquor duties and toddy rentals. Record profits were realised alongside record rates of drunkenness. The backlash that followed was fierce and unyielding. The fallout from the Act was an important factor that induced the Bhandaris to turn away from toddy tapping in western India. An abstinence movement swept across the Bombay Presidency in 1886 as drinkers boycotted country liquor, accusing the newly launched *abkari* system of 'sucking the blood of the people'.[46] The Raj responded decisively and forcefully. It harassed strikers and jailed the most radical dissidents. Only in the 1890s did the anti-liquor strikes finally subside as prices stabilised somewhat.

The Madras Abkari Act of 1886 was introduced in this context. It followed in the provincial government's decision in 1884 to centralise the administration of alcohol production and trade with the approval of the Government of India and the Secretary of State. Like the Bombay Abkari Act, it attempted to rationalise alcohol policy in order to achieve the twin goals of temperance reform and revenue maximisation. The state thus introduced a system of taxation that brought the country's liquor industry under a greater degree of control and intervention, ostensibly to 'restrict the strength of the country spirit so as to prevent its competing unduly with (liquor) on which the full rate of import duty (had) been paid'.[47] The reforms introduced a fixed duty on every tree that was tapped, corresponding to fixed duties payable on every gallon of spirit issued from the distilleries, a law previously applied only to arrack manufacturers.

As with the manufacture and distribution of country liquor, retailers of imported foreign liquor had to pay a fixed duty and licence fees that were either fixed or variable, depending on the type of licence they held. However, the duties they paid were not credited to provincial treasuries, as with country liquor, but to the Government of India's customs account. Any policy measure affecting the importation and distribution of imported liquor would warrant the central government's attention and involvement thereafter. The Act brought Madras city and the adjoining countryside, which had previously been administered under separate systems, under uniform alcohol excise laws. Its subsequent extension to the entire province was justified on the grounds that it had been implemented in Bombay and would therefore succeed in 'securing proper control and repressing drunkenness' in Madras.[48]

As with the Bombay Abkari Act, the Madras Abkari Act immediately brought forth a wave of protest from toddy tappers and contractors, who bore the brunt of the burden it imposed. Following the Act's introduction, an association of toddy tappers in Madras town appealed against the new laws. They sought to cancel the order directing toddy drawers to take out a separate licence. The deputy commissioner of salt and *abkari* revenue surmised that this last request arose in response to the additional burden on tappers already being subjected to municipal taxes.[49] As it turned out, however, the state ultimately rejected the appeal because the tappers did not have any valid grounds of complaint. By 1893, government officials themselves were remarking that the Act had wrought significant hardship on poorer classes of drinkers. In districts like Malabar, excise officials raised the concern that toddy taxation must be moderate or the labouring classes would be 'deprived of their food'.[50] The 'stringent measures adopted in recent years for concentrating the distillation of liquor in a few central places and for limiting sales to licensed places,' they pointed out, had 'increased the price of liquor and reduced the consumption so much that the complaint is now made that the poorer classes suffer hardship in being deprived of toddy.'[51] The cyclical, self-fulfilling logic that sustained alcohol policy thus continued being put to the service of the Raj.

Colonial Alcohol Policy the Basis for Prohibition

On 28 October 1921, the Madras Young Women's Christian Association and the Madras Temperance Federation sent representatives to welcome a special guest who had just arrived at Central Station. The guest in question was 'Pussyfoot' Johnson, the enigmatic American reformer who had acquired a sterling international reputation for his temperance work. Coming on the heel of prohibition's introduction in America, Johnson's visit to Madras city inspired a slew of presentations by Indian temperance societies. The Good Templars of Madras attended his public lectures with their temperance manifesto. The Madras Temperance League was enthusiastic that the American example would spur India's anti-alcohol movement on to even greater heights. The Total Abstainers' Fraternity described Johnson's visit as 'providential encouragement'.[52] Gilbert Slater, however, did not share their enthusiasm for 'the weird figure'. Indians and Americans, he would later complain, shared 'a pathetic faith in the virtue of passing laws against supposed moral delinquencies'.[53]

Indeed, legislating against supposed moral delinquencies would prove challenging in a context wherein all kinds of alcohol could be obtained with ease, limited only by one's imagination and purse strings. Colonial policy, with its underlying assumptions and prejudices, had resulted in a drinking landscape that was cleaved along caste, class and gender lines. Each alcohol industry had its own client base, modus operandi, and pricing and taxation strategies, as distinct from one another as day from night. As it took shape over the staggered period of British imperialism in India, colonial alcohol policy developed as one that was highly discriminatory. It differentiated between the country liquor and foreign liquor industries on the one hand and between country liquor varieties on the other. Owing to the association that had gradually developed between country liquor and untouchability, policy measures sought to distance toddy and arrack from European society. This had the effect of giving rise to new drinking subcultures that warranted further state intervention along the lines of reasoning that had produced them in the first place.

The country liquor industry was closely associated with the underclasses of society across southern India. Consumed by labourers, cultivators, bricklayers, coolies, coachmen, cart drivers, cooks, butlers, Chetikara (poorer classes of Eurasians) and fishermen, toddy lubricated almost every aspect of subaltern life. As it was deliberately priced to ensure that it remained affordable to the Indian working classes, toddy often proved to be the only alcohol that this demographic could afford. By the beginning of the twentieth century, the most popular variety of toddy consumed in the Presidency of Fort St George was coconut toddy. Though illegal, peasants often received 'toddy money' in lieu of, or in addition to, their wages. One study noted that working-class men often likened their drinking to the preference among Brahmins to indulge in oil baths on Saturdays.[54]

Besides being consumed directly as alcohol, toddy – as an agent of fermentation – was also an important ingredient in pickled vegetables and leavened bread. Women from toddy-tapping caste communities were frequently involved in these activities. Indeed, toddy frequently figured not just as alcohol but also as food among the Indian underclasses. It was a common cultural practice among the working classes in the Tamil and Telugu districts to mix it with rice to make a meal, while labouring communities in Malabar consumed it for breakfast. Moreover, society valued palm toddy for its medicinal utility, particularly in treating gonorrhoea.[55] Toddy consumption peaked in hot weather and plummeted during cholera outbreaks, while the reverse was true for arrack.

Great regional variation also characterised country liquor production in the province. Toddy was derived from date palms in the northern districts, from the coconut and palmyra varieties in the southern districts, and from the coconut palm on the western coast, just as there were variations in how various communities went about the work of toddy production. As A. R. Venkatachalapathy has shown, toddy was served in earthen pitchers, which were kept separate for patrons belonging to different caste communities, although a degree of reallocation also took place as circumstances warranted.[56] Arrack shops did away with this pretence altogether. Instead, they used porcelain and glass cups to serve their customers, which was made possible because arrack shops came under a greater degree of governmental scrutiny and regulatory measures before toddy shops did. The length of time that the average customer spent over his drink also differed between toddy and arrack shops. According to an excise report, toddy drinkers lingered for several hours to chat and socialise. Arrack drinkers, on the other hand, preferred to down around one and a half drams of liquor, often with mutton chops on the side, before leaving the premises quickly.[57] Toddy, with its lower alcoholic content, gave rise to binge drinking and supported expressions of conviviality, becoming a social leveller in the process. In contrast, arrack – with its vastly greater concentration of alcohol per dram – was difficult to stomach in larger quantities. It also carried negative connotations of alcoholism, with the effect that drinkers preferred to be more discreet about their fondness for the strong spirit.

While most districts demonstrated a marked fondness for toddy, a few showed rising rates of arrack consumption. In North Arcot, for instance, arrack consumption was more common. In fact, it was such an integral aspect of Telugu Balija Naidu culture that it inspired its own saying: 'If a man is born a Balija, he must crack open an arrack bottle.'[58] In contrast, drinking across all communities was markedly lower in South Arcot. In yet other districts, the experience of colonialism fostered entirely new drinking cultures. In the Nilgiris, toddy had not been as popular as elsewhere in the province even before the onset of colonialism.[59] Due to climatic and soil conditions, coconut and palm trees were sparsely distributed in the highlands. Moreover, the few toddy shops on the highland plains were gradually displaced as English-style taverns sprang up to absorb the surplus beer being manufactured by the newly launched breweries. The local Badaga community's preference for fresh milk and toddy before colonialism subsequently shifted to a taste for beer and arrack, owing to the proliferation of licensed shops in the district.[60]

With growing affluence and better connectivity between the metropole and the colony, various fine malts and imported wines entered the subcontinent in the twentieth century. Advertised in English newspapers and periodicals, beer, ale and porter entered the subcontinent from Europe. Due to surging demand, unrestricted trade and well-oiled collection and storage machinery, foreign liquor imports increased from 687,766 gallons to 801,088 gallons in the five years between 1899 and 1904.[61] Merchants kept large stocks of brandy, gin, vermouth, beer, whiskey and champagne for sale in the province's cities and towns. Imported foreign liquor catered to all segments of European society from sailors and soldiers up through the highest echelons of colonial government. Besides alcohol imported from Britain, France, Germany and Spain, large quantities of wine and spirits also arrived in Madras from the ports of the Straits Settlements, Batavia and Ceylon.[62] Crate loads of liquor shipped from Portuguese Goa and the French possessions of Mahé and Pondicherry augmented them. Several disputes arose between the British and French colonial authorities over alcohol revenues owing to smuggled liquor entering the province from Mahé between the late nineteenth and early twentieth centuries. When the British tried to tax wine imported into Pondicherry and Karical through Madras, the French protested on the grounds that wine, being their national beverage, should be allowed free entry.[63] Eventually, Pondicherry's wines and spirituous liquors were granted duty-free status in the Presidency of Fort St George to improve relations with French colonial authorities.

The rapid growth of club life between the late nineteenth and mid-twentieth centuries opened up a space of elite sociability, lubricated by the finest wines and whiskeys. Some of the most influential clubs included the Adyar Club, the Malabar European Club and the Mylapore Club. Historian S. Muthiah presents us with the fascinating vignette that the Madras Cricket Club prioritised alcohol expenditure over even its food budget for the first hundred years of its history.[64] Imbibing the choicest of liquors was a hallmark of sophistication in the Indian Civil Service, so much so that there were real dangers of overdoing it. Paul Jayaraman, a civil servant in Malabar, wrote in his memoirs that a senior British officer had warned him about alcoholism soon after his appointment. Several marriages had crumbled under the weight of 'unrestrained' drinking, not to mention the massive drink-related debts that British officers were known to accumulate.[65]

The demand for imported foreign liquor was especially pronounced in the province's cities and towns, which presented lucrative opportunities for enterprising individuals. Several Indian businessmen, one of whom was Trichinopoly's G. Chinniah Pillay, made their fortunes in the imported foreign liquor business. Pillay ruled over a vast and sprawling liquor empire that spanned eight districts of the province and comprised mainly beer and wine. His turnover was so great that he could afford to pay an annual rent of 240,000 rupees, a fortune in those days.[66] Operating out of Madras city, another merchant, P. Rungiah Chetty, acquired a reputation for being one of the finest 'direct importers of wine and spirits from the best distilleries and vineyards in Europe'.[67] Beyond catering to the tastes of Indian and British officials in the province's cities, imported foreign liquor also found its way into the villages, aided by the opening up of the Indian railways. By 1909, the landowning elites of a village in Salem district had set up their own club to bring in imported foreign liquor from Madras, taking advantage of a newly opened railway line to do so.[68]

Medicated or tonic wines acquired a degree of social acceptance that even the finest of spirits could not rival in the first few decades of the twentieth century. This particular class of alcohol was prized for its purported medicinal properties in the homes of upper-class Indians and Europeans. The issue of how medicated wines should be treated for licensing purposes had first sparked controversy in Britain where it had prompted legislative intervention that such wines would have to contain quinine in the proportion of one grain to the fluid ounce before sellers could reasonably claim exemption from licensing laws.[69] While the beef wines that graced British tables and medicine cabinets failed to find a foothold in Indian society, the likes of Wincarnis, Hall's Wine and Drakshasava certainly did. An Ayurvedic concoction with low alcoholic content, the last of these was seen as a health elixir. Unlike Wincarnis and Hall's Wine, preparations like Drakshasava could lay claim to a degree of cultural authenticity, thus causing a great deal of anxiety for advocates of temperance reform and the nationalist leadership alike.

Besides imported liquor, several breweries were established in the province to meet the demand for the relatively more affordable, locally manufactured foreign liquor. The British Brewing Corporation, founded in 1902, catered to elite segments of society in Madras city. The army readily absorbed the brews produced by the Bangalore Brewery Company. The company, which opened its doors to business in 1889, supplied beer to camps spread across the province as far north as Bellary. The Nilgiri highlands housed several breweries, each catering to a specific consumer profile, in keeping with colonial alcohol policy. Situated between Coonoor and Ootacamund, the Rose and Crown Brewery Company made a distinction between English beers, manufactured from the finest Kent and Bohemian hops, and native beers, brewed from cane sugar or jaggery. Castle Brewery catered exclusively to the European planter community that was spread out over the Nilgiri hills.[70] The Nilgiri Brewery manufactured 'native' beers for local taverns. In the highlands, the tavern replaced the toddy shop that was so ubiquitous elsewhere in the province.

The production of native hill beers triggered health concerns on the grounds that the manufacturing process used insufficient barley malt and hops. This concern was so severe that it prompted the closure of Llangollen Brewery. The admixture of beer and spirits in taverns was a related malpractice that was held responsible for inciting drunk and disorderly behaviour amongst the Badagas in the Nilgiri Hills. Excise officials promptly intervened with revised manufacturing instructions and reassured the public that minimum nutritional standards would be maintained. This was accompanied by the decision to import malt from the Punjab's Rewari region to manufacture higher grades of beer – that is, English beers – while locally grown barley continued to produce beer that was supplied to the taverns.[71] Elsewhere in the Rampa hills of present-day Andhra Pradesh, the colonial policy of restricting the Adivasis' access to toddy, whilst leasing out tapping rights to contractors, played a major role in fomenting local discontent that eventually culminated in the tribal Rampa Rebellion of 1922 against the British.[72]

Country liquor consumption had reached such high levels in the Presidency of Fort St George by 1915, particularly in Madras, Salem and Malabar, that a committee was appointed to investigate the situation. It found that, notwithstanding the numerous temperance efforts that had brought about toddy and arrack shop closures and relocations, arrack consumption had more than doubled between 1900 and 1916. Where previously, pricing measures had been held responsible for a similar change in drinking cultures, the committee connected this 'abnormal rise' to the dynamic of conspicuous consumption. In colonial understandings – or, more accurately, misunderstandings – toddy's popularity as the working-class alcohol of choice had prompted middle-class drinkers to switch to arrack.[73] Misunderstandings, because the change in consumer preferences equally owed to the economic and ecological changes sweeping the province, their effects most visible in certain districts. The surge in international demand for Malabar coconuts in the 1920s translated into a situation wherein toddy production quickly reached surplus levels. The preference for arrack that was observed earlier supported a distinct new drinking culture as the arrack industry absorbed the excess toddy. Dilip Menon argued that the emergence of the arrack shop as a social institution marked the transition to more 'modern' drinking cultures as the hitherto vital link between drinking and specific periods of traditional celebration was subsequently broken.[74] Regular public drinking, especially of arrack, thus became commonplace in Malabar.

Alongside the upper-caste contempt for country liquor as the signifier of inferior social status, imbibing foreign liquor acquired a degree of social acceptance owing to its association with Europeans and upper-class Indian society. With its 'Bacchanalia in brahmin homes', Madras city evidenced the highest incidence of foreign liquor consumption among the upper crust of Indian society.[75] Indeed, the domestic consumption of foreign liquor emerged as a new drinking subculture among the upper castes, who often outwardly professed to be teetotallers. Missionaries in Madurai remarked that the Brahmins were 'to a large extent, consumers of liquor', although they drank secretly.[76] A leading newspaper in Karnataka suggested that 'liquor should be sold undiluted' so that 'Brahmins who have hitherto been holding aloof from liquor shops, might enjoy the pleasure of drinking as well'.[77] Like Tanjore's Pattunulkarar community, several castes that publicly denounced drinking continued to imbibe on the sly.

The British governor of the Madras Presidency between 1934 and 1940, Lord John Erskine, mused that the upper-caste Hindu aversion to alcohol was 'somewhat surprising' in view of the 'bacchanalian conduct' of most of their Hindu gods.[78] The tension that the governor observed between Brahmanical and non-Brahminical cultures is evident in Hindu lore and actual practice. The Tiyyas worshipped the Hindu god of destruction, Siva, as their clan deity. The reason for this was their belief that the deity had accepted an offering of toddy from one among their kin.[79] Bearing out the scholarly observation that 'blood, fertility, alcohol and action are all hallmarks of the goddess', Mariamman temples in early twentieth-century Tanjore propitiated the goddess with toddy first thing in the morning.[80] Ironically, some Shanars in Tinnevelly offered hard liquor to a British officer they believed had become a demon upon his death.[81] Ramnad's Saiva Maravars propitiated the folk guardian deities, Karapanasamy, Bhadrakaly and Maduraiveeran, with liquor, meat and fruit, all of which the devotees consumed with great relish after the ceremony. These intersections between alcohol and local cultures would influence legislator Rao Bahadur M. Raman to later state his opposition to the Madras Prohibition Act. Toddy, he argued, could not be banned as it was 'an object of good omen' for the Hindus.[82]

* * *

This chapter has shown that local drinking cultures, as well as official imperatives and discourses, informed the Madras Abkari Act, the forerunner of the Madras Prohibition Act. The East India Company had had to manage the problems and opportunities presented by country liquor in a context wherein European demand for alcoholic drinks could not be easily or adequately met. This situation had informed a proto-alcohol policy of sorts that sought to insulate and distance the country liquor industry – with its lowly caste profile – from 'respectable' society.

Premised upon pre-existing ways of knowing Indian society and the frameworks they had nurtured, the Abkari Act wrought all sorts of regulations. Alcoholic proof strengths, the quantities and types of liquor that could be bought and sold, the places in which this could be done and definitions of problematic drinking all came under the purview of state scrutiny and legislation. Far from decreasing, however, rates of alcohol consumption actually increased, as did the varieties of alcohol that drinkers could obtain. As with the Company's approach, the policy stance of the Raj fostered drinking cultures and subcultures that were cleaved along class, caste and gender lines.

The colonial government's revenue-oriented policy stance prompted protest from missionary groups and the British public for regulatory checks and balances in the governance of alcohol. Responding to the pressure under broader circumstances that greatly affected the extent to which it could flex its muscles, it formulated an alcohol policy that alternated between different forms of power.

Owing to the sheer diversity of the voices that influenced its development, colonial alcohol policy was motivated by contrarian aims. It thus routinely fell short of providing good governance as it claimed to do. However, it did produce circumstances that enabled and justified subsequent exercises of governmentality. This situation would provide the basis for the emergence of a nationalist alcohol policy that promised to do better and that claimed to know how to go about it.

The stage was thus set for another round of prohibitioning.

Notes

1. Henry Davison Love, *Indian Records Series: Vestiges of Old Madras 1640–1800, Traced from the East India Company's Records Preserved at Fort St. George and the India Office and from Other Sources*, vol. 2 (London: John Murray, Albemarle Street, 1913), p. 22, https://archive.org/details/vestigesofoldmad00loveuoft/page/n5/mode/2up (accessed on 12 February 2023).

2. James Forbes, *Oriental Memoirs: A Narrative of Seventeen Years Residence in India* pt 68, vol. 1 (London: Richard Bentley, 1834), p. 24. Two other works that referenced Forbes's account of toddy include Ralph Barnes Grindrod, *Bacchus: An Essay on the Nature, Causes, Effects, and Cure of Intemperance* (London: J & H.G. Langley, 1840), p. 193; and *The Biblical Repertory and Princeton Review*, vol. 13 (London: Peabody, 1841), p. 484.

3. Gilbert Slater, *Southern India, Its Political and Economic Problems* (London: G. Allen & Unwin, 1936), p. 182. See also John Statham, *Indian Recollections* (London: Samuel Bagster, 1832), p. 29; William Tennant, *Indian Recreations: Consisting Chiefly of Strictures on the Domestic and Rural Economy of the Mahomedans and Hindoos*, vol. 2 (London: C. Stewart, 1804), p. 283; and Thomas Pennant, *View of Hindoostan*, vol. 1 (London: 1798), p. 139, for similar descriptions.

4. Julia Charlotte Maitland, *Letters from Madras, during the Years 1836–1839* (London: Jon Murray, 1861), p. 74. Maitland was married to a British civil servant.

5. W. N. Chipperfield, *The Madras Quarterly Journal*, vol. 9 (Madras: Adelphi Press; London: Robert Hardwicke, 1866), p. 348.

6. Chris Nierstrasz, 'In the Shadow of the Company: The Dutch East India Company and Its Servants in the Period of Its Decline (1740–1796)', in *TANAP Monographs on the History of Asian-European Interaction*, ed. Leonard Blussé, pp. 102–111 (Leiden: Brill, 2012).

7. Captain William Symson, *A New Voyage to the East Indies* (London: H. Meere, for A. Bettesworth, and E. Curll, 1715), p. 34. Although the account in question was in fact a pastiche of passages lifted from other contemporaneous writings, the book's reference to arrack shows that interest in Asian liquor varieties had gained traction in the West by 1715.

8. Josiah Conder, *The Modern Traveller*, vol. 3: *India* (London: James Duncan, 1830), p. 54. I also referred to the seventeenth-century account furnished by the Italian traveller Pietro Della Valle that toddy was 'not unpleasing to

the palate'. See *Travels of Pietro Della Valle in India: From the Old English, Translation of 1664*, originally published in 1892, reprint digital edition (Cambridge: Cambridge University Press, 2010), p. 62. An important exception is the account provided by Dr Scudder, the American missionary posted in Ceylon, who questioned Forbes's account of toddy when he wrote: 'I do not recollect that I ever was in so vile a place, so far as drunkenness was concerned and among so many drunkards … the principal cause of drunkenness among them is toddy.' See also 'Value and Uses of the Palmyra Tree', *Missionary Herald* (1839), pp. 24–25.

9. Peter Burne, *The Concordance of Scripture and Science Illustrated, with Reference to the Temperance Cause, with a Prefatory Letter by Dr Lees, on the Philosophy and Philology of the Question* (London: Arthur Hall & Company, 1847), p. 19.

10. Letter of Fr. Bouchet in LEC, Tome XIII, MDLCLXXXI, pp. 45, 50, and 87, quoted in S. Jeyaseela Stephen, *Caste, Catholic Christianity and the Language of Conversion* (Delhi: Kalpaz Publications, 2008), p. 75.

11. John Fryer, *A New Account of East-India and Persia: In 8 Letters Being 9 Years Travels, Begun 1672 and Finished 1681* (London: n.p., 1698), p. 53.

12. Rev. William Arthur, *A Mission to the Mysore: With Scenes and Facts Illustrative of India, Its People, and Its Religion* (London, 1847), p. 415.

13. *The Chingleput, Late Madras, District: A Manual Compiled Under the Orders of the Madras Government* (Madras: Government Press, 1879), p. 310.

14. *Wesleyan Methodist Magazine* (London: 1871), p. 47.

15. David H. Kling, *A History of Christian Conversion* (Oxford: Oxford University Press, 2020), p. 554.

16. Edward Balfour, *The Cyclopædia of India and of Eastern and Southern Asia Commercial, Industrial and Scientific, Products of the Mineral, Vegetable, and Animal Kingdoms, Useful Arts and Manufactures*, vol. 2 (London: Bernard Quaritch, 1885), pp. 23–24. See also Arthur Frederick Cox, *A Manual of the North Arcot District in the Presidency of Madras* (Madras: Government Press, 1881), p. 286.

17. *Times of India*, 17 May 1902.

18. Anthony D. King, *Colonial Urban Development: Culture, Social Power and Environment* (London: Routledge, 1976), p. 73.

19. Charles Allen, *Plain Tales from the Raj: Images of British India in the 20th Century* (London: Hachette, 2015), p. 71.

20. Erica Wald, *Vice in the Barracks: Medicine, the Military and the Making of Colonial India, 1780–1868* (Basingstoke: Palgrave Macmillan, 2014),

pp. 126–127, for a discussion of climatic considerations in colonial constructions of drunkenness. See also Harald Fischer-Tiné, 'The Drinking Habits of Our Countrymen: European Alcohol Consumption and Colonial Power in British India,' *Journal of Imperial and Commonwealth History* 40, no. 3 (2022), pp. 383–409.

21. Henry Marshall, *Contribution to a Natural and Economical History of the Coco-nut Tree* (London: 1832), pp. 19–20.

22. J. Talboys Wheeler, *Madras in the Olden Time: Being a History of the Presidency from the First Foundation to the Governorship of Thomas Pitt, Grandfather of the Earl of Chatham, 1639–1702* (Madras: Higginbotham, 1861), pp. 70–71.

23. *Alexander's East India and Colonial Magazine,* vol. 10, July–December 1835 (London: R. Alexander, 1835), p. 37.

24. William Benjamin Carpenter, *The Physiology of Temperance and Total Abstinence: Being an Examination of the Effects of the Excessive, Moderate and Occasional Use of Alcoholic Liquors on the Healthy Human System* (London: H.G. Bohn, 1858), p. 104.

25. *British and Foreign Medico-Chirurgical Review,* vol. 5 (London: 1850), p. 92.

26. Ibid.

27. David Scott, 'Colonial Governmentality', *Social Text* 43 (1995), pp. 191–220.

28. Kaviraj, 'On the Enchantment of the State', p. 284.

29. See for instance, Sabyasachi Bhattacharya, *The Financial Foundations of the British Raj: Ideas and Interests in the Reconstruction of Indian Public Finance 1858–1872* (New Delhi: Orient Balckswan, 2005). See also Sabyasachi Bhattacharya, 'Laissez Faire in India', *Indian Economic and Social History Review* 2, no. 1 (1965), pp. 1–22. Bhattacharya and others have presented the argument that colonial economic policy was primarily profit-driven, with little place for the provision of welfare.

30. Michel Foucault, 'Truth and Power', in *Power/Knowledge: Selected Interviews and Other Writings, 1972–1977,* ed. C. Gordon, pp. 109–133 (New York: Pantheon Books, 1980), especially pp. 112–113.

31. Nicholas B. Dirks, *Castes of Mind: Colonialism and the Making of Modern India* (Princeton: Princeton University Press, 2001), pp. 43–60.

32. Alexander William Crawford Lindsay, *Report on the Mysore General Census of 1871* (Mysore: Government of Mysore Press, 1874), p. 66.

33. *The Encyclopaedia Britannica: A Dictionary of Arts, Sciences, and General Literature*, vol. 15 (London: n.p., 1894), p. 186. See also Sir Cements Robert Markham, *Travels in Peru and India: While Superintending the Collection of Chinchona Plants and Seeds in South America, and Their Introduction into India* (London: J. Murray, 1862), p. 423.

34. Christopher Bayly, *Empire and Information: Intelligence Gathering and Social Communication in India, 1780–1870* (Cambridge: Cambridge University Press, 1996), pp. 170–172. See also Nivedita Menon, 'Thinking about the Postnation', *Economic and Political Weekly* (7–13 March 2009), pp. 70–77.

35. Hardgrave, *The Nadars of Tamilnad: The Political Culture of a Community in Change* (Berkeley and Los Angeles: California University Press, 1969), pp. 145–146.

36. *Asiatic Review* (London, 1896), pp. 427–428.

37. W. Francis, *Nilgiri District Gazetteer* (Madras: Government Press, 1908), pp. 286–287, TNA.

38. *Report on the Administration of the Madras Presidency* (London: Superintendent, Government Press, 1880), p. 20.

39. Italics mine. H. A. D. Phillips, *Our Administration of India: Being a Complete Account of the Revenue and Collectorate Administration in All Departments, with Special Reference to the Work and Duties of a District Officer in Bengal* (Bombay: Thacker; Madras: Higginbotham, 1886), pp. 107–108.

40. Gladstone's speech quoted in *Asiatic Review* (London, 1895), pp. 23–24.

41. *Report of the Second Decennial Missionary Conference Held at Calcutta, 1882–83, with a Missionary Map of India* (Calcutta: J.W. Thomas, Baptist Mission Press, 1883), p. 435. See also Geoffrey A. Oddie, *Social Protest in India: British Protestant Missionaries and Social Reforms, 1850–1900* (Delhi: Manohar, 1979), pp. 205–206. Besides the missionaries, some segments of the Indian Civil Service also expressed strong reservation about the government's excise policy. Sir William Wilson Hunter, a Scottish-born historian, for instance, wrote that the profit-driven system had contributed to an unchecked degree of alcoholism in society.

42. *The Missionary Herald of the Baptist Missionary Society* (London: Baptist Mission House, 1893), p. 393.

43. *The Administration of Bengal under Sir Andrew Fraser 1903–1908* (Calcutta: Legare Street Press, 1908), p. 118.

44. *Transactions of the Royal Botanical Society*, vol. 7 (London: Botanical Society of Edinburgh, 1863), p. 164.

45. William Wilson Hunter, *Bombay, 1885 to 1890: A Study in Indian Administration* (Bombay: Government Press, 1900), p. 379.

46. G. M. Sathe, *Native Newspaper Reports, Bombay* (Bombay: Government of Bombay, 1886), pp. 12–13. See also Mark Lawrence Schrad, *Smashing the Liquor Machine: A Global History of Prohibition* (Oxford: Oxford University Press, 2021), p. 204.

47. P. Ramanatha Iyer and P. Raghava Iyer, *The Civil Court Manual (Annotated), Madras* (Madras: Modern Printing Works, 1919), p. xi.

48. Abkari Act of 1886, quoted in P. Ramanatha Iyer and P. Raghava Iyer, *The Civil Court Manual, Madras* (Madras: Modern Printing Works, 1919), p. x.

49. G.O. No. 923, 923 A, Revenue Department, 22 September 1887, TNA.

50. S. Srinivasa Raghavaiyangar, *Memorandum on the Progress of the Madras Presidency during the Last Forty Years of British Administration* (Madras: Government Press, 1893), p. clxxiv. Raghavaiyangar thus cited the opinion of excise officials in his account of alcohol policy in the Madras Presidency.

51. Ibid.

52. Tarini Prasad Sinha, *'Pussyfoot' Johnson and His Campaign in Hindustan* (Madras: Ganesh & Co., 1922), p. 370.

53. Gilbert Slater, *Southern India, Its Political and Economic Problems* (London: G. Allen & Unwin, 1936), p. 336.

54. A. Moffat, *The Drink Traffic in the Madras Presidency* (Madras: G.A. Natesan & Co., 1909), pp. 11–12.

55. Abhilas Chandra Mukerjie, *A Report on Toddy Taxation* (Calcutta: Bengal Secretariat Press, 1895), p. 53.

56. A. R. Venkatachalapathy, *In Those Days There Was No Coffee: Writings in Cultural History* (New Delhi: Yoda Press, 2006), p. 68.

57. G.O. No. 606, Revenue Department (Mis.), 14 March 1932, TNA. A dram typically converts to about 3.7 millilitres.

58. *The Madras District Manuals, North Arcot*, vol. 2 (Madras: Government Press, 1894), p. 276, TNA. See also *South Arcot District Gazetteer* (Madras: Government Press, 1906), pp. 102–103, TNA, for a discussion of how this district differed in its treatment of country liquor.

59. Francis, *Nilgiri District Gazetteer*, pp. 286–287.

60. Edgar Thurston, *Badagas and Irulas of the Nilgiris: Paniyans of Malabar; a Chinese-Tamil Cross; a Cheruman Skull; Kuruba or Kurumba; Summary of Results (Madras Government Museum Bulletin)*, vol. 2, no. 2 (reprint edition) (New Delhi: Asian Educational Services, 2004). See also Paul Hockings,

'Ancient Hindu Refugees: Badaga Social History, 1550–1975', in *Studies in Anthropology*, vol. 6 (The Hague: Mouton Publishers, 1980), p. 46.

61. *Statistics from the Report of the Administration of the Abkari Revenue in the Madras Presidency*, 1899–1900 and 1903–1904, quoted in the *Indian Review* (March 1905), p. 170.

62. *Report on the Administration of the Madras Presidency, during the Year 1880–1881* (Madras: Government Press, 1881), p. 129. For an overview of the liquor types that were imported into the province, see, for instance, Harald Fischer-Tiné, 'Liquid Boundaries: Race, Class, and Alcohol in Colonial India,' in *A History of Alcohol and Drugs*, ed. Harald Fischer-Tiné and Jana Tschurenev, pp. 90–115 (London: Routledge, 2013), especially pp. 93–94.

63. Ibid.

64. S. Muthiah, *The Spirit of Chepauk: The MCC Story, a 150 Year Sporting Tradition* (Chennai: EastWest Books, 1998), p. 482.

65. Paul M. Jayaraman, *Facets of My Life under the British Raj* (Colombo: MD Gunasena & Co., 1936), p. 31, Jayaraman Papers, MSS Eur C509, India Office Records, London (IOR).

66. Arnold Wright, *Southern India: Its History, People, Commerce, and Industrial Resources* (reprint edition) (New Delhi: Asian Educational Services, 2004), p. 491.

67. Ibid.

68. Moffat, *The Drink Traffic in the Madras Presidency*, p. 3.

69. *British Medical Journal*, vol. 1 (London, 1889), p. 151.

70. W. Francis, *Madras District Gazetteer* (Madras: Government Press, 1923). According to Francis, the brewery was established in 1826.

71. Ibid.

72. Sumit Guha, *Environment and ethnicity in India, 1200–1991* (Cambridge: Cambridge University Press, 1999), pp. 209–210.

73. *The Hindu*, 22 June 1917.

74. Dilip Menon, 'From Pleasure to Taboo: Drinking and Society in Kerala', *India International Centre Quarterly* 22, nos. 2–3 (1995), pp. 143 –156.

75. John Matthai, *Excise and Liquor Control* (Madras: Authors Press and Publishing House, 1924), p. 43, IOR.

76. Letter from Burnell, 24 March 1859, Madura Mission, quoted in *Missionary Herald*, vol. 55 (1859), p. 228.

77. *Mysore Vrittanta*, 2 November 1889, Native Newspaper Reports (NNPR) (October–November 1889), p. 458.

78. Letter from Erskine, Governor of Madras, to HRH, 27 July 1938, pp. 2–3, Erskine Papers, files 5–7, MSS EUR D596, IOR.

79. Quoted in A. M. Abraham Ayrookuzhiel, *The Sacred in Popular Hinduism: An Empirical Study in Chirakkal, North Malabar* (Charlottesville: University of Virginia, 1983), p. 18.

80. See the Madras Prohibition Bill, Madras Legislative Council Proceedings, vol. 2, 1938, appendix 10, pp. 310–311, TNA. See also T. Richard Blurton, *Hindu Art* (Cambridge, MA: Harvard University Press, 1993), p. 157. Mariamman is an especially fearsome form of the goddess worshipped in Tamil Nadu. *Amman* comes from the Tamil *amma*, meaning mother.

81. Edgar Thurston, *Ethnographic Notes in Southern India* (Madras: Government Press, 1906), p. 297.

82. Madras Prohibition Bill, Madras Legislative Council Proceedings, vol. 2, 1938, appendix 10, pp. 310–311, TNA.

2

Congress Nationalism, Provincial Politics and Prohibitioning

Reforming Politics and Reform as Politics

The commissioner of excise asked his subordinates to gather information about the liquor Indians preferred most in the Presidency of Fort St George in 1905. He also wrote to laboratories to clarify whether toddy was indeed 'a completely innocuous liquor containing a large proportion of food material'.[1] Major Charles H. Bedford's report concluded that most of the toddy being consumed in the province was at an advanced fermentation stage. Samples sent for laboratory testing had revealed a high proportion of fusel oil – a known cause of indigestion, dysentery and rheumatism. With the hydrometer's use in testing the proof strength of alcoholic drinks in mid-eighteenth-century England, utilising technology to regulate alcohol had become an exercise in building public trust.[2] The hydrometer's subsequent use to test and establish the proof strengths of different country liquors in India was comparable but much more significant in its impact. It demonstrates the colonial state's determination to penetrate an indigenous industry in order to bring it into alignment with Western scientific technologies, processes and practices. Remarkably, the Congress leadership would similarly show interest in ascertaining toddy's nutritional properties. As the president of the Prohibition League of India (PLI), Rajaji wrote to the heads of the Tropical School of Medicine in Calcutta and the Pasteur Institute in Coonoor in 1931. He sought to verify that 'to drink beer in order to ensure efficient enzyme action in the body (was) as unnecessary as to drink toddy in order to ensure a sufficient supply of Vitamin B'.[3]

The colonial government and the nationalist leadership were similar in their attempts to make the country liquor industry amenable to governance through the language and technologies afforded by Western scientific modernity.[4] Armed with the information that the country liquor that Indians were drinking fell short of the minimum desired quality standards, the colonial state couched its intervention in the industry in a discourse of paternalism. Alcohol policy enabled the state to charge more for 'good' country liquor, whilst criminalising 'illicit' alcohol sales. By fixing proof strengths and the purity of the alcohol at scientifically backed levels, the state attempted to reconcile its revenue and reform objectives. Whereas the colonial state sought country liquor's nutritional profile to justify its continued provision, the nationalist leadership used this information to strengthen its prohibition demand. Alcohol policy thus informed a nationalist discourse that, 'even as it challenged the colonial claim to potential domination, also accepted the very intellectual premises of modernity on which colonial domination was based'.[5]

Alcohol policy was entwined with the workings of the state in the Presidency of Fort St George from the get-go. The colonial government progressively increased taxes in the province between the late nineteenth and mid-twentieth centuries, with the consequence that revenue from alcohol excise would account for almost a third of the total provincial revenue.[6] Between the Madras Abkari Act of 1886 and the Madras Prohibition Act's introduction in 1937, alcohol policy became a key site of key political competition and, hence, consensus-building. As it developed within the paradigm of political contestation between colonial and nationalist elites, it also bore the imprint of a growing coalescence between political rivals, owing to key shifts within the field of operation of colonial power. However, the dynamic between the colonial state and nationalist elites was not the only factor influencing the demand for prohibition as it took shape in this period. Instead, it emerged as a multifaceted site of consensus-building at the national and provincial levels. Between the late nineteenth and mid-twentieth centuries, interactions between several concurrent developments left their mark on prohibition's development as an idea, demand and, subsequently, as a policy. These included the role played by key political personalities and their ideologies, the opportunities and constraints wrought by structural changes at the all-India level, the responses they produced in the provinces and the international temperance movement.

One of the most crucial domestic developments that provided a push towards prohibition was neither as singular nor as readily recognisable as a policy measure. Instead, it was a series of intellectual shifts in Indian thinking about the state that came about as a consequence of policy changes. From the early nineteenth century onwards, Indian elites either rejected the European model of the state or sought to reform politics in the image of that state.[7] The latter school of thought, which eventually won out, was influenced by two major developments. First, sati's emergence as a site of social reform had provided a major platform for debates on state intervention in society to crystallise.[8] Consequently, the related questions of whether the state should intervene in society at all and what the limits of that intervention ought to be had become especially polarising. Second, political centralisation after 1857 had brought with it a growing awareness among Indian elites that the British Raj would need to accommodate their demands for liberal rules of governance. The reforms that had followed in the aftermath of Queen Victoria's Proclamation had given more Indians than ever before the opportunity to engage with the formal workings of the state.

The establishment of the Indian National Congress came in this context in 1885, months before the passing of the Madras Abkari Act. This watershed moment opened the door for further developments that paved the way for prohibition's emergence as a political programme of immense significance. With the founding of the Congress, the stage was set for the emergence of a powerful critique of the colonial state and the creation of a discursive space in which the rules for the subsequent exercise of state power in society could be rewritten. The nationalists would inherit, adapt and channel pre-existing ideations of the state through their politics.[9] The intellectual undercurrents and political developments they were responding to became the nucleus of prohibitioning throughout the early to mid-twentieth century.

The Congress took a keen interest in the colonial state's alcohol policy from its inception. European missionaries, as well as Indian religious and caste-based organisations, had spearheaded temperance initiatives previously, which had aligned well with the state's preference for relegating reform-related issues that did not serve its interests to the realm of 'the social'. The strategy enabled the state to ignore them or downplay their importance.[10] In marked contrast, the Congress's zero-tolerance stance provided a powerful impetus for the subsequent politicisation of temperance. Prohibition thus became entwined with an overarching contestation over the state in India, although 'the alcohol question' never entirely left the realm of 'the social' either, owing to its intersections with caste and gender. The ensuing tensions did two related things. First, they produced responses to prohibition by the Congress that, like the colonial state, alternated between liberal and more coercive forms of governmentality. Alternating between mobilising the domains of the social and the political – in a context wherein prohibition became integral to both – meant that the Congress necessarily needed to also alternate between different tactics of power. Second, the situation simultaneously necessitated and limited consensus-building, thus creating an unstoppable momentum towards prohibition.

The first moment of convergence between temperance and Congress politics occurred when the British prohibitionist and member of parliament William S. Caine attended the Allahabad session of the Congress in 1888. The Congress stalwart Bipin Chandra Pal was so energised by Caine's insistence on the urgency of a concerted global anti-alcohol response that he subsequently took up the cause of temperance with great enthusiasm in his speeches and writings. Caine initiated the Anglo-Indian Temperance Association (AITA) in London that same year. The organisation played a crucial role in exerting pressure on the British parliament to prioritise the regulation of drinking amongst Indians as part of its alcohol policy. The AITA's efforts ultimately produced a 'ponderous inquiry' into liquor consumption in 1889 and a study investigating cannabis use among Indians four years later.[11]

Subsequent Congress party conferences mooted several resolutions that aimed to curb the liquor traffic as part of its overarching efforts to eradicate vice in the subcontinent. The organisation pressed the colonial government to grant the right of local voters to determine the number and type of liquor shops that could be open in their neighbourhoods, pointing to the passing of Local Option Bills in Britain in 1860 and in Canada in 1878 as important precedents.[12] Although the Congress criticised the colonial state for its lack of action on opium and cannabis addiction as well, it was alcoholism that dominated the Congress's prohibition efforts as it became evident over the early twentieth century that drinking was to India what opium was to China.

Although the politicisation of temperance in colonial India features in the literature as a matter of British procrastination and Congress initiative, prohibition as a political idea and demand equally developed in response to provincial developments.[13] The nineteenth century had brought forth the steady growth of associational life in the Presidency of Fort St George. Local grievances caused by increased missionary activity and administrative centralisation had invigorated public life, prompting the formation of associations that had broached the necessity of state-directed alcohol reform even prior to the Congress's establishment. Following the Indian Councils Act of 1861, the Madras Legislative Council was established as an advisory body to address local grievances, foremost among them the lack of Indian political representation. The establishment of the Madras Maha Jana Sabha and the revival of the Madras Native Association in the late nineteenth century constituted the first real attempts at establishing the foundations of the rationalised state along Western lines in southern India.[14] Collectively, these developments had invigorated public life in the province, creating fertile ground for the subsequent politicisation of temperance.

During the Swadeshi movement in 1905, the Congress concentrated on undermining the economic dominance of the Raj, a task to which alcohol readily lent itself as key target. Indeed, foreign cloth and liquor emerged as the most iconic symbols of an avaricious colonial state, with the movement emphasising the importance of Indian self-help and *atmashakti* – self-reliance – in place of the corrupting false modernity that it charged colonialism as having brought to India. Nationalist discourse thus pivoted on a fundamental *ghar–bahir* dichotomy wherein India's cultural and spiritual superiority elevated it above the materially advanced West.[15] According to this discourse, the challenge was acquiring the essence of Western modernity – including the workings of the modern state – while retaining the innate cultural–moral superiority that distinguished India. As a taxable commodity that sustained the colonial economy, alcohol represented an exploitative foreign state's onslaught on the Indian body politic in this discourse. The nationalists denounced all kinds of alcoholic drinking as un-Indian and anti-national; the ensuing agitation caused profits from the imported liquor industry especially to plummet in Bombay and Assam.[16] Even as alcohol thus became synonymous with British cultural imperialism and economic exploitation, prohibition aligned perfectly with the logic of *swadeshi* as an expression of opposition to both.

The concurrent introduction of landmark temperance legislation provided the momentum for the emergence of a spirited debate on alcohol policy. The colonial government had followed the deeply unpopular Abkari Act of 1886 with reforms that had tried to fuse public awareness about temperance with health promotion under sustained pressure for action from the Congress. With the Morley–Minto Reforms of 1909, the organisation had become better represented in the Indian legislative council. This enabled it to raise demands for increased imperial spending on health and sanitation, areas of government policy that it was following with a great deal of interest in this period. In 1910, Gopal Krishna Gokhale demanded that provincial governments should be allocated more funds for spending on sanitation. The sanitary commissioner in the Madras Presidency concurred with his views that spending on sanitation was grossly inadequate.[17] Owing to the appalling sanitary conditions that presented in toddy and arrack shops, this became a matter of concern for alcohol policy too. Although the immediate response from colonial officials was that nothing further could be done about provincial expenditure on health and sanitation, pressure from the Congress translated into new exercises of colonial governmentality in the following years. In 1915, the Madras government sanctioned a bill that approved temperance education in schools and published instructional teaching materials designed to bring it into alignment with academic subjects like moral education, hygiene and general knowledge, although 'no further reference to the subject appear[ed] in later reports'.[18] Short-lived as they were, such initiatives helped to ensure that the state-directed regulation of drinking remained on the agenda as a matter of political dialogue.

Prohibitioning was filtered through the Congress's growing interest in evolving a more inclusive and accessible public health policy following the First World War. The organisation sought greater government spending on the promotion of temperance in the provinces, along with passing resolutions that supported the promotion of indigenous systems of medicine and critiquing the colonial government's compulsory vaccination schemes.[19] In the southern province, the Abkari Act inspired debate all through the Home Rule movement, thus bolstering the demand for prohibition.

Stories of Indian soldiers drinking to cope with the grim realities of the battlefield found their way into the subcontinent during and after the First World War, which dovetailed with the nationalists' criticism of the colonial state's lack of ethical responsibility in its alcohol policy.[20] Country liquor evidenced the most marked reduction in rates of consumption in this period. In contrast, the consumption of beer and imported foreign liquors amongst a segment of Indian society, ranging from soldiers to members of the Indian Civil Service, did not show any sign of decrease between 1916 and 1918.[21] For its part, the colonial government doubled down on proving its commitment to its alcohol policy. Between 1918 and 1919, the rental prices of beer shops increased by a staggering 45 per cent from the previous year in Madras city, prompting the closure of 23 shops 'to prevent competition' with toddy.[22]

The ideological convergence between the Theosophical and Home Rule movements, due to the political personalities who led both, informed the patently elitist bent of the prohibition demand as it developed in this context. Annie Besant warned that alcoholic drinks ought to be shunned owing to an apparent risk of spiritual contamination between those who produced liquor and those who consumed it, as 'persons concerned in the making of these drinks [were] not the most thoughtful, refined or cultured of human beings'.[23] Yet Besant made an exception for French wines, which were presumably not as harmful as their country liquor counterparts.

Even though the figures show that it was the consumption of imported alcohol that was on the rise in this period, both the colonial state's alcohol policy and the nationalists' prohibition demand foremost discriminated against country liquor. The situation became so dire that it prompted the *Swadeshabimani* Malayalam newspaper to comment that 'as the indigenous industry of manufacturing country liquors [had] too many restrictions put upon it, the industry will be extinct and the people who lived by [it] will have to wander about without any means of livelihood'.[24] The president of the Madras Temperance League echoed this criticism when he pointed out that discriminating only against country liquor would earn the resentment of the working classes, who were frequently both its consumers and producers.[25]

The South Indian Liberation Front, otherwise known as the Justice Party, was established in the Madras Presidency in 1916 amidst these developments. Like the Congress, the Justice Party too had expressed support for prohibition, at least initially. The similarities did not end there. Party leaders like E. V. Ramasamy 'Periyar' and A. P. Patro, the latter responsible for the excise portfolio, had in fact started their political careers with the Congress.[26] During his visit to Madurai two years after the Justice Party's establishment, Bipin Chandra Pal exhorted Congress workers to fight against the scourge of drinking. The very next year, Yakub Hassan summoned a meeting in Madras city to discuss prohibition's technical and theoretical aspects. Until this point in time, the Congress had been concerned with pushing for temperance initiatives without a concrete plan for prohibition. All of this would change in the 1920s. The stage was set for prohibition's emergence as part of an overarching nationalist critique of the colonial state's alcohol policy, which was exercised in and through the provinces.

Province, Nation and Prohibition as an Idea in the 1920s

Prohibitioning in the 1920s developed in response to two key developments. The first was the Government of India Act of 1919. The Act subjected excise administration to a greater degree of debate and deliberation by bringing the alcohol question closer to the grasp of provincial administration than it had ever been before. Second, and relatedly, the Act brought forth political responses in the Madras Presidency that catalysed the progress towards prohibition. Filtered through the ideological lens of key political personalities, these intersecting developments eventually shaped prohibition's emergence as a powerful idea and core agenda of the Congress's Constructive Programme at the all-India level.

Based on the recommendations of a report by Edwin Montagu, the then secretary of state for India, and Lord Chelmsford, India's viceroy at that time, the Act of 1919 effectively provincialised excise administration. 'A means of enlisting Indians to work for imperial ends' from the British point of view, it sought to stave off the nationalist demand for home rule by providing Indians with a degree of 'responsible government'.[27] More significantly, it introduced a system of dyarchy. The exercise of state power in the provinces was thus divided between the most strategically significant departments, now known as 'reserved' subjects under the control of executive councillors, and 'transferred' subjects, comprising the most under-funded portfolios like health, education and excise, which subsequently became the responsibility of elected minsters.[28] The elected ministers depended on the revenue portfolio, which was handled by the executive councillors, for funds to implement their envisioned programmes. This aspect of dyarchy necessitated consensus-building as the issue of government spending on temperance reform – or lack thereof – wrought lengthy debates on the state's responsibility and obligations. The avenue for these debates were the provincial legislatures which the reforms also introduced, along with a limited form of electoral representation. Dyarchy thus effectively sounded the AITA's death knell. Whereas the organisation had previously directly lobbied London, it was now rendered redundant as excise administration passed into the hands of provincial political actors.

At the same time, a distinct political ethic of prohibition took root in this period. Indeed, the Congress leadership's conceptualisation of prohibition cannot be discussed without reference to its ideological resonance, which influenced the more practical aspects of its implementation. As the key political personality whose personal experiments with 'truth' would shape several underlying principles, assumptions and strategies of Indian nationalism, M. K. Gandhi's views on the state and prohibition had far-reaching implications for both. Aspects of his experiments with diet and lifestyle had a direct and tremendous bearing on the Congress's brand of governmentality, expressed through its approach to government policy.[29]

Although Gandhi was sceptical of state power, he accepted that the struggle for independence was essentially a struggle for the state. For him, 'the good state' was a minimal coercive political authority whose task was foremost to serve society. It would accommodate the wishes of all segments of India's heterogeneous population and intervene in society to secure its moral and material well-being, crucially, without using force. To this end, Gandhian nationalism as Congress nationalism sought to mobilise the domain of the social.

Gandhi's determination to bring the ethics of his brand of nationalism into alignment with the pursuit of Indian independence led to his calling off the Non-Cooperation movement following the outbreak of violence.[30] Drawing upon earlier Indian political thinking, he posited self-restraint, or rule over oneself – *swaraj* – as the fundamental prerequisite for national self-rule. He extended his critique of Western modernity by arguing that the state's exercise of power was inversely related to internal government, which came down to government by the individual. State intervention only became necessary, as it had in the West, as the individual had failed at self-governance.[31] For Gandhi, therefore, governmentality was the very crux of the duty that a democratic state owed to its citizens.

However, the Congress leader was unequivocal in endorsing maximum state authority where banning drinking was concerned. Of course, alcohol directly threatened his vision of bodily self-governance. He was convinced of the necessity of prohibition for the poor, who he believed needed to be governed against their baser instincts and appetites.[32] Gandhi wrote that 'one of the most greatly felt evils of the British Rule is the importation of alcohol … the enemy has spread throughout the length and breadth of India, in spite of the religious prohibition'.[33] Indian state power, informed by *satyagraha*, would overcome the corruption brought about by the Western state in this line of reasoning. In this, Gandhi too – like the colonial state he was so critical of – alternated between sovereign and coercive forms of governmentality. As he increasingly came to see state-directed prohibition as the only way forward, the Congress also committed itself to mobilising the domain of the political.

As a product of the dichotomous discourse on which nationalism was premised, prohibition became crucial for its furtherance as well. Congress nationalism posited two domains: the corrupt, masculine-external world whose control needed to be wrested from the effects of Westernisation, and the feminine-moral internal world whose sanctity needed to be protected and preserved at all cost.[34] According to this logic, Indians already possessed the moral strength required for abstemiousness. They just needed to be re-socialised into it; the moral decline caused by colonialism and the fondness for drinking that it had thus brought about were but superficial.

In putting forth these views, Gandhi tapped into the elite worldviews and cultural frames of reference that characterised much of the nationalist leadership. Upper-caste leaders like Gandhi, who hailed from an affluent Gujarati Modh Bania family, along with the Tamil Brahmin Rajaji, saw abstemiousness as synonymous with Indian culture as their backgrounds predisposed them to assume and expect its universality. Indeed, they often talked about prohibition in terms of purity and pollution, thus revealing the hand of caste in informing its underlying ethos.

An outcrop of the Congress's growing enchantment of the state was that it constructed parallel institutions and practices of governance enabled by constitutional shifts, foremost among them the Act of 1919.[35] Through this process, the party emulated the model of the modern Western state whilst simultaneously basing the alternative state it sought on a discourse of opposition to the colonial state. With dyarchy, the Congress took over the AITA's activism in India. It was in this context that Gandhi called for the boycott of toddy and liquor shops during Non-Cooperation agitation, which resulted in the widespread destruction of toddy palm and coconut trees. Shortly after the movement's launch, the Ahmedabad session of the Congress passed a resolution appealing to all Congressmen to support prohibition. The Bardoli Programme, which the Working Committee of the Congress unfurled in February 1922, established anti-alcoholism as a key aspect of the organisation's Constructive Programme of social amelioration. Significantly, it also committed the Congress to a more intrusive brand of governmentality. The programme set out that the organisation would henceforth conduct house-to-house visits to persuade drinkers to give up drinking rather than rely solely on public picketing efforts.[36] Toddy and liquor shop picketing was nevertheless 'a daily affair' in the Telugu districts of Krishna, West Godavari and Guntur, where it was more successful than the picketing of shops selling foreign cloth.[37] The Congress-led agitation for the local liquor option system, which had steadily gained momentum over the course of the previous decades, was eventually introduced through the provincial legislatures that same year.[38]

Corresponding with these domestic national developments, the Volstead Act of 1919, which was passed in America, legitimised prohibition as an exercise in modern Indian statecraft against the Raj. The policy's introduction in 1920 by a powerful Western democracy that had previously kicked off the shackles of British rule added another layer of legitimacy to prohibition as a modern policy with global relevance. Simultaneously, however, Congress leaders rationalised Indian prohibition as superior to that of the West. When the policy eventually failed in America, as its repeal made clear in 1933, the nationalist leadership maintained that it would succeed in India. As Rajaji put it, 'in England or in America one might feel that any law like this is an interference with personal liberty. In India, they may not feel so, as long as we stick to our faith, to our traditions and to our culture.'[39] Prohibition thus became pivotal to imaginings of an 'alternative modernity' that emerged through 'a creative dialogue' between a future based on rationalist humanism and universalism on the one hand and a glorious past on the other.[40]

However, the Congress leadership did not harbour any illusion that the provinces of British India would need to be won over first. As dyarchy had transferred the initiative for excise administration to the province, the policy's relevance needed to be proven there before any meaningful change could be effected at the all-India level. To this end, Gandhi held public meetings in 1927 in Bangalore, Madurai and Pudukkotai, wherein he outlined prohibition's significance for the nation.

The Justice Party and Prohibition in the Madras Presidency

The Justice Party formed the first popular ministry in the Madras Presidency under A. Subbarayulu Reddiyar's chief ministership in December 1920. The Raja of Panagal subsequently became chief minister and remained in power until the end of 1926, when the Justice Party lost the provincial elections. As no party secured a clear majority in these elections, an 'independent ministry' supported by a faction of the Congress was set up under P. Subbaroyan's leadership. The Justice Party returned to power in the elections of 1930 and remained in office until 1937, when it was ousted by the Congress.

Unlike other aspects of the Justice Party's proposed social programme like the promotion of inter-caste marriage, which was complicated by upper-caste non-Brahmin resistance, prohibition enjoyed widespread upper-caste support. Officially, the party toed a pro-prohibition stance as it aligned with its 'dream of constituting a unified non-Brahmin fraternity'.[41] Like stalwarts of the all-India non-Brahmin movement, Shahu Chhatrapati and

Keshavrao Jedhe, who had been teetotallers, Pitti Theagaraya Chetty, the Justice Party's founder, was publicly committed to prohibition's introduction and the elimination of toddy addiction in the weaving community. The Madras Cosmopolitan Club even took an oath of teetotalism on Chetty's death anniversary to honour his commitment to prohibition.[42] To this end, the Justicites included prohibition in their first list of proposed reforms.

However, historians have cast doubt on the Justice Party's actual commitment to prohibition, with grounds to support this view.[43] In 1921, an open letter from a member of the public to Chetty set out that 'alcohol is a corroding poison' and asked, '[W]hat have you done by way of its annihilation or prohibition? The thinking section of the non-Brahmin community is watching you, Sir, whether you contribute anything to the moral advancement of the community whose leadership you claim!'[44] As excise minister, Patro opposed the closure of foreign liquor shops on election days in 1926, fearing that such a course of action would cause 'considerable inconvenience in places like Ootacamund and Madras, with a large European population that takes little or no interest in municipal elections'.[45] Likewise, he emphasised that a liquor shop should be allowed to continue in its existing location in Madras city, despite several petitions that sought its relocation, as it was a foreign liquor shop that served the needs of European residents. When a dispute arose between the colonial excise establishment and the Corporation of Madras over the latter's right to close toddy and arrack shops in the districts where they were situated, he responded by reiterating the argument that such decisions were not within the corporation's jurisdiction. This prompted the *Swadesamitran* newspaper's wry comment that 'both the ministers and the bureaucracy desire to exercise authority as they like and are not willing to promote the interests and rights of the people. This is a characteristic of dyarchy. One is a white bureaucracy and the other is a black one. But both are bureaucracies.'[46]

Facilitated by the workings of dyarchy, the Justice Party's alliance with the colonial government translated into an admittedly conservative approach in matters that were inimical to British interests, a list that included prohibition. Yet the Justice Party ministries also initiated several partial experiments with prohibition during their terms in office. Prohibition was introduced among the Nilgiris hill tribes in 1924. A year-long ban on arrack followed four years later in Tanjore, Ramanathapuram, Tirunelveli and Salem. Twenty-two toddy shops and eleven arrack shops were closed in parts of Tiruchengode, Rasipuram and Namakkal districts by 1930.[47] Although they were but piecemeal measures introduced to appease public opinion, these experiments played a role in sustaining the political momentum towards prohibition in the province. Moreover, as most of them were unfurled in the Tamil districts, the Tamil Nadu Congress Committee (TNCC) was particularly drawn into the debate on prohibition.

The provincial Congress committees locked horns as much with the Justice Party, which warned that Congress raj would translate into a Brahmin raj, as with the British over policies like prohibition. The key factor that influenced the TNCC's approach to prohibition in the 1920s was its immediate rivalry with the Justice Party. As the Congress in Kerala was not allowed to interfere in the internal affairs of the princely states of Cochin and Travancore, the scope of the Kerala Provincial Congress Committee's (KPCC) work was effectively limited to Malabar.[48] The KPCC subsequently brought pressure to bear on toddy and liquor shop renters not to renew their licences, organised programmes like Prohibition Week, which featured rallies and mass demonstrations on the policy's importance, and mooted the formation of the North Malabar Prohibition League.

Congress-led prohibition agitation was most pronounced in the Tamil and Telugu districts. The TNCC, which Rajaji dominated, took the Justice Party to task for its tardiness in pushing the prohibition agenda. The Andhra Provincial Congress Committee (APCC) joined the TNCC in this endeavour.[49] Rajaji had supported Subbaroyan's ministry partly in the hopes that the latter would support prohibition's introduction. His hopes notwithstanding, the Justicites voted for a motion that would have brought about a significant cut in excise expenditure instead during the first budget session of the Madras Legislative Council in March 1927. The TNCC duly voted against the motion. For his part, Subbaroyan ruffled more than a few feathers in the Congress with his statement that prohibition was a central subject, the enforcement of which was the central government's responsibility.[50] A bulletin published by the Congress Publicity Committee promptly charged that the Justicites had done nothing substantial to deal with intemperance:

On the part of the Minister, Sir A.P. Patro, there has been too much of talking and too little of tackling. On the other hand, this party has put every obstacle in the way of genuine temperance reformers by its active support of the ruthless policy of repression of prohibitionists and picketeers, during the palmy days of non-cooperation, by its prohibition

of health officers in the mofussil carrying on temperance propaganda …
The party will go to the electorate on Dr. Natesa Mudaliar's motion and
say that they are pledged to prohibition within 20 years. If they do so,
please ask them when this 20 years is supposed to begin.[51]

Like the Justice Party, the TNCC was disorganised and needed a strong
political agenda in the 1920s. Dominated as it was by Brahmins, it lacked a
broad support base, which played into the hands of the Justicites. Unlike the
APCC, a 'permanent and powerful political institution at the district level',
the TNCC could not count on extensive or even consistent public support.[52]
These factors wrought practical limitations on its ability to force changes in the
provincial government's approach to prohibition. Intra-party disagreements
were most evident in the aftermath of the Non-Cooperation movement,
which yielded its most disappointing results in the Madras Presidency. It was
clear by this point that the party was fairly split between the agitators led by
Rajaji, who had initially opted for *satyagraha*, and the constitutionalists, led
by Srinivasa Iyengar, Rangaswami Iyengar and S. Satyamurti, who preferred
to work within the framework of the Raj. The division was so stark that the
Congress appeared to hold two separate parties with mutually incompatible
ideologies within it.[53] These differences gradually caused the development of
rival political strategies, jockeying for influence, and mass defections by non-
Brahmin party cadres from the TNCC. Periyar's departure from the party is
a case in point.

Disgruntled with this state of affairs, Rajaji left to establish an ashram
in Tiruchengode, Salem. At the ashram, Rajaji – like the Justicites before
him – settled on prohibition as an agenda that would appeal to the upper
castes and, hence, increase his political relevance. He subsequently cultivated
himself as the Congress Party's public face of prohibition at the national and
provincial levels. At the national level, he founded the PLI to coordinate
all the temperance, abstinence and prohibition organisations in India. At
the provincial level, Rajaji became the most vociferous critic of any plan
or proposal that even appeared likely to delay prohibition's introduction.
His colleague S. Satyamurti believed that prohibition could be more easily
brought about through consensus-building with the colonial government
than Rajaji's agitational tactics. As chairman of the Madras Legislative
Council, Satyamurti had supported the Justice Party ministry's proposal to
introduce prohibition after a period of twenty years.[54] This prompted sharp
rebuke from Rajaji, who wrote demanding answers: 'What is this resolution

of yours, asking for a total prohibition programme spread over 20 years? It is most depressing to one like me who wants prohibition now ... Please withdraw it!'[55]

Alongside these developments, the non-Brahmin movement's cultural arm presented a formidable challenge to the Congress's prohibition campaign. Periyar and Rajaji were political rivals for most of their lives, although both had started their careers as dedicated Congressmen. Unlike Rajaji, Periyar became an ardent champion of caste eradication. He led the charge in securing temple entry protests for Dalits and acquired fame as a hero of the Vaikom Satyagraha in neighbouring Travancore state for his participation and subsequent arrest. Periyar had also been a dedicated prohibitionist. At the height of the Non-Cooperation movement, Erode's deputy collector had issued an order prohibiting his presence wherever toddy shop sales took place in the district. The Tamil newspaper that reported the incident denounced the order for hindering the leader's 'divine propaganda against drink'.[56] Periyar had, in fact, presided over Congress meetings that resolved to boycott toddy shop auctions in 1921.

However, from the mid-1920s onwards, the hero of Vaikom became the Congress Party's arch-nemesis instead.[57] He pioneered a radical brand of cultural politics, showcasing his rejection of upper-caste hegemony. The movement spawned the mass publication of Self-Respect propaganda tracts, the most influential of which were the weekly *Kudi Arasu* (Republic) and *Puratchi* (Revolt) newspapers.[58] In place of Brahmanical texts and traditions, the movement encouraged revolutionary practices like the Self-Respect wedding, which dispensed with priests and Vedic chants. Moreover, the movement adopted the term 'Adi Dravida' as a radical, counter-hegemonic alternative identity to the derogatory 'Paraiyar' (Pariah).

Historians have shown that Periyar attacked the upper-caste stigma attached to liquor and meat consumption as signifiers of inferior social status through 'creative mutations' of Gandhian mobilisation.[59] Whereas Congressmen encouraged *khadi* production and teetotalism amongst the poor, the Self-Respect movement emphasised the importance of reclaiming alcoholic drinking as an emblem of a proud Dravidian identity instead. During a conference against untouchability in 1929, Periyar questioned the scorn with which the upper castes perceived Adi Dravida dietary practices when he asked: 'Who doesn't drink liquor? Who does not consume meat? Are they the ones who drink all the liquor that is produced?'[60] Indeed, *Kudi Arasu* asserted that the omnivorous diet was optimal; besides being healthy, it was also 'modern'.[61] Self-Respect commentaries delved into diverse aspects of diet, including how to eat, when to eat and what to eat to sustain a wholesome Dravidian lifestyle. Significantly, these publications also quoted Western medical opinion to legitimise their claims, thus demonstrating a commitment to align the Dravidian movement with internationalism.

Before long, Periyar's advocacy of non-Brahmin dietary practices converged with his criticism of the Congress's prohibition programme. He was unequivocal in declaring that toddy would never leave south India.[62] Whereas the Congress's discourse of teetotalism emphasised abstinence from alcohol as steeped in Indian traditions and culture, Self-Respect literature emphasised the place of alcoholic drinking in non-Brahmin cultures and traditions. To this end, the *Kudi Arasu* newspaper pointed out that 'there is no greater danger to ancient custom or immemorial usage than the "total prohibition campaign" now in fashion'.[63] Here was a critique of the Congress's envisioned governmentality. Mocking the Congress's prohibition campaign as a 'drama' of sorts, he wrote that the party would introduce it only to further its selfish agenda.[64] In his assessment, prohibition was but a distraction that would divert the Indian public's attention from problems like unemployment, which he argued the policy would most certainly exacerbate. Describing a picketing incident that took place in Tiruppur, Periyar pointed out that those who had attacked the toddy shops and those who had been attacked had been part of the same caste; the only point of this exercise was that it had brought praise for Rajaji as a mediator between the rival groups.

Nonetheless, Periyar's stance on alcohol was informed more by politics and less by ideological fervour. Like his colleagues in the Justice Party, and formerly in the Congress, he personally abhorred alcohol, which, in his own words, was more despicable than human excrement.[65] As late as in 1932, his Erode Plan of Socialism had included, among other things, the demand for total prohibition. The non-Brahmin movement's critique of prohibition in the Madras Presidency was inextricably entwined with the context of political competition that informed it and that it fuelled in turn. Although the Justice Party became increasingly redundant, Periyar's leadership of the non-Brahmin movement supplied a virulent language of opposition to prohibition that the Congress would find impossible to ignore. In fact, Periyar would remain one of the foremost political critics of prohibition in the Madras Presidency even after he assumed control of the Justice Party, which became the Dravidar Kazhagam under his leadership.

Prohibition and the Foundations of the Nationalist State in the 1930s

All through the 1920s, the Congress's prohibition programme had remained rather vaguely defined. The next decade saw sustained efforts to firm up the programme and, hence, the demand for the policy. Indeed, prohibition developed as a key political programme closely associated with the nationalist organisation's increasing engagement with the state. In the 1930s, Indian nationalist thought became increasingly dominated by the view that defeating the Raj would necessitate Indians acquiring the essence of the Raj's power: a modern state that could engineer a modern society.[66] Jawaharlal Nehru's increased prominence within the Congress in this formative decade of constitutional change was primarily responsible for laying the foundations of the nationalist state. Nehru emphasised the pursuit of science and technology over culture and religion. He sought industrial development and socialist democracy where Gandhi prioritised *gram swaraj*. Whereas Gandhi was sceptical of the state, Nehru embraced it. He argued that only state-directed economic planning would eradicate poverty; the Congress would take the first steps in this endeavour under Nehru's leadership in the late 1930s and early 1940s.[67]

In line with the Nehruvian vision of the state, the 1930s saw the intensification of the nationalist leadership's efforts to parallel the Raj in its institutional organisation, effectively transforming itself into a Congress raj in the process. The Congress negotiated constitutional reforms, drafted an independent constitution based on the Nehru Report, addressed communalism, sought the creation of a constituent assembly and first raised its demand for complete independence in this decade. The high command came into existence with the aim of achieving greater centralisation.[68] Prohibition's development in this decade again closely reflected the contours of its political context. The policy contained within it both the kernel of *satyagraha* that had sustained the Congress's agitational politics previously, and a growing resolve that the organisation would do whatever it needed to – including cooperate with the Raj where necessary – to seize the state and secure the nation's well-being; that is, put into effect its alternative brand of governmentality.

Given his ideological commitment to prohibition and instrumental role at both the provincial and all-India levels of nationalist organisation, Rajaji's contributions to prohibitioning in this context cannot be overstated. He accepted leadership of the PLI as general secretary – a position that a

Briton, Revd Herbert Anderson, had previously held. The change of hands held immense symbolic significance as the Congress now formally assumed responsibility for the policy's realisation. The Congress executive committee accepted Rajaji's scheme for national prohibition in April 1929. This was a programme that crucially depended on the provinces' cooperation and action; every province would have a prohibition unit answerable to the provincial Congress committee, just as every district would have organisers who would establish anti-drink societies in the provinces' towns and villages. These societies had the mandate to picket liquor shops, discourage bidding at liquor auctions and set up sources of 'alternative' – that is, sober – entertainment.[69]

The All-India Prohibition Committee, comprising Vallabhai Patel, Rajendra Prasad, M. A. Ansari and Rajaji, oversaw these efforts. Supported by a monthly grant from the Congress Working Committee, the committee regularly issued memoranda and proposals urging provincial Congress committees to work towards achieving prohibition. Concerned with the policy's scope and timing, it first demanded that complete prohibition should be the goal instead of the colonial government's stance of regulation. Second, the committee demanded immediate prohibition, whereas both the colonial government and regional political rivals were committed to a gradual and staggered introduction. Collectively, these organisational efforts had the effect of centralising the Congress's efforts, bringing prohibition-related initiatives at the provincial level into alignment with directives at the national level. Consequently, prohibition became crucial to the moment of 'ideological reconstruction', that is, when the party placed the ideals of a national state at the forefront of national liberation.[70]

The Congress's thrust for consensus notwithstanding, political elites did not all agree on the policy's urgency or desirability. As the All-India Congress Committee found out, several prominent politicians instead agreed with the colonial government in favouring regulation over prohibition. B. R. Ambedkar raised concerns about prohibition's practicability in Bombay when he said that policymakers would need to consider how to 'make good the losses' that were bound to occur due to the policy.[71] As late as 1936, the Muslim League's Bashir Syed Ahmed advised that prohibition should not be a priority for the party when there were bigger concerns like the federation issue to consider.[72] T. B. Sapru, a former Congressman who had helped mediate the Gandhi–Irwin Pact, said that he had 'serious doubts' about the moral or spiritual gains that could be expected from prohibition, just weeks before the policy's introduction in the Madras Presidency.[73]

These circumstances meant that Congress leaders were acutely aware that prohibition did not enjoy universal support even in elite Indian circles, which increased their determination to build consensus in the direction of proving prohibition's feasibility.

Indeed, there were several instances wherein Rajaji was concerned that the colonial government would construe the provincial Congress committees' response to prohibition as indication of the party's indifference to the policy. He wrote to Nehru expressing concern that 'the great expectations that people all over the world entertain in regard to our prohibition agitation are likely to be disappointed if our Congress committees will not rise to the occasion'.[74] Ever the pragmatist, Nehru did not make his views on prohibition public in this period, likely due to deference for Gandhi. He would, however, be sceptical of the policy in the years following independence. At any rate, Rajaji's concern about the party's apparent lack of enthusiasm prompted Nehru to issue a circular to all the provincial Congress committees stating that 'Mr. Rajagopalachariar feels that many Congress committee are not interesting themselves sufficiently … I trust that you will agree with me in thinking that this campaign has not only considerable social and economic value but also political value and a nation-wide agitation will undoubtedly help our cause greatly.'[75] It was of vital importance that the leadership presented a united front to the party on its constructive programme, particularly prohibition, which was controversial to begin with.

Indeed, a few months before prohibition's introduction in 1937, Rajaji again became disillusioned with the provincial Congresses' lack of progress towards prohibition's introduction. He wrote to all the Congress working committees emphasising that it was 'incumbent' upon the Congress ministries to bring about total prohibition in their respective provinces within three years. Concerned about the policy's financial implications, Rajaji appealed for the provincial ministries' cooperation in pressing the central government to release funds for its enforcement. It was difficult for him 'to be always singing a song of "no money"', he wrote, the constant repetition of which would make prohibition 'very unpopular'.[76]

More embarrassingly, the Congress's surveillance networks revealed more than a few errant Congressmen profiting from alcohol sales on the sly. A few months before the prohibition's introduction in the Madras Presidency, Rajaji wrote to a party cadre from Madras city expressing disappointment that the latter had leased out his coconut gardens for toddy tapping. Although he was aware that it meant loss of much income to give up the business, he reminded his colleague that they should be careful not 'to give a handle for enemies to say that we are not sincere'.[77] A member of the Council of State similarly wrote to Gandhi emphasising the extent of the problem. Noting the abundance of drinks at a dinner party thrown by a Congressman, he questioned, 'when the Congress is pledged to prohibition, when the prohibition campaign is launched in the Congress provinces, is it right for a Congress member to arrange for drinks?'[78] Although the extent of such indiscipline within the organisation cannot be precisely determined as it was an issue that the party leadership sought to keep under wraps, the Congress papers reveal several instances wherein its volunteers were found to have private business dealings with toddy and liquor vendors.[79] The view that 'programmes proclaimed from above were at odds with the way politicians worked lower down' was more accurate of the Congress's prohibition stance than arguably any other aspect of its Constructive Programme.[80]

As the Congress took rapid strides towards becoming more cohesive, the colonial government responded with political reforms aimed at rendering the organisation irrelevant. It dealt with nationalism with a two-pronged strategy that brought coercive tactics into alignment with constitutionalism. Alongside the imprisonments of key political leaders like Gandhi, Nehru and Patel, it introduced the Government of India Act of 1935, which superseded the Montagu–Chelmsford Reforms of 1919. The Act of 1935 provided the direct impetus for prohibition. It abolished dyarchy at the provincial level and allowed popularly elected provincial legislatures to emerge. British governors enjoyed critical emergency powers in the provinces and could still veto any policy they deemed a threat to imperial interests. At the same time, the Act of 1935 proposed dyarchy at the central level, with the governor-general exercising direct control over subjects like defence and foreign affairs. The Act laid the framework for creating a national federation comprising two levels: a central executive level and parliament and, subordinate to it, the provinces and princely states. It expanded political franchise from 3 per cent previously to 14 per cent of the population, who now obtained the right to vote. The Act also provided separate electorates for Muslims, Sikhs, Christians and other religious minorities, but denied them to the Depressed Classes. Under the semblance of devolving power, it sought to ensure that real power remained with the colonial state. The British calculated that enabling locally elected Indian governments to enact policies of provincial preoccupations would 'weaken the grip of any all-India movement'.[81] The provincial elections of 1937 served to concretise these plans.

Between the late 1920s and mid-1930s, all the provincial Congress committees in the Madras Presidency had moved away from a stance of agitational politics to constitutionalism. However, this was most marked where the TNCC was concerned. There were several reasons for this turn of events, including the rise to prominence within the party of influential non-Brahmin Congressmen who were able to garner the support of a more significant segment of the province's non-Brahmin demographic than before; the success of the Civil Disobedience movement, which increased the party's support base; and a corresponding decline in the political fortunes of the Justice Party, whose lack of internal cohesion increasingly strained its alliance with the British. By the mid-1930s, the Congress in Madras thus had greater cohesion than its counterparts in most other provinces. However, 'in becoming so comprehensive in character, the party moved away from confrontation and towards cooperation with the Raj inside the constitutional framework the British had established'.[82] Prohibitioning at the all-India level would take its cue from the consensus-building processes that had developed at the provincial level.

However, by this point in time, three main factions presented within the Congress at the all-India level. The first, led by Rajaji, favoured constitutionalism, whilst the other two factions supported agitational politics and focusing on the constructive programme, respectively. Having played a prominent role in steering the course towards constitutionalism in the Madras Presidency, Rajaji argued that the time was ripe for a constitutional battle for the state at the all-India level too. He was pivotal in persuading Gandhi that such a course, enabled by the Act of 1935, would establish 'prestige and confidence among the masses' and hence 'give [the Congress] the power'.[83] The Justice Party's inability to establish a lasting mandate beyond its immediate goal of securing non-Brahmin representation ultimately sealed its fate. Lord Erskine would remark in 1937, a few months before prohibition's introduction, that 'the population were tired of them ... the Justice party at the last election was really groping about for a new policy and it is therefore not altogether surprising that it failed to find one'.[84]

Various aspects of prohibition would bear the imprint of the cumulative developments in the 1920s and 1930s. In combination with the Nehruvian emphasis on planning, Gandhi's enthusiasm for *gram swaraj* – rural self-sufficiency – would influence the *neera* campaign as part of prohibition's ameliorative programme. Alongside its ideological underpinnings, prohibition developed as a pragmatic policy stance owing to provincial political dynamics, intersections that presented between politics at the provincial and all-India levels and key shifts within the Congress, all of which were interacting with major constitutional developments. Doubts and disagreements persisted about prohibition within the Congress, reflecting elements of agitational politics, the Constructive Programme and constitutionalism as the three major factions present within the organisation at that time. Throughout all this, the tension between the commitment to self-restraint as *swaraj*, and a grudging acceptance of the necessity of state intervention, remained. In other words, the tension between alternating forms of governmentality persisted. The Congress organisation insisted that prohibition was a democratic intervention that had the support of the Indian people and, to this end, focused on proving public consensus on the policy.[85]

* * *

Colonial alcohol policy and the responses it elicited were continuously interacting with historical contingencies specific to the context of late colonialism. A constellation of domestic and international developments interacted in the interwar period to politicise the alcohol question. These included the rise and development of Indian nationalism, the provincialisation of excise, religious revivalism and reform, the global temperance movement, economic depression and the outbreak of war. The most important of these was the Congress organisation's role in leading the agitation for change in alcohol policy. Prohibition did not just figure as a crucial focal point of anti-colonial mass mobilisation, but was rather absorbed into the Congress's bid to wrest control of the state and dispense good governance, where the British had apparently failed to.

Notes

1. *Indian Excise Committee* (1905), reports received from Major C. H. Bedford, V26/3232, p. 12, IOR.
2. William J. Ashworth, 'Between the Trader and the Public: British Alcohol Standards and the Proof of Good Governance', *Technology and Culture* 42, no. 1 (2001), pp. 27–50, especially p. 30.
3. Letter from C. Rajagopalachari to Dr. R.N. Chopra, Tropical School of Medicine, Calcutta, 29 May 1931, pp. 1–2, C. Rajagopalachari Papers;

see also, D. No. 86, Letter from Rajagopalachari to Director of Pasteur Institute, Coonoor, 23 May 1931, Nehru Memorial Library, New Delhi (NML), and Letter from Pasteur Institute, Coonoor to C. Rajagopalachari, 6 November 1931, p. 23, C. Rajagopalachari Papers, NML.

4. For a discussion of the influence of Western scientific discourses and practices in informing colonial and nationalist policies, see Gyan Prakash, 'Science between the Lines', in *Subaltern Studies IX*, ed.Shahid Amin and Dipesh Chakrabarty, pp. 59–82 (Delhi: Oxford University Press,1996), especially p. 60. I refer to Prakash's discussion that 'scientific reasoning became the organising metaphor of the Western-educated elite'. See also David Arnold, *Science, Technology and Medicine in Colonial India* (Cambridge: Cambridge University Press, 2000); Biswamoy Pati and Mark Harrison (eds.), *The Social History of Health and Medicine in Colonial India* (London: Routledge, 2009); and Sarah Hodges, *Contraception, Colonialism and Commerce: Birth Control in South India, 1920–1940* (London: Taylor & Francis, 2017).

5. Chatterjee, *Nationalist Thought and the Colonial World*, p. 30.

6. David Washbrook, 'Country Politics: Madras 1880 to 1930', *Modern Asian Studies* 7 (1973), pp. 475–531. See also Frederick Grubb, *Fifty Years Work in India: My Temperance Jubilee* (London: H.J. Rowling and Sons, 1942), p. 11, IOR.

7. Kaviraj, 'On the Enchantment of the State'.

8. Lata Mani, *Contentious Traditions: The Debate on Sati in Colonial India* (California: California University Press, 1998), pp. 129–131. See also Andrea S. Major, *Sovereignty and Social Reform in India: British Colonialism and the Campaign against Sati, 1830–1860* (London: Routledge, 2010), pp. 26–28.

9. Kaviraj, 'On the Enchantment of the State'.

10. Viswanath, *The Pariah Problem*, pp. 5–7.

11. James H. Mills, *Cannabis Britannica: Empire, Trade, and Prohibition 1800–1928* (Oxford: Oxford University Press, 2003), pp. 54–57. See also Lucy Carroll, 'The Temperance Movement in India: Politics and Social Reform', *Modern Asian Studies* 10, no. 3 (July 1976), pp. 417–447.

12. B. S. Baliga, *Compendium on Temperance and Prohibition in Madras* (Chennai: Government of Madras, 1960), pp. 23–25.

13. Colvard, '"Drunkards Beware!"', especially pp. 176–179. See also Chandra, Mukherjee, Mukherjee, Mahajan and Panikkar, *India's Struggle for Independence*, pp. 142–145.

14. R. Suntharalingam, *Politics and Nationalist Awakening in South India, 1852–1891* (Tucson, Arizona: University of Arizona Press, 1974). I refer to Suntharalingam's argument that the period after 1845 had marked a watershed in the province's political history, heralding political demonstration through public meetings 'in which the wider implications of an act of public policy were debated'. An important development in this regard was the establishment of the Madras Native Association in 1852.

15. Partha Chatterjee, 'Colonialism, Nationalism, and Colonialized Women: The Contest in India', *American Ethnologist* 16, no. 4 (1989), pp. 622–633.

16. Charles Andrew Orr, *A Study of Indian Boycotts* (Ann Arbor: University of Michigan Press, 1940); *Report of the Foreign Liquor Committee, 1908–09* (Bombay: Bombay Government Press, 1909), pp. 12–13. See also Marc Jason Gilbert, 'Empire and Excise: Drugs and Drink Revenue and the Fate of States in South Asia', in *Drugs and Empire: Essays in Modern Imperialism and Intoxication*, ed. James H. Mills and Patricia Barton, pp. 116–-141 (London: Palgrave Macmillan, 2007).

17. Mark Harrison, *Public Health in British India: Anglo-Indian Preventive Medicine 1859–1914* (Cambridge: Cambridge University Press, 1994), p. 188.

18. Satyavati S. Chitambar, *Systematic Scientific Teaching on Temperance and Hygiene in Indian Schools* (Lucknow: n.p., 1929), pp. 10–11.

19. The resolutions were passed in 1918 and 1920. Arnold, *Science, Technology, and Medicine*, pp. 183–184. See also Joseph S. Alter, *Gandhi's Body: Sex, Diet, and the Politics of Nationalism* (Philadelphia: University of Pennsylvania Press, 2011), pp. 12–14; and Sanjoy Bhattacharya, Mark Harrison and Michael Worboys, *Fractured States: Smallpox, Public Health and Vaccination Policy in British India 1800–1947* (London: Orient Blackswan, 2005), pp. 110–114.

20. Dwight B. Heath, *The International Handbook of Alcohol and Culture* (London: Bloomsbury, 1995), p. 133.

21. *Swadeshimitran*, 22 March 1918, NNPR (April–June 1918), p. 560

22. *Report of the Indian Excise Committee, 1918–1919* (Bombay: Government Press, 1919), p. 7, IOR.

23. Annie Besant, *The Influence of Alcohol* (Madras: Theosophical Publishing House, 1892), pp. 9–10.

24. *Swadeshabhimani*, 22 March 1918, NNPR (January–March 1918), p. 560. See also Colvard, "'Drunkards Beware!'", p. 116, for an overview of the favourable tariff structure that the colonial government introduced for imported and Indian-made foreign liquor.

25. Quoted in *Swadeshimitran*, 12 November 1935, NNPR (October–December 1935), p. 657.

26. Patro was an elected member of the Madras Legislative Council.

27. Anil Seal, 'Imperialism and Nationalism in India', in *Locality, Province and Nation: Essays on Indian Politics, 1870 to 1940*, ed. John Gallagher, Gordon Johnson and Anil Seal, pp. 1–28 (Cambridge: Cambridge University Press, 1973), p. 10.

28. The portfolios of the transferred half were subject to scrutiny by the reserved half and the governor could override the decisions of both the ministers and the executive council. The Act of 1919 thus ensured that the colonial government retained control over matters that substantially affected imperial power in India.

29. For a discussion of Gandhi's experiments with diet and the body in general and their impact on Congress nationalism, see Alter, *Gandhi's Body*, pp. 82–85.

30. Shahid Amin, *Event, Metaphor, Memory: Chauri Chaura, 1922–1992* (Berkeley and Los Angeles: University of California Press, 1995), pp. 24–26.

31. Anthony J. Parel, *Pax Gandhiana: The Political Philosophy of Mahatma Gandhi* (Oxford: University of Oxford Press, 2018), pp. 115–117.

32. David M. Fahey and Padma Manian, 'Poverty and Purification: The Politics of Gandhi's Campaign for Prohibition', *The Historian* 67, no. 3 (2005), pp. 489–506.

33. *The Collected Works of Mahatma Gandhi*, vol. 1 (Delhi: Government of India, 1958), p. 59.

34. Partha Chatterjee, 'Empire and Nation: Indian Thought on the Role of the State in the Narrative of Modernity', *European Journal of Sociology* 46, no. 2 (2005), pp. 116–136.

35. Kaviraj, 'On the Enchantment of the State'.

36. K. B. Saxena, *Swaraj and the Reluctant State* (Delhi: Aarkar Books, 2020), p. 71.

37. B. Kesavanarayana, *Political and Social Factors in Andhra, 1900–1956* (Hyderabad: Navodaya, 1976), p. 124.

38. B. S. Baliga, *Madras District Gazetteers: Ramanathapuram* (Chennai: Government of India, 1957), p. 806. Dewan Bahadur M. Ramachandra Rao had pushed the Local Option Bill in the Madras Legislative Council in 1922. Punjab had passed the Bill in 1921.

39. Premier and Minister for Finance, C. Rajagopalachari's speech to the Legislative Assembly of Madras, 1 September 1937, p. 133, fortnightly

report for the second half of August, Public and Judicial Department Records (P & J) 4249/1937, IOR.

40. K. N. Panikkar, *Colonialism, Culture, and Resistance* (Oxford: Oxford University Press, 2007), pp. 24–26.

41. V. Geetha and S. V. Rajadurai, *Towards a Non-Brahmin Millennium: From Iyothee Thass to Periyar* (New Delhi: Bhatkal & Sen, 1998), p. 209. See also Foreign and Political Department, F. No. 100/37-G., Resolutions regarding reforms passed at a meeting of members of the South Indian Liberal Federation at Trichinopoly, December 1919, in National Archives of India, New Delhi (NAI). The Justice Party was formerly known as the South Indian Liberal Federation.

42. W. V. S. Krishnaswamy Naidu, *Cosmopolitan Club Centenary Celebration Souvenir* (Madras: The Cosmopolitan Club, 1973), p. 292, TNA, Chennai.

43. I refer to the arguments that David Arnold and Sarah Hodges have presented. Whereas Hodges is generally sympathetic to the party's commitment to social reform, Arnold's analysis veers towards cynicism. See David Arnold, *The Congress in Tamilnad: Nationalist Politics in South India, 1919–1937* (London: Curzon Press, 1977), p. 65; and Hodges, *Contraception, Colonialism and Commerce*, p. 43.

44. Letter from a member of the public, named P. P. Lingam, published in *The Hindu*, 25 July 1921.

45. G.O. No. 177, Revenue Department, 25 January 1932, p. 3, TNA.

46. *Swadeshimitran*, 17 May 1926, NNPR (April–June 1926), p. 633.

47. *Madras Excise Revenue, 1931–1932* (Madras: Government Press, 1932), p.18

48. E. M. S. Namboodiripad, *Kerala, Society and Politics: An Historical Survey* (New Delhi: National Book Centre, 1984), p. 161. See also P. K. K Menon, *The History of Freedom Movement in Kerala: 1885–1938* (Trivandrum: Government of Kerala, 1970), p. 240.

49. P. Yenadi Raju, *Rayalaseema during Colonial Times: A Study in Indian Nationalism* (New Delhi: Northern Book Centre, 2003), p. 251.

50. K. V. Ramanathan (ed.), *The Satyamurti Letters: The Indian Freedom Struggle through the Eyes of a Parliamentarian*, vol. 2 (New Delhi: Dorling Kingsley, 2008), p. 76.

51. *The Congress Bulletin* (New Delhi, June 1930), All India Congress Committee (AICC), file 23, NML.

52. Washbrook, 'Country Politics', pp. 508, 516, 519. See also Christopher Baker, *The Politics of South India, 1920–1937* (Cambridge: Cambridge

University Press, 1976), pp. 250–252; and Arnold, *Congress in Tamilnad*, pp. 142–145.

53. David Arnold, 'The Politics of Coalescence: The Congress in Tamilnad', in *Congress and the Raj: Facets of the Indian Struggle, 1917–47*, ed. Donald Anthony Low, pp. 259–288 (London: Heinemann, 1977), pp. 262–263.

54. Satyamurti would later go on to advocate for independence before the achievement of prohibition, stating that he much preferred a free nation of drunkards to a slave nation of teetotallers.

55. Letter dated 9 December 1925, quoted in Ramanathan, *The Satyamurti Letters*, p. 101.

56. G.O. No. 1982, Revenue Department (Mis., Confl.), 3 September 1921, appendix: letter from the Inspector, Erode Circle, R.C. No. 678, TNA.

57. Frustrated by Gandhi's refusal to accede on the principle of proportional representation for Dalit communities and the dominance of Brahmins within the Congress, Periyar staged a spectacular walkout from the party's Kanchipuram session in 1925. K. Veeramani (ed.), *Collected Works of Periyar EVR* (Chennai: Periyar Self-Respect Propaganda Institution, 2007), pp. 163–165. See also Geetha and Rajadurai, *Towards a Non-Brahmin Millennium*, p. 220.

58. Of these, *Puratchi* was more concerned with politics, whilst *Kudi Arasu* engaged with all manner of subjects, ranging from constitutional matters to mass culture.

59. Geetha and Rajadurai, *Towards a Non-Brahmin Millennium*, pp. 292–295.

60. *Kudi Arasu*, 17 February 1929.

61. *Kudi Arasu*, 12 April 1936.

62. *Kudi Arasu*, 24 October 1937.

63. *Revolt*, 4 August 1929, in *Revolt: A Radical Weekly in Colonial Madras*, ed. V. Geetha and S. V. Rajadurai (Chennai: Periyar Dravidar Kazhagam, 2008), p. 333. This particular quotation is taken from an article in a book entitled *The Right of Temple Entry*, which was compiled by E. V. Ramasamy in 1933. The article's author was P. Chidambaram Pillai, a leading Self-Respecter and legislator from the princely state of Travancore.

64. *Kudi Arasu* compilation, vol. 12, January–June (1931) (Chennai: Periyar Dravidar Kazhagam, 2008), p. 303.

65. *Kudi Arasu*, 24 October 1937.

66. Kaviraj, 'On the Enchantment of the State'.

67. Aditya Balasubramanian, *Toward a Free Economy: Swatantra and Opposition Politics in Democratic India* (Princeton: Princeton University

Press, 2023), pp. 155–157. I refer to Balasubramanian's argument that Rajaji's decision to start the Swatantra Party was not just informed by the alternative vision for state-directed planning that he and like-minded colleagues shared, but more by the fear that such planning was being led by a communist Nehru.

68. The 'Congress system' comprised a president and working committee (the All-India Congress Committee) and the annual Congresses. Beneath the high command, there stood the provincial Congress committees and beneath them, the city, district and taluk/ward, and village Congress committees.

69. Rajmohan Gandhi, *Rajaji: A Life* (New Delhi: Penguin Books, 1997), pp. 109–111.

70. Kaviraj, *The Imaginary Institution of India*, pp. 18–21.

71. Bombay Legislative Council Debates, vol. 19, pp. 838–840, dated 10 March 1927, in Babasaheb Ambedkar, *Writings and Speeches from the Bombay Legislature, Simon Commission and Round Table Conferences*, vol. 1 (New Delhi: Maharashtra Government Press, 1979), pp. 163–164.

72. Proceedings of the Legislative Council of the Government of Madras, Official Report, vol. 81 (Madras: Government Press), p. 266.

73. Letter from T. B. Sapru to Subbaroyan, 28 September 1937, Sapru Papers, 28 September 1937, pp. 989–990, in *Towards Freedom Struggle, 1937–47*, vol. 1: *Documents on the Movement for Independence in India*, ed. P. N. Chopra (1937) (New Delhi: Indian Council of Historical Research, 1937), pp. 990–991.

74. Letter from C. Rajagopalachari to Nehru, 26 August 1929, receipt no. 1556, All-India Prohibition Campaign, AICC Papers, NML.

75. Congress Working Committee Papers, file nos. 2–4, 28 August 1937, I-26/3269, p. 2, AICC Papers, NML.

76. Copy of circular sent by Nehru to all the Congress members of the Central Legislature and Congress Ministries of seven provinces, 12 March 1938, R. no. 4–5, pp.1–2, C. Rajagopalachari Papers, NML.

77. Confidential letter from C. Rajagopalachari to P. G. Ganapathy Naidu, Committee Member, Royapuram Congress Sabha, AICC Papers, files no. 1–2, 5 June 1937, NML.

78. *Harijan*, 19 March 1938.

79. See, for instance, AICC Papers, files no. 1–2.

80. Anil Seal, 'Imperialism and Nationalism in India', p. 2.

81. Quoted from Bracken, the Chief Secretary of State, 5 December 1934, TNA, SF 930, 17 December 1935, p. 3, in Arnold, 'The Politics of Coalescence', p. 282.

82. Arnold, 'The Politics of Coalescence', pp. 259–260.

83. Rajagopalachari to Gandhi, 21 April 1934, H. Poll 4/4/1934.

84. Letter from Erskine to HRH, 14 April 1937, Erskine Papers, file 7, IOR.

85. M. K. Gandhi, *Navajivan*, 31 July 1921, quoted in Ranajit Guha, *Dominance without Hegemony: History and Power in Colonial India* (Cambridge, MA: Harvard University Press, 1997), p. 148.

3

The Development of a Prohibition Culture and Ideal

Civil Society and Prohibition

While politics at the national and provincial levels converged to produce prohibition as a political idea and demand, thereby influencing its policy features along the way, it was the concurrent development of a vibrant prohibition culture that imbued the policy with moral force as the demand of the Indian people. Prohibition become an ideal as it filtered through society before crystallising in the provinces as a policy. Indeed, civil society activism reinforced the Congress's demand for the policy as it took shape, bringing a distinct casteist and gendered worldview into alignment with teetotalism-as-patriotism.

Reflecting 'a convergence of modern science with a synthesis of Victorian morality and established merchant/Bania and Brahman pious norms',[1] social movements across India had surfaced certain elitist values that gradually became cultural norms between the late nineteenth and mid-twentieth centuries. As they often included the threat of social exclusion, movements that originated and developed within caste communities proved remarkably effective in persuading large numbers of people to turn away from drink – more so, arguably, than state-led prohibition subsequently was. However, there was a key difference between earlier movements and the distinct culture of prohibition that took root between 1920 and 1937. Although the latter was overtly political in its orientation and outlook, it was embedded in a discourse that elevated it above the domain of politics. As an influential Tamil newspaper put it, 'the political issue need not be mixed up with this. Go to your villages and organise compacts so that there may not be any drunkard therein.'[2] Prohibition thus became a transcendental national goal for large segments of the population, who thus also alternated between mobilising themselves in the domains of the political and the social.

Although the Indian middle classes were not a monolithic bloc, certain broad similarities are discernible in how they responded to the circumstances of their times. They emerged as a distinct social grouping by championing religious reform, weighing in on colonial governance and articulating their views of domesticity. Of course, alcohol was entangled in all of these issues. Newspapers and civic associations became their chief mouthpieces on society as they intervened to reinforce traditional hierarchies of gender and caste, often blocking – in the process – the underclasses from participating in the public sphere.[3] The middle classes thus came to constitute colonial India's civil society. In the Madras Presidency, middle-class individuals in Malabar aspired to be 'custodians of dominant cultural values' through their 'constant vigil' to distinguish themselves from working-class individuals.[4] Moreover, caste hierarchies frequently converged with class power. Tamil Brahmins brought their elaborate rules of purity and pollution from the villages to the cities when they migrated.[5] As the urban Brahmin middle class thus grew, spatial organisation in the cities came to bear the imprint of a hierarchical social order – one in which the Depressed Classes were systematically excluded and pushed to the margins of society. Prohibition emerged as an ideal amidst, and in response to, these circumstances.

In various combinations, interactions between caste, class and gender produced a national culture of prohibition that propped up the nascent nationalist state in southern India. Alcohol became crucial to civil society activism across India in the interwar period not only due to its intersections with public and private spheres but also because it threatened to blur the distinctions between them. Public drinking was disturbing enough as it was to the middle classes, to say nothing of domestic drinking. Both, however, were rapidly gaining ground in the interwar period, thus fuelling middle-class anxieties about domesticity, corruption of culture and loss of respectability. The war against alcohol thus needed to be waged in both public and private spheres. The contestations that ensued over alcoholic drinking had the effect of enshrining prohibition as a civic responsibility in which all Indians had a part to play.

In the Presidency of Fort St George, the period between 1920 and 1937 saw the growth of a distinct prohibition culture that developed in response to circumstances unique to that province. For one, provincial drinking cultures that are partly traceable to shifts in colonial excise policy aided its development.[6] Equally, it reflected a growing sense of impatience with the lack of political momentum achieved towards prohibition. As it took shape, this culture of prohibition imbued demands for the policy's introduction with a sense of urgency as caste-based respectability and patriotic responsibility were brought into alignment with one another. Corresponding with the Congress's efforts at mobilisation, civil society engagement with the public sphere helped to identify the Indian underclasses as the primary target population of state-directed reform. This aspect of prohibitioning thus simultaneously drew upon and further reinforced entrenched social identities along the lines of class, caste and gender. Notwithstanding the observation that 'the Brahmins were the most handicapped in the race for Westernisation … especially so in the South, where the majority of them were vegetarians and abstained from alcoholic liquor', elite segments of Indian society also evidenced a tendency to aspire towards club membership and stocked bottles of fine liqueur at home as outward signifiers of modernity.[7] Tippling had acquired a degree of social acceptance that had to be overthrown in order to prove the nationalist claim of being different but still modern.

As a crucial site of civil society activism, prohibition spawned an elaborate national culture that supported the related projects of unyoking modernisation from Westernisation, reclaiming the domestic sphere and elevating the status of the middle classes, who frequently engaged with prohibition in highly selective ways. As it developed, the hegemonic discourse of prohibition as national culture targeted the bodies of people from the lowest caste and class groups. It thus constituted 'a hierarchical organisation of values, accessible to everybody, but at the same time the occasion of a mechanism of selection and exclusion'.[8]

Religion, Reform and the Contest for Abstemiousness

It was 'only natural' to embrace prohibition in India, Rajaji proclaimed, as 'Muhammedans and most of the Hindu communities [were] prohibited by religion or by social usage from drinking alcoholic liquors'.[9] The nationalists tried to claim legitimacy for prohibition as an exercise of moral state power by looking to society. And there were grounds for this view. Between the late nineteenth and mid-twentieth centuries, anti-alcoholism had become inextricably entwined with upper-caste social movements that had drawn liberally from Western models of scientific rationality and Enlightenment ideals. These movements envisaged a modern society based on elite Indian cultural norms and traditions.[10] Bengal's first association to solely focus on anti-alcoholism, the Surapan Nivarani Sabha had been founded by Rajnarayan Basu in the mid-nineteenth century. Formerly a heavy drinker himself, Basu had been concerned about the growing popularity of drinking among college-going youth. The Arya Samaj denounced alcoholic drinking and meat-eating as sins of the highest order. Inspired by the Brahmo Samaj, the Prarthana Samaj, established in Bombay in the 1860s, likewise condemned alcoholic drinking and raised alarm that members of its society drank 'indiscriminately' and in the company of Europeans.[11] Commitment to teetotalism as part and parcel of spiritual purity had thus emerged as a reformist ideal with a distinctly upper-caste Hindu bent.

Notwithstanding the observation that reform was slow to start in southern India as social innovation by Madras Brahmins would mean the extinction of the privileges that separated them from the benighted lower orders, there were several important reformist initiatives that were pursued in the province from the mid-nineteenth century onwards.[12] Most were concerned with caste. Dalit uplift movements gained ground with the establishment of organisations like the Hindu Progressive Improvement Society in 1852. When a branch of the Brahmo Samaj was established in southern India as the Veda Samaj, its members pledged to abstain from alcohol in every form.[13] G. Subramania Iyer, founder of *The Hindu* newspaper, promoted the cause of teetotalism through the Hindu Social Reform Association. In Kerala, Sree Narayana Guru likened liquor to poison and warned his followers not to manufacture, sell or drink it. He was concerned with the structural discrimination confronting toddy-tapping castes like his own community, the Ezhavas. The organisation that he set up, the Sree Narayana Dharma Paripalana Yogam (SNDP), subsequently expounded the importance of social uplift, the pursuit of which also translated into rejecting alcohol production and consumption.

Islamic literary writings in southern India show little tolerance for alcoholic drink or drinkers, corresponding with mainstream Islamic religious teachings on alcohol.[14] Temperance organisations echoed the religious–literary injunctions against alcohol in Islam. John Matthai was an economist and temperance reformer who wrote about alcohol consumption in the Madras Presidency. He deducted the numbers of Muslims and Brahmins in the province when he tried to estimate the size of the local drinking population in 1924.[15] Drinking, however, was commonplace among

Brahmins in parts of the province. Muslims were often involved in the liquor trade, whilst excise administration reports noted that 'lower classes of Mohammedans', employed as coolies and workmen, frequented toddy and arrack shops alongside their Hindu counterparts.[16] Whilst the Mappilas of the west coast were apparently 'a very sober class of people', the Muslims on the east coast were not so particular, with the *jutka-wallah*s particularly being singled out as 'inveterate drinkers'.[17] Alcoholic drinking among middle- and upper-class Muslims is more difficult to ascertain owing to its being such a social taboo. The *Jaridah-i-Rozgar*, a Muslim newspaper that was published out of Hyderabad, hinted at precisely this tension when it recommended the establishment of an exclusively Muslim temperance society. Apparently, it would bring 'shame' to the religion if Muslims who drank publicly owned up to the habit.[18]

Alongside the engagements that alcoholic drinking thus brought about among Muslims and Hindus, a particularly close relationship developed between temperance and Christianity. Dalit communities, which often bore alcohol-related social stigma as either drinkers or liquor producers, saw religious conversion as offering a path out of caste-based discrimination. As with the global temperance movement, Christian missionaries across India stressed that temperance and spiritual redemption went hand in hand, although they soon found that this was easier said than done. Several cultural clashes occurred when Christianity encountered local drinking cultures, as experiences from the northeast of India, in particular, would show.[19]

Local rice beers, in particular, had worked deeper inroads into local cultures, traditions and economies in Manipur, Mizoram and Nagaland. Colonial alcohol policy sought to restrict the consumption of indigenous beers – although rather inconsistently – across regions in northeastern India under the rubric of temperance as good government. In this context, Christian missionaries, particularly the American Baptists, played a pivotal role in introducing the ideal of prohibition, which they did by forging a close association between teetotalism and Christianity.[20] As tribal communities embraced Christianity in ever-increasing numbers, prohibition became intertwined with religious responsibility even as it was becoming enshrined as patriotic responsibility elsewhere.[21]

Indeed, the last decades of the nineteenth century were marked by a Christian revival in the West, resulting in the establishment of several new evangelical societies in the Madras Presidency. These included the Society for the Propagation of the Gospel, the London Missionary Society, the Church Missionary Society, the Wesleyan Mission and the Free Church Mission of Scotland. The Jesuits of the New Madura Mission became concerned with the 'problem' of drinking and emphasised strict teetotalism as an aspect of lifestyle. The London Missionary Society and the Danish Missionary Society were committed to promoting sobriety among European soldiers and sailors in the province. The South India Temperance Union (SITU), which sought the promotion of complete voluntary abstemiousness, was established in Madras in 1838, catalysed by the belief that beer, wine and other fermented drinks needed to be 'wholly discarded'.[22] By 1840, the organisation had branches in Bangalore, Mysore, Bellary, Vizagapatam, Madura, Coimbatore and Kumbakonam. In Dindigul, the Panjampatti parish priests organised local temperance groups, while parishioners initiated 'vigilance committees' that kept a close watch on known alcoholics in their congregation.[23]

European and American missionaries in India spearheaded temperance initiatives that were matched by the efforts of native organisations like the Indian Christian Temperance Association (ICTA) of Madras. By 1922, the ICTA had built several temperance halls that served the city's poor and emphasised complete abstemiousness as the path of the righteous. Its meetings were sponsored by the Danish Missionary Society, although Indians from a range of socio-economic, ethnic and age backgrounds often attended them. The ICTA organised meetings in vernacular Indian languages and English in open, public spaces like temple courtyards in Tanjore and Tiruvannamalai. In 1912, the province's Indian Christian Association started a monthly Anglo-vernacular magazine, the *Madras Temperance Herald*, which subsequently enjoyed wide circulation in India, Burma and Ceylon. Motivated by the concern that 'to drink was to associate with the devil in more ways than one', Bible women in the Telugu districts often distributed copies of the good book as the antidote to drinking.[24] The Bishop of Madras emphasised the correlation between temperance and the material wellbeing of Indian converts to Christianity when he said:

> Here are 50 million people ... branded as Untouchables. A great deal of their poverty and degradation arises from intemperance. In one of our Mission districts in the Telugu country, I found that the Tamil missionaries had persuaded nearly all of converts ... to give up strong drink. The result was very remarkable.[25]

Of course, conversion did not necessarily engender teetotalism or even temperance in practice. Indian Christians often acquired notoriety for being as – if not more – bibulous than their apparent cultural counterparts, the Europeans. In 1911, Revd L. P. Larsen of the Madras church warned that alcoholic overindulgence was gaining a worrying degree of acceptance amongst Indian Christians, while a sizeable community of Roman Catholics on the Malabar west coast, who converted from the ranks of the Vellalar, Paraiyar and Chakkiliyar communities, continued to drink 'large quantities of toddy and arrack'.[26] It was partially to guard against the temptations posed by communion wine that the rebel Anglican pastor and founder of the independent Hindu Church of Lord Jesus, A. N. Sattampillai, insisted on sacrificial nourishments that were 'not offensive to any class of people'.[27] Likewise, Samuel Vedanayagam Pillai, a Vellalar Christian government official, condemned alcoholic drinking and advocated strict vegetarianism for Indian Christians. Pillai drew upon Hindu mythology and the Tamil moral treatise *Thirukkural* to initiate new converts into a culture of abstemiousness.[28]

Notwithstanding their attempts at Indianising temperance, the movement's close association with Christianity became problematic for the province's Hindu reformers who interpreted it as part of an overarching missionary assault on Hinduism. The fact that there was 'not a single active Temperance Association in south India worked only by natives who are Hindus' was identified as a cause for concern in 1902.[29] The Theosophists drew parallels between spiritual purity and abstemiousness in their exhortations to young men to consume 'healthy, nourishing, and non-stimulant articles of food, such as are mentioned in the regulations of Vedic Brahmacharya'.[30] Led by the Theosophists, the Madras Vegetarian Society sought to create public awareness about 'the diseases, the drink-craving, and expenses' arising from meat consumption.[31] Raghupathi Venkata Ratnam Naidu, president of the Madras Brahmo Samaj, compared nautch dancing with liquor consumption by 'cultivated' men, denouncing both as 'disgraceful blemishes on Indian society'.[32] In 1919, Justice Sadasiva Iyer condemned drinking as a characteristic of 'weaker' cultures. He said that

> liquor containing alcohol in weak quantities may not be impure drink to a Western body or to one of the drinking classes of India. But if a Mussalman ... begins to drink, it is a very impure action for him. So also when a Brahmana sage ... begins to indulge in alcoholic liquors, his action is impure.[33]

In doing so, Iyer referenced the logic of caste wherein caste rank and the threat of pollution were directly related. Despite the colonial government's efforts to keep 'the social' insulated from politics, contestations that played out in and through this domain directly shaped prohibition as a demand as the latter took shape.[34]

Informed by these elite concerns and values, temperance organisations played a pivotal role in prohibitioning by influencing the development of a distinct prohibition culture. They often raised specific demands that greatly influenced government policy. In 1907 and 1912, Indian temperance delegations appealed the secretary of state for further changes in colonial excise policy. Notably, the Indian Temperance Association had sent a memorandum to the viceroy demanding further reduction in the number of liquor shops and hours of liquor sales, the setting up of tea and coffee stalls in areas with high drinking traffic, the introduction of temperance education in schools and transfer of control over the auction system of liquor licensing to Indian advisory committees. Barring licensing matters, the colonial government accepted the demands, which formed the basis of the policy changes that it introduced between 1912 and 1925.[35]

Policing Public Drinking

Social movements and temperance organisations undertook efforts to promote abstemiousness that dovetailed with civil society engagement with public drinking establishments. Plebeian liquor shops where drunk and disorderly behaviour could be seen came under particular scrutiny in the province's cities in the interwar context. This was due to the increasing politicisation of the alcohol question, which intersected with civil society anxieties about urban space. The visibility of working-class drinking establishments prompted civil society engagement with the (re)location of toddy and liquor shops. The ensuing measures targeted working-class individuals as much as they did the spaces where alcohol could be procured. Collectively, these developments heralded the emergence of a national culture of prohibition as they enshrined ridding society of alcohol as a universal responsibility.

In the Madras Presidency, cities like Madurai and Bezwada offered up the greatest shows of public support for the Congress's anti-liquor campaigns, while Madras and Tanjore acquired the unenviable distinction of having the largest concentration of toddy shops and proportion of toddy drinkers. Bouts of drunken and disorderly behaviour were keenly felt and protested, particularly in the provincial capital of Madras city, which recorded a large number of arrests annually in connection with public drunkenness. The Madras Town Nuisances Act of 1889 provided the legal framework for these arrests. The Act had issued a stern warning that 'whoever is found drunk and incapable of taking care of himself, or is guilty of any riotous, disorderly or indecent behaviour in any street or thoroughfare ... shall be liable to a fine'.[36] It was also reported that men who became 'unruly' after one drink too many in Madras town had to be removed from public thoroughfares until they regained their senses.[37] Drunk and disorderly behaviour could thus warrant punitive state action even in the absence of an identifiable victim. Whilst individuals could be thus managed, the establishments that facilitated their drunken and disorderly behaviour could not be removed so easily. The city's toddy shops were identified as the source of most urban lawlessness and the worst displays of public drinking and drunkenness in all the province. This was an incredibly jarring problem for civil society as the provincial capital housed numerous police stations, not to mention the British governor's residence.[38]

Madras city experienced tremendous population growth between 1871 and 1931. The most significant rate of growth took place between 1921 and 1931, when a phenomenal annual increase of 22.8 per cent was recorded, attributed as it was to a 'migration of despair'.[39] Alongside Brahmin migration from the villages, poor agricultural conditions and lowered crop prices had prompted large numbers of landless Dalit labourers to flock to the city in search of a better life. These migrants settled in the city's oldest sectors, where sanitation, garbage disposal and water supply systems were unable to keep up with urban growth and where, therefore, 'mortality rates were most striking'.[40] The inhabitants of the town centres were generally more educated, wealthier and of higher caste status, while Dalit communities who supplied most of the city's physical labour needs 'lived outside the urban localities ... where their mud huts and low rank were better tolerated'.[41] The presence of these migrants triggered alarm amongst the upper-caste elite. Krishnaswamy Iyer, who later became advocate-general of the Madras Presidency and subsequently played an important role in drafting the Indian Constitution, referenced just this sentiment when he addressed a public meeting in the city. If 'every man is conditioned by his surroundings,' he asked, what would happen if those in 'a high position in the scale of civilisation' were forced to live cheek by jowl with the 'degraded, wallowing in filth and drunkenness and vice?'[42] Toddy and arrack were generally not consumed in homes but designated shops. Due to its public nature, country liquor consumption especially played into fears of social contamination.

Colonial urbanism in the subcontinent was frequently constituted through the simultaneous intermingling with, and opposition to, 'the rural'. Indian cities surfaced the most pronounced social anxieties over the regulation of civic spaces as they saw the 'intense use of space by all social classes'; indeed, street life was characterised by great risk in colonial and nationalist constructions of public space.[43] Certain neighbourhoods that the authorities saw as being especially prone to bouts of drunken and disorderly behaviour were singled out for regular police patrols.

Unlike drinking in industrial neighbourhoods, which was a tolerated evil, the concern that public drinking – with its lowly caste associations – was eating away at the moral fabric of the city's residential neighbourhoods provoked protest against toddy and liquor shops in this context. In Madras city, the toddy shop's role as an institution of working-class male sociability went hand in hand with its importance as a site of migrant sociability. Working-class migrant males in the West have historically tended to have a social life revolving around plebeian establishments and temporary dwellings that present a jarring contrast to the nuclear family as the model of urban stability. The city toddy shop, with its uncomfortable associations of the unruly world of the rural, became even more dangerous as a site where the lifestyle of the Depressed Classes encroached into the norms of upper-caste Indian family life. It was reported, with palpable shock, that not only men but also women and children were increasingly patronising these establishments.[44] The visibility of public drinking was deeply troubling for the middle classes as it made it evident that it was 'not possible to divide the city into Brahmin, non-Brahmin and Harijan sectors'.[45] Drawing comparisons between Madras city and Calicut, the *West Coast Spectator* newspaper asked 'why the customers of a tavern should be allowed to use the street in front of it ... the frontage of toddy shops is invariably taken possession of by customers of the Dalit persuasion especially – and the scenes that take place beggar description'.[46] There was noticeable alarm that vice was spilling out from these shops to the streets, where it threatened the ways of life of respectable society and contaminated urban life.

Working-class drinking establishments became charged sites of civil society engagement as they threatened to violate the rules of social mixing. The fact that they could sometimes pass off as respectable places rendered them especially dangerous as they increased the risk of social contagion. A letter about a toddy shop in Saidapet cautioned that it looked so 'grand' that it could have been mistaken for a milliner's or draper's firm by day. Quite a different situation, however, apparently unfolded at night:

> What a hideous crowd of men and some women too, and what a nasty stench! It was a toddy vendor's hell. Inside the place, the wretches heard music, vocal and instrumental, arranged for in such places by the vendors to attract men, when they drank. Some abused the passers by and some spoke highly of themselves. It was all babel![47]

The liberal consumption of alcohol during festive periods also surfaced serious concern among the city's residents. A letter published in *The Hindu* remarked that public drinking and drunkenness was so widespread amongst the working classes and a growing segment of the middle class as to warrant 'the temporary closing of all liquor shops in certain parts or wards of the city during the Deepavali day, if not all the shops in the city'.[48] The League of Youth, founded in 1924, sprang into action with its temperance work among urban slum dwellers with the aim of 'doing away with the conditions of living disfiguring City life'.[49]

Civil society demands for liquor shop relocations – if not complete closures – were expressed with increasing frequency over the 1920s and 1930s. Complaints about public drinking and the disruption it wrought on the electoral process reported that the majority of voters in parts of the city turned up intoxicated at polling stations and proceeded to 'vote for themselves, in most cases, for their mothers, wives and brothers and so on'.[50] As these drinkers reportedly presented polling officers, candidates and their agents with all kinds of troubles, they requested 'the strictest orders throughout the Presidency' to close all the public taverns during election periods.[51] Toddy and arrack shops were indeed closed on election days to prevent the poor from abusing their civic rights and responsibilities, while foreign liquor shops, on account of their 'foreignness', were exempted from this law.[52]

Unsurprisingly, the location of toddy and arrack shops thus also became a matter of political debate. In 1926, a city toddy shop was singled out for mention during a legislative council meeting. The shop, which was apparently located 'in one of the most crowded thoroughfares in the City of Madras' and near a tramway line, was found to have routinely sold toddy to adolescent boys after closing hours. When temperance activists tried to hinder these clandestine sales, toddy renters apparently 'descended to the level of throwing filth on these workers'.[53] As well-intentioned members of the public saw toddy and arrack shops as posing danger to public spaces in more ways than one, they raised demands through their political representatives for these establishments to be relocated, if not removed altogether. In other words, they were asking and authorising the state to move against liquor establishments on their behalf.

These developments had the effect of altering existing drinking cultures. Owing to the unsavoury associations that were thus drawn between public drinking and the dross of society, drinkers who could afford to do so increasingly drank in elite spaces like clubs or refreshment rooms that consequently grew in popularity. Alternatively, they drank in the privacy of their homes. It was reported that alcohol could not be 'openly indulged' in Madurai by the early twentieth century, owing to the social stigma attached to public drinking.[54] Due to the increased demand for their services, railway refreshment rooms and English public houses rose in popularity. The proliferation of prestigious drinking establishments prompted the remark that 'the conveniences and facilities afforded' to the Indian upper classes by spaces that were 'well-built, well-managed, well-lit and in several other ways made luring and attractive' enabled their not-so-secret indulgence.[55]

Domestic Drinking, the Home and Prohibition as Women's Work

Women's bodies and the condition of the family home together constituted a highly charged ideological category in colonial India. Debates relating to women and domesticity not only brought forth a gendered nationalist discourse but also enabled it to make inroads into various aspects of Indian society. The colonial state interpreted the *zenana* and the domestic practices of Indian women as indicative of India's unpreparedness for self-rule. The nationalists, on the other hand, fused anxieties about the state of the Indian home with concerns about the integrity of the national domestic space in legitimising their claim to political power. The home thus carried 'the contradictory political burden of standing in for the nascent Indian nation as well as of marking domestic space as evidence of an authentic India rooted in [an implicitly] Hindu past'.[56]

As guardians of the home, women featured prominently in the alcohol policy of, first, the colonial state and, subsequently, the nationalists. They also directly influenced the development of a national prohibition culture through their involvement in various aspects of the politics of governing alcohol. Social class and caste mapped onto gender, influencing the diverse viewpoints that subsequently came to inflect prohibition discourse. Women from different social strata exploited the space available to them as guardians of the home to articulate their respective positions on alcohol, in the process further reinforcing the close association that the global temperance movement had forged between women and anti-alcoholism.[57] While drinking within the confines of the family home blurred the lines between private and public, the anti-liquor movement bridged public and private, the politics of anti-colonialism and the Indian family home in crucial ways. As an internally differentiated category, women played a crucial role in negotiating these overlapping spheres of civil society activism.

'Public attachment to notions of women as child producers and protectors' has meant that women's drinking has globally attracted more attention than men's relationship with alcohol.[58] The colonial state adopted the stance that Indian women who drank were abnormal; they existed beyond the pale of respectable middle-class society. Indeed, official observations of Indian women drinkers in the late colonial period 'dwelt with particular horror on the public nature of their drunkenness'.[59] They frequently emphasised these women's class and caste status to drive home the message that their drinking was an aberration. Excise manuals established that women who drank regularly drank toddy in particular. The Korabar, Lambadi and Enadi women of the lowest castes apparently frequented toddy shops where they drank 'equally with the men of their caste if they [could] afford to do so'.[60] Women of the Dher community, who were employed as cooks; Odda women, who worked as wage labourers in roadworks; and Korchowar women, who washed the streets and wove baskets, all drank frequently – in the colonial gaze, to the point of engaging in drunken brawls. Officials reported that around a fourth of the children from these communities also drank toddy regularly.[61] *Sasilekha*, a Telugu literary journal, voiced civil society concerns when it proposed that 'liquor should not at all be sold to women'.[62] Colonial authorities, however, dismissed such concerns on the grounds that in the towns at least, the 'few' women who frequented the shops were usually of 'bad character'.[63] While they conceded in principle the importance of discouraging women from gathering at toddy and arrack shops, they laid the blame for women's public drinking on factors other than the presence of the shops themselves.

The visibility of women's public drinking in India violated the gendered division between public and private spheres, which was imbued with an especially pronounced cultural–national resonance in the context of anti-colonial agitation. The nationalist leadership inherited the prejudice with which the colonial excise establishment viewed women drinkers. It similarly denounced women who drank as the 'other' of the Indian motherland's chaste and respectable women. M. K. Gandhi was appalled that indentured labour had reduced women, 'who would never have touched wine in India', to the pitiable state of 'lying dead-drunk on the roads'.[64]

If women's public drinking thus touched a raw nerve among elite segments of society, they found the spectre of their drinking within the confines of the family home – where it could not be policed – even more alarming. The spectre of domestic drinking, which threatened the breakdown of the family unit, became a key factor informing civil society engagement with alcohol. In the Telugu district of Godavari, the domestic consumption of toddy became so common that women apparently drank without inhibition and gave it to their children too, who subsequently went to school 'smelling of drink'. A headmaster reported having had to dismiss 'even Brahmin boys' from school when he found them 'reeling in the street'.[65] The impact of women's drinking on the development of a distinct prohibition culture was remarkable, to say the least.

In 1926, Rajaji expressed concern that owing to the combined pressure wrought by famine and temperance organisations, toddy shop renters in Tiruchengode had lowered toddy and arrack prices such that '*even* womenfolk resort[ed] to drink'.[66] He found the spectre of women's public drinking so reprehensible that he demanded immediate prohibition in Salem and Coimbatore to address the situation and appease public opinion on the matter. When the desirability of criminalising alcohol sales to working-class women was raised for discussion, it was met with the colonial government's response that such a course of action would lead to even more harmful outcomes like triggering a spike in liquor sales at brothels or in women of dubious character resorting to alternative, more deleterious sources of intoxication. Ultimately, the excise commissioner recommended the enforcement of restricted toddy sales to women only 'in special areas where it [was] thought to be necessary', a position that translated into the tacit reinforcement of the status quo.[67] Women's employment in liquor shops was banned, although exceptions were made in this regard too. Renters' family members, for instance, were exempted from this law. Prohibitioning enabled and would subsequently continue to enable prohibition by presenting exemptions and exceptions to the policy.

The country liquor problem was largely seen as a public drinking problem, as opposed to the imported varieties of liquor that had made inroads into upper-class and upper-caste Indian homes by the late nineteenth century. There was an important distinction made between public drinking and domestic drinking on the basis of class and caste. Whilst public drinking emerged as an area of concern owing to its associations with the working class, Depressed Class segments of Indian society, the Indian middle classes saw domestic drinking as a crisis that struck too close to home for comfort. As a medical officer in Bengal put it, it was the 'more demoralising habit of private drinking indulged in by nearly nine-tenths of the Bengalis instructed at our English colleges and schools', rather than the occasional imbibing at formal gatherings, that prompted civil society engagement with drinking in that province.[68] In the Presidency of Fort St George, temperance societies published a series of temperance pamphlets targeting children and conducted regular home visits so that Hindu women who had 'no opportunity to hear lectures and improve themselves, could benefit by attending these meetings along with their children'.[69]

Medical missionary and temperance advocate Ethel Landon was responding to just these concerns when she remarked that 'brandy and wines of European manufacture are gaining an undeserved popularity among the better classes ... Hindus are freely using them in their homes.'[70] Brandy was a common home remedy in 'acute illnesses', whilst elite Indian women were freely administered wine or spirits after childbirth, a practice that especially fuelled middle-class anxieties about the private sphere.[71] Temperance manuals reflected and reproduced these anxieties, with a particularly graphic cartoon warning that 'a drunkard's house will not prosper ... his children will be akin to piglets. If the wife too joins in drinking, their house is nothing but a pig sty ... If even their children join in, then we ourselves do not know what to compare it to' (Figure 3.1).[72]

There was another class of alcohol that was enjoyed within the confines of the domestic sphere and that was associated almost entirely with Europeans and the wealthiest segments of Indian society. With their apparent health benefits and steep prices, the latter rendering them inaccessible to the vast majority of the population, medicated wines acquired a degree of respectability that more pedestrian classes of alcohol could not lay claim to. They became particularly susceptible to substance abuse as they contained

Figure 3.1   Family ruined by alcohol

Source: Y. G. Bonnell, *Kudumba Matuvilakku Sastiram* (Domestic Temperance Science Manual) (Madras: Minerva Press, 1916), p. 35.

high concentrations of spirit, prompting the *Karnataka Prakasika* to comment that while Germany had banned the sale of alcohol to the mentally unsound, drunkards and underage persons, English 'medicines' in India were 'calculated to create a taste for liquor' in the most vulnerable segments of the population.[73] Rajaji would later attack the ease with which medicated wines, such as Hall's Wine, could be procured. He argued that enfeebled men and women were easy victims for liquor merchants who fooled their customers into buying wines they marketed as miracle medicinal potions, inducing addiction that way. These wines could be 'dangerous and positively injurious', he warned, for new mothers who were recovering from the trauma of childbirth.[74] Indian tonic manufacturers were running advertisements in local newspapers, while multinational corporations were cashing in on the growing Indian middle-class demand for alcohol with therapeutic properties.[75]

At any rate, the imperative of reclaiming Indian bodies from the scourge of alcohol, beginning with the home, led to all sorts of attempts at Indianising dietary habits. Reformers drew parallels between drinking and smoking, warning that *beedi* smoking had become 'fashionable' among non-Brahmins and Brahmins alike, even though it served no 'warming' purpose in tropical

India.[76] The upper castes similarly resisted the 'incursion' into Tamil society of coffee as they saw it as challenging established norms of domesticity, at least to begin with.[77] In a context wherein the colonial state was promoting coffee as a temperance drink, the inaugural Congress conference in Avanashi, Coimbatore, declared that 'coffee, tea and similar drinks should be given up'.[78] In the place of toddy and arrack which could 'tear and burn up the organs', or the Western imports of coffee, tea and Ovaltine – all of which were commonplace in middle-class households in Madras – the leader of the nationalist and labour movements, T. Kalyanasundaram, proposed buttermilk. He asked why put corrupting substances in one's body when one could instead drink *neermor*, a wholesome and authentically Indian drink.[79]

In a context wherein such concerns were fast gaining ground, temperance developed as women's work in India as well. Prevalent cultural norms, nationalist discourse and the practical aspects of Congress mass mobilisation all converged to bestow upon women particularly the responsibility of fighting for prohibition's introduction. According to nationalist discourse, women could defend their homes from alcohol-induced violence and loss of income by participating in liquor shop picketing and boycotts. However, they were also defending India-as-home, in the process bridging private and public spheres in discursive as well as practical ways. To this end, the early twentieth century saw increased interest in social uplift for women, spearheaded by organisations like the Bharat Stri Mandal and the Women's India Association. The spectre of the sex worker bringing India's dishonour to the streets that Gandhi conjured up stood in stark contrast to women who took to the streets demanding the closure of toddy, arrack and liquor shops. In the context of the national movement, even women who were otherwise located beyond the pale of domesticity could acquire respectability through their involvement in liquor shop picketing, a sacred duty that instantly 'purified' them and reaffirmed their status as guardians of the domestic sphere. After meeting Gandhi in Mayuram – a small town in Tanjore – the *devadasi* Ramamirtham Ammaiyar subsequently joined the Congress and took up liquor shop picketing with great enthusiasm in 1921. Ammaiyar would subsequently be bestowed the honour of being the first woman in southern India to court arrest for liquor shop picketing.[80]

Gandhi had earlier remarked that the future of the Non-Cooperation movement in Madras rested with two women in Erode: Periyar's mother and wife. Kasturba Gandhi was an ardent advocate of prohibition, lending her support to toddy and liquor shop boycott campaigns in several instances.

As the first woman president of the Congress, Sarojini Naidu presided over these momentous events in the history of India and was also involved in the women's association Rashtriya Stri Sabha in Bombay; the *sabha* subsequently espoused prohibition's introduction as one of its key goals. Naidu herself had grown up with the shadow of alcoholic drinking by a woman who had been close to her in her family home. Her nurse, Gangu, would apparently get drunk, leave and return to the household at periodic intervals.[81]

The drive towards prohibition found support amongst an emergent class of educated, reform-minded women. It inspired spirited discussion amongst women's associations and clubs between the late nineteenth and mid-twentieth centuries. As the president of the Madras Legislative Council, S. Muthulakshmi Reddi played a pivotal role in swaying public opinion in support of prohibition. In 1927, Reddi demanded immediate prohibition on the grounds that Hindu women, who already did not enjoy inheritance rights, suffered immeasurably on account of their husbands' alcoholism. The first woman magistrate of India, Margaret Cousins, recommended that women's appeals to offenders for drunkenness would be more effective than men's.[82] The All-India Women's Conference, which Cousins co-founded, resolved to work towards prohibition in 1931. The conference declared to this end that 'in view of the many evils caused by intoxicants, this conference emphasises the need for increasing activity in the campaign for prohibition of drink and drugs'.[83]

Middle-class women also pressed the government for liquor shop closures and relocations. In 1929, the Mother's Union of Purasawalkam passed a resolution demanding the relocation of a toddy shop from Purasawalkam High Road because it was located too close to the girls' school and Christian College hostel. Another petition requested the removal of a toddy shop from its premises at Thatha Muthiappen Street, Madras city, as it was near 'a respectable residential quarter' as well as a Muslim girls' school and a Madras Corporation boys' school. The children were apparently frightened to pass by the toddy shop to go to their homes in the evenings on account of the toddy drinkers sitting on the road.[84] After prohibition was introduced, Reddi would recall that previously, 'our girls and inmates of our Home could not pass by the Lattice Bridge road immediately after dark ... men used to pass by ... fully drunk, shouting in all sorts of obscene language'.[85]

At the height of the Non-Cooperation movement, women brought pressure to bear on public organisations and charities to supply free milk and fruit drinks as counter-attractions to alcohol during village festivities, where there was a potentially unrestricted supply of liquor.[86] Anti-liquor agitation played an important role in bridging the worlds of the public sphere of politics and the private sphere of the home in the politics of women such as Durgabai Deshmukh and Duvvuri Subamma. If women had thus participated in large numbers in liquor shop picketing during the Non-Cooperation movement, the Civil Disobedience movement marked a turning point in their mobilisation against alcohol. The outbreak of violence during liquor shop picketing during the Non-Cooperation movement prompted Gandhi's insistence in 1930 that women, with their supposed virtues of patience and forbearance, would take charge of all anti-liquor and foreign cloth boycott protests subsequently. Their ability to endure suffering without retaliating, Gandhi believed, would elevate *satyagraha* as a moral force in the world's eyes. Mary Campbell, a British temperance worker who was in Delhi at that time, wrote about the courage with which 1,600 women in that city alone courted arrest for their involvement as liquor shop pickets.[87] Following Gandhi's arrest in the Civil Disobedience movement, a plethora of women's organisations, including the Desh Sevika Sangh, the Nari Satyagraha Samiti, the Mahila Rashtriya Sangh, the Ladies Picketing Board and the Swarajya Sevika Sangh, were established to coordinate picketing and other aspects of *satyagraha* protest.

As key mediums of civil society engagement with the public sphere, Indian vernacular and English language newspapers played an important role in concretising the association between prohibition and women. The *Sutantira Sangu* appealed for women to join hands against this greatest of 'sins' when it declared that 'many women should come forward in the Tamil land also ... Picketing of toddy shops is essential to exorcising the demon of drink from this country.'[88] Trichy's *Chandramarutham* newspaper argued, on the other hand, that although *swadeshi* was a noble goal, everyone had the right to purchase what they wanted; women's 'peaceful' picketing would serve only to annoy the buyers and sellers of foreign cloth and liquor.[89] As much as the Muslim newspaper *Alma-E* appreciated the intent of Indian ladies who were engaged in picketing liquor shops, it declared that it would be better for them 'to exert their energies in a more appropriate and useful direction'.[90] In doing so, the newspaper reflected the concern that Muslim women's mobilisation in the public sphere was coming at the expense of the cultural institution of purdah.

While women's participation in prohibition politics played a significant role in creating the impression that public consensus for the policy had been reached, women were anything but a flattened discursive category.[91] Notwithstanding the nationalist leadership's claims, it is possible to overstate women's enthusiasm for temperance and prohibition, which could not be taken for granted in situations when self-interest militated against national interests. Women of all classes also expressed opposition to the policy when it came at the expense of their households. It must be pointed out here that Parsi women offered up the most coordinated resistance to prohibition's introduction in Bombay. A meeting of 2,000 women in Framji Cowasji Institute Hall under the leadership of Lady Dhunbai Cowasji Jehangir opposed prohibition on the grounds that it had outlawed a legitimate source of livelihood that the Parsi community had long engaged with. The women gathered expressed 'indignation' at the economic losses suffered by the community, including Parsi widows.[92]

Under different circumstances, working-class women in the Madras Presidency's Salem district opposed the government's planned relocation of toddy and arrack shops far from their husbands' places of work. These women appealed to the excise establishment to reconsider the policy measure on the grounds that 'if their men-folk must drink, they preferred them to get their drink at convenient centres after doing a full day's work and earning up to their maximum capacity'.[93] The alternative, they pointed out, would be to walk long distances to get their drinks, which would mean being late for work the next day. At any rate, the report met with predictable public cynicism. The *Swadesamitran* newspaper remarked, with more than a hint of sarcasm, that the women of Salem district had come forward 'to display their magnanimity deeming the financial condition of the Government to be of greater importance than the welfare of their own families!'[94]

The Development of a National Culture of Prohibition

The various strands of civil society engagement with colonial alcohol policy converged to produce a vibrant national culture of prohibition in the interwar period. It bore the imprint of the concurrent developments amidst which it emerged, although its sum was greater than all its constituent parts. The prohibition culture reflected the anxieties of the Indian middle classes as they related to drinking, which led to their supporting prohibition as the only solution for the alcohol menace. There was a strong religious–cultural orientation at its core, which found alignment with Congress nationalism.

Ridding the nation of alcohol became a sacred, patriotic mission given these circumstances. Although this culture of prohibition imagined the policy in terms of what it would mean for the Indian nation, it foremost reflected the demands and dimensions of civil society activism in the provinces.

Prohibition's political and cultural aspects thus became inextricably entwined, with the one reinforcing the other. The robust culture of prohibition that took root in the provinces bolstered the nationalists' politics of anti-alcoholism. In turn, the Congress contributed to further developing this culture of prohibition-as-patriotism as it stepped up its efforts in this direction. The production and circulation of images, symbols and vernacular idioms relating to prohibition gave the policy enduring meaning and significance by embedding it in local cultures. The concept of 'cultural hegemony' is helpful in understanding the development of prohibition culture in India. Antonio Gramsci saw cultural hegemony as a constant process through which elite groups in society maintain hegemony. By perpetuating their desired values, norms and ideology, he argued, these groups achieve hegemonic consensus in the sphere of culture – a brand of consensus that often reproduces and reifies differences in wealth and power, whilst also opening a space where counter-hegemonies can be produced.[95] As it developed, the national culture of prohibition that took root in the provinces reproduced prevailing social inequalities and acquired staying power owing to the context of anti-colonial mass mobilisation, thereby influencing prohibitioning in the long run. The hierarchies that influenced civil society engagement with alcoholic drinking were further reinforced in the process. With its Dalit, working-class associations, country liquor and the people with whom it was associated became the foremost targets and, hence, casualties of this prohibition culture.

Three aspects of this culture enabled prohibition to be enshrined as an ideal. First, it legitimised a much greater degree of surveillance and intrusion into the lives of drinkers than the religious reform movements that it subsumed. By fusing patriotism with prevailing classist and casteist prejudices, the culture of prohibition not only rationalised and normalised such intrusion, but also idealised it. Beyond absolving those who participated in the nationalist project of policing drinkers and drinking establishments from any guilt, it celebrated them as patriots, hence encouraging others to also follow in their footsteps. It thus nurtured the development of disciplinary society. Second, this culture of prohibition had a tremendous impact on society as it was able to harness the power of visuality. Just as the global temperance movement deployed vivid illustrations and imagery,

Indian prohibition culture used emerging technologies and media forms to normalise state-directed intervention in society. Finally, as this goal was expressed in local languages, literatures and popular cultures, it brought forth the emergence of vernacular cultures of abstemiousness that sought to edge out non-elite drinking cultures. In the process, the circulation of prohibition-related messaging thus brought forth an unprecedented degree of ideological alignment between the province and the nascent Indian state.

As the foremost mouthpiece of civil society engagement with the public sphere, the press constituted one of the main media forms around which a community of patriots was forged. Aided by rising rates of literacy from the late nineteenth century onwards, print journalism 'enabled change, allowing certain texts and forms of information to spread more quickly and widely' to influence political opinion.[96] Newspapers like *The Hindu*, *Indian Patriot*, *South Indian Mail*, *Indian Review* and *Madras Standard* boasted considerable readership rates among the English-educated middle classes. Upper-caste nationalist Indians owned vernacular dailies like the Malayalam *Mathrubhumi* and the Tamil *Swadesamitran* which reflected their stance on various aspects of government policy, including prohibition.[97] Founded by Konda Venkatappaya, a Brahmin and leading light of Congress nationalism, the Telugu newspaper *Krishna Patrika* ran a regular editorial column on prohibition. Its commentaries launched a frontal attack on alcohol's supposed assault on culture.

The nationalist press provided a powerful conduit for the emergence of a sustained critique of the state's alcohol policy. Vitriolic columns and editorials condemned the government's excise policy, while celebrating the progress of the Congress leadership's anti-liquor campaign.[98] The competition engendered by the auction system was not without its share of public criticism. The *Swadesamitran* newspaper raised concerns about the ethical implications involved in a laissez-faire approach to the liquor trade when it argued that 'the present system of selling each arrack or toddy shop to the highest bidder once a year has worked such mischief in increasing the number of shops and in inducing the shopkeepers to undersell one another'.[99] As long as the licensing of liquor shops was in the hands of the colonial state and the auction system was in vogue, *The Hindu* pointed out, 'there will be no diminution in the general promotion of the liquor traffic'.[100] Women's magazines like the Kannadiga *Karnataka Nandini* and children's journals like the Telugu *Bal Bharti* regularly carried stories, poems and editorials on prohibition. Print journalism thus played a vital role in propagating the image of an idealised citizen-in-training who unreservedly supported the prohibition cause, regardless of class, caste, gender or age.

The *Krishna Patrika* published an editorial in 1927 commenting that it was sheer folly not to introduce prohibition in India where drinking had apparently been considered immoral from 'time immemorial', when even 'Western' countries like America and Russia were implementing the policy.[101] The Tamil newspaper *Sutantira Sangu* published poems that equated drinking with the loss of chastity, the decline of the vernaculars and the destruction of temples, thus reflecting civil society's anxiety about alcohol's place relative to the public and private spheres.[102] *The Hindu* ran a regular column entitled 'The Drink Demon', wherein it critiqued various facets of colonial excise administration. Owing to these cultural constructions, alcohol consumption went from being an aspect of social malaise to becoming an especially insidious cultural imposition. Although the association of alcoholism with demonic attributes has precedents in the West, the use of the vernacular in the Indian context produced a markedly different outcome.[103] It demonised the country liquor industry in particular.

Vernacular media exploited cultural references and symbolism to a far greater degree in driving home prohibition's urgency and importance. The local word for toddy was frequently used to reference alcohol in these media forms, thus reflecting the networks of circulation that country liquor had carved in local cultures. In fact, toddy is called *kal* or *kallu* in three of the four main south Indian languages spoken in the province: Tamil, Telugu and Malayalam. 'Even if you drink buttermilk under *echala mara* [the toddy palm], people will not believe it is buttermilk,' sets out a Kannadiga idiom. Likewise, *Kallu mannandoi babu, kanlu teravendoi* (Give up toddy, open your eyes) is a popular Telugu poetical expression from the pre-independence era that is variously attributed to the poet-patriot Garimella Satyanaryana or a song from the film *Gruhalakshmi*.[104] An influential poet whose writings were essential in reaching the people of the Tamil districts with the message of Gandhian nationalism, Subramania Bharati was equally unsympathetic towards toddy and toddy drinkers. He wrote:

> Breathes there a votary of liberty
> That would be content with aught else?
> Lives there a seeker after rare nectar
> That would take a fancy to toddy?[105]

The compound Tamil word *kallarakkan*, comprising *kalla* (toddy or cunning) and *arakkan* (demon), was used with increasing frequency in the interwar period to refer to alcoholic drinking.[106] The term conveyed the meaning that toddy drinking was a social menace, one that was stealthily but steadily advancing in society. As country liquor thus became synonymous with alcohol, it rendered the country liquor industry the foremost casualty of prohibition. With prohibition's introduction in the province, the poet Namakkal Ve. Ramalingam Pillai sang songs of jubilation welcoming the death of the toddy demon, which in his imagination threatened the very essence of Tamil cultural purity.[107]

The prohibition culture that developed encompassed discernible classist as well as casteist dimensions. It shows us two things. First, it demonstrates a prevailing sentiment – a consensus of sorts – that the middle-class domestic idyll was increasingly coming under threat due to the rise in drinking. Second, it shows that even as many among the upper crust of society came to associate 'a gentleman's drink' with sophistication and cosmopolitanism, they were convinced they themselves were above the need for prohibition. Prohibition, they argued, was essential for the labouring classes who could not control – govern – themselves.

In a Telugu play that the colonial government deemed subversive enough to ban in the 1930s, a Brahmin father–son duo – the British collaborator Poornayya Sastri and his young nationalist son Sundaram – discuss caste and class, alcohol and independence. Sundaram asks his father why the latter is contemptuous of caste inter-dining. When Sastri replies that castes like the Malas and the Madigas are to be shunned as they eat meat and drink toddy, Sundaram retorts that the British also ate meat and drank intoxicating liquors which are worse than toddy.[108] Although Western culture was clearly inferior in this critique, the Europeans' superior class status in the context of colonialism had conferred an undeserved status on drinking. The message here was that prohibition was the only panacea for such cultural impositions.

Likewise, in the Tamil short story 'Banker Vinayaka Rao', the protagonist, Rao, is a wealthy banker and elected member of the legislative council who is initially dismissive of the Congress's prohibition programme. Rao's family has a maidservant whose husband is addicted to toddy. His wife wonders why the government cannot simply ban drinking to protect the poor. Rao responds that were it not for their addiction, their maid would be enjoying the benefits of middle-class life, thus depriving their family of a servant.

Rao only realises the error of his thinking when his only son, a regular at refreshment rooms, dies in a car accident while driving under the influence. He subsequently champions the cause of prohibition.[109] Alcoholic drinking thus propped up an oppressive class structure in such commentaries – prohibition, its only cure.

The vivid illustrations and cartoons that graced the pages of vernacular popular magazines and journals often depicted scenes of society joining hands with the Congress to overcome drunken debauchery. As part of the rich 'visual vocabulary of nationhood' that was disseminating through Indian society at this time, this aspect of prohibition culture left a visceral emotional impact on its audience.[110] It was a deeply gendered discourse that sought to evoke a sense of pride in those who intervened to reform drunkards and, conversely, a sense of shame in those who persisted with their drinking; the latter were often stripped of not only their masculinity but also their humanity. In 1931, the Tamil magazine *Ananda Vikatan* published a cartoon on the importance of bringing this demographic and its supposed misdeeds to light. It showed a Congress volunteer holding a lantern to an unkempt, half-naked savage crouching in the morass, the latter clutching a liquor bottle to his chest. The caption read that 'the toddy demon has become a most cunning, secretive demon. But how much longer can he survive, hiding in nooks and crannies like this?'[111] The longer text applauded prohibition as essential and urgent. First, toddy thus absorbed the attributes the upper echelons of Indian society bestowed on the people with whom they associated it with. Second, it became part of a discourse that legitimised an unprecedented degree of surveillance and intrusion into the lives of drinkers. State and civil society were allied in the project of prohibition that was thus constructed as civic responsibility. The cartoon's intended meaning was that only the shining light of Congress-led prohibition could save the downtrodden Dalit labourer from himself (Figure 3.2).

The visual aspect of prohibition culture acquired cinematic flair with the advent of the talkies in the 1930s. Cinema emerged as an especially compelling medium through which public opinion could be moulded in the service of patriotism, with the middle classes constituting the majority of the theatre-going audience in the 1930s and 1940s.[112] The theme of social uplift took centre stage in most cinematic renditions. Two Tamil films in particular deserve mention for their overt focus on toddy drinking. The film *Vimochanam* (Redemption) was released in 1939 amid the euphoria surrounding prohibition's introduction in Salem. Its protagonist, Arumugam,

Figure 3.2   The 'toddy demon' and the shining light of Congress redemption
Source: *Ananda Vikatan*, 16 November 1931, Madras, p. 736.

is a hardened toddy addict who sells his wife's jewellery to feed his habit. Forced to brew his own liquor with prohibition's introduction, Arumugam is convicted for his crime, which adds immeasurably to his wife's woes. The family's troubles are attributed not to prohibition but to Arumugam's drinking; its redemption comes as the film concludes when Arumugam has a change of heart and becomes a teetotaller. Similarly, the most popular Tamil film of the 1930s, *Thyagabhoomi* (Land of Sacrifice), sought to address several social inequalities while propagating prohibition.[113] Celebrities like Tamil singers K. B. Sundarambal and M. V. Mani recorded film songs endorsing the Congress campaign, while others like M. M. Chidambaranathan became involved in picketing toddy and liquor shops, thus forging a close relationship between cinema and nation, both on-screen and off-screen. Prohibition was thus rendered a sacred mission – an ideal.

* * *

The nationalist response to alcohol policy, and Congress-led mass mobilisation against the excesses of the colonial state more broadly, influenced Indian public opinion and brought forth the emergence, circulation and entrenchment in society of a virulently anti-alcohol reformist discourse. The consensus that gradually emerged was the notion that the colonial state had failed to provide effective solutions for intemperance. The predominantly upper-caste, middle-class segments of Indian society played a particularly prominent role in lobbying for responsible state intervention in society. Temperance came to be much maligned in this civil society discourse as the limited policy stance of a self-seeking Raj. In contrast, prohibition was enshrined as the policy stance of a responsible Indian government and the sacred patriotic responsibility of all its citizens-in-training. Women featured prominently in the discourse of prohibition and were actively involved in mobilisation efforts

Figure 3.3 Death to the demon bottle

Source: *Ananda Vikatan*, 16 November 1931, Madras, p. 799.

for the policy's introduction. Vernacular mass media forms of the 1920s and 1930s contributed significantly to the production of a vibrant culture of prohibition. Prohibition was no longer just a policy demand. Instead, it took shape as a powerful ideal as to what the nationalist state could do and what Indian society could become as a result. Prohibitioning thus had the effect of bridging aspirations for modern Indian statehood with aspirations for modern Indian citizenship (Figure 3.3).

Notes

1. Susan Bayly, *Caste, Society and Politics in India from the Eighteenth Century to the Modern Age* (Cambridge: Cambridge University Press, 2001), pp. 183–184.
2. *Sutantira Sangu*, 26 January 1930, NNPR (January–March 1930), p. 54.
3. The very notion of the *bhadralok*, or respectable gentleman, was premised upon and legitimised through reference to its 'other', the *chhotolok*, or 'little people', in Bengal. See, for instance, Partha Chatterjee, *Empire and Nation: Essential Writings 1985–2005* (New York: Columbia University Press, 2010), p. 122. See also Chatterjee, *Nationalist Thought and the Colonial World*, pp. 133–134; and Sanjay Joshi, *Fractured Modernity: Making of a Middle Class in Colonial North India* (New Delhi: Oxford University Press, 2001), pp. 24–28.
4. K. Sreejith, *The Middle Class in Colonial Malabar: A Social History* (London: Routledge, 2021), pp. 162–164.
5. See, for instance, C. J. Fuller and Haripriya Narasimhan, *Tamil Brahmans: The Making of a Middle-Class Caste* (Chicago: University of Chicago Press, 2014), pp. 65–80.
6. Dilip Menon, *Caste, Nationalism and Communism in South India: Malabar, 1900–1948* (Cambridge: Cambridge University Press, 1994), pp. 135–137.
7. M. N. Srinivas, *Caste in Modern India* (Bombay: Asia Publishing House, 1970), p. 49; *The Hindu*, 17 November 1904. I refer to *The Hindu*'s editorial's comment that 'those who imitate the Europeans are the higher classes, the classes which once religiously eschewed liquor, but which now seek a little exhilaration from wine'. See also Mrinalini Sinha, 'Britishness, Clubbability, and the Colonial Public Sphere: The Genealogy of an Imperial Institution in Colonial India', *Journal of British Studies* 40, no. 4 (October 2001), pp. 489–521.

8. Michel Foucault, *The Hermeneutics of the Subject: Lectures at the College de France, 1981–1982*, ed. Frédéric Gros, trans. Graham Burchell (New York: Palgrave Macmillan, 2001), p. 173.

9. C. Rajagopalachari (ed.), *Prohibition: The Official Organ of the Prohibition League of India*, no. 17 (July and October 1930), p. 2, NML.

10. Chatterjee, *Nationalist Thought*, pp. 107, 133–134. See also Bayly, *Caste, Society and Politics*, pp. 252–256.

11. Speech delivered at Prarthana Samaj meeting in 1878, quoted in K. Damodaran, *Indian Thought: A Critical Survey* (Berkeley: California University Press, 1967), p. 371.

12. Charles H. Heimsath, *Indian Nationalism and Hindu Social Reform* (Princeton: Princeton University Press, 1964), pp. 111–112. See also Kenneth W. Jones, *The New Cambridge History of India: Socio-Religious Reform Movements in British India* (Cambridge: Cambridge University Press, 2006), pp. 162–163.

13. Ibid.

14. Ronit Ricci, *Islam Translated: Literature, Conversion, and the Arabic Cosmopolis of South and Southeast Asia* (Chicago: Chicago University Press, 2011), pp. 106, 119.

15. Matthai, *Excise and Liquor Control*, p. 43, IOR.

16. Abhilas Chandra Mukerjie, *A Report on the System of Abkari Administration w.r.t. the Taxation of Toddy in the Presidency of Madras, 1895* (Calcutta: Bengal Secretariat Press, 1895).

17. *Madras Christian College Magazine*, vol. 27 (Madras, 1910), p. 22.

18. *Jaridah-i-Rozgar*, 7 April 1888, in Native Newspaper Reports (1889), TNA.

19. See, for instance, Kyle Jackson, *The Mizo Discovery of the British Raj: Empire and Religion in Northeast India, 1890–1920* (Cambridge: Cambridge University Press, 2023), pp. 150–154; and Tezenlo Thong, *Colonization, Proselytization, and Identity: The Nagas and Westernization in Northeast India* (London: Springer, 2016), pp. 38–40. The missionaries in northeast India belonged mainly to the American Baptist or Presbyterian Welsh denominations. In Mizoram, missionaries walked a theological tightrope between accommodating the rice beer, *zu*, and endorsing teetotalism, while the missionary emphasis on alcohol avoidance caused an all-round reduction in social gatherings among some tribes. In Nagaland, the insistence by American Baptist missionaries that native brews were fundamentally

irreconcilable with Christian living had prompted the first attempts at prohibition in 1894.

20. Jackson, *The Mizo Discovery*, p. 153.
21. Christians are the majority community in contemporary Nagaland and Mizoram, and are roughly evenly matched with the Hindus in Manipur.
22. *Journal of the American Temperance Union*, vols. 1–4 (1837), p. 109.
23. A. Wilson, 'History of Missionary Work in Dindigul A.D. 1838–1938', unpublished master's thesis, Madurai Kamaraj University (1991), TNA.
24. Marine Carrin and Harald Tambs-Lyche, 'The Santals, though Unable to Plan for Tomorrow, Should Be Converted by Santals', in *Christians and Missionaries in India: Cross-Cultural Communication Since 1500*, ed. Robert Eric Frykenberg, pp. 274–294 (New York: Routledge, 2003), especially p. 289.
25. Rt. Rev. the Lord Bishop of Madras, quoted in 'Depressed Classes', *Indian Review*, January 1911, p. xiv.
26. 'Tribes and Tribal Customs, Diet and Food Customs in South India', p. 4, J. L. H. Williams Papers, section 4, MSS EUR C 796/12, IOR.
27. A. N. Sattampillai, *A Brief Sketch of the Hindu Christian Dogma* (Palamcottah: Shanmuga Vilasam Press, 1890), p. 12, quoted in Ulrike Schröder, 'No Religion, but Ritual? Robert Caldwell and the Tinnevelly Shanars', in *Ritual, Caste, and Religion in Colonial South India*, ed. Michael Bergunder, Heiko Frese and Ulrike Schröder, pp. 131–160 (Halle: Verlag der Franckeschen Stiftungen, 2010), especially pp. 154–155.
28. Mayuram Vedanayagam Pillai, *The Life and Time of Pratapa Mudaliar*, trans. Meenakshi Tyagarajan (New Delhi: Katha, 2005), p. 249.
29. *Voice of Progress* (Madras: K. Viresalingam, Chintamani Press, 1902), p. 12. This was a monthly journal managed by the Madras Hindu Social Reform Association. See also Suntharalingam, *Politics and Nationalist Awakening*, p. 35.
30. Mahadeva Sastri, *The Basic Truths of Vedic Religion* (Madras: Theosophist Office, 1912), p. 4.
31. *Madras Vegetarian Society* (Madras: Theosophist Office, 1914), p. v.
32. Heimsath, *Indian Nationalism and Hindu Social Reform*, p. 259.
33. T. Sadasiva Iyer, *Problems of Social Reform* (Madras: India Printing Works, 1919), p. 32.
34. Viswanath, *The Pariah Problem*, pp. 5--7.
35. Baliga, *Compendium on Temperance and Prohibition in Madras*, pp. 4–7.

36. *The Madras Code* (Madras: Government Press, 1888), p. 298.

37. Mukerjie, *A Report on Toddy Taxation*, p. 53.

38. *Indian Social Reformer,* 10 July 1898, p. 6. See also Y. G. Bonnell, *Kudumba Madhuvilakku Saastiram* (Domestic Temperance Science Manual) (Madras: Minerva Press, 1916), p. 47.

39. See Susan Lewandowski, 'Urban Growth and Municipal Development in the Colonial City of Madras, 1860–1900', *Journal of Asian Studies* 34, no. 2 (1975), pp. 341–360, especially p. 349. I refer in particular to Lewandowski's argument that between 1871 and 1910, migration from adjoining rural areas contributed to 70 per cent of Madras city's population growth.

40. Ibid.

41. Susan M. Neild, 'Colonial Urbanism: The Development of Madras City in the Eighteenth and Nineteenth Centuries', *Modern Asian Studies* (1979), pp. 217–246, especially p. 230.

42. V. Krishnaswami Iyer, 'Transcript of Speech Delivered at a Public Meeting in Madras City (1912)', in *Depressed Classes,* (New Delhi: Gitanjali Prakashan, 1977 [1912]), pp. 123–130. Iyer was an active member of different advisory boards and educational institutions such as the Madras Sanskrit College. See also Radhika Singha, 'Punished by Surveillance: Policing "Dangerousness" in Colonial India, 1872–1918', *Modern Asian Studies* 49, no. 2 (2014), pp. 241–269; and Shaikh, *Outcaste Bombay*, pp. 134– 135. Singha argues that the most pronounced social anxieties arose over the unruly behaviour of *badmash*es in rural India. These anxieties, however, became even more pressing in the context of rural migration to the cities, particularly where the policing of drunkenness was concerned.

43. Douglas E. Haynes, *Rhetoric and Ritual in Colonial India: The Shaping of a Public Culture in Surat City, 1852–1928* (Berkeley: University of California Press, 1991); King, *Colonial Urban Development*; Nandini Gooptu, *The Politics of the Urban Poor in Early Twentieth-Century India* (Cambridge: Cambridge University Press, 2001); Prashant Kidambi, *The Making of an Indian Metropolis: Colonial Governance and Public Culture in Bombay, 1890–1920* (London: Routledge, 2016); Dipesh Chakrabarty, 'Of Garbage, Modernity and the Citizen's Gaze', *Economic and Political Weekly* 27 (1992), pp. 541–547, especially p. 543. Chakrabarty's work has shown that Indian street or bazaar life was characterised by profound ambiguity and risk in colonialist and nationalist articulations of public spaces. It was a dangerous

place for 'respectable' segments of society to seek protection from, as whatever did not belong to the 'inside' was found there, 'cheek by jowl, in assorted collection, violating rules of mixing'.

44. Bonell, *Kudumba Madhuvilakku Saastiram*, p. 47. See also Kidambi, *The Making of an Indian Metropolis*, pp. 211, 150–153; and Sudipta Kaviraj, 'Filth and the Public Sphere: Concepts and Practice about Space in Calcutta', *Public Culture* 10, no. 1 (1997), pp. 83–85.

45. Suntharalingam, *Politics and Nationalist Awakening*, p. 31.

46. *West Coast Spectator*, 31 August 1916, NNPR (August–December 1916), p. 125.

47. *Indian Social Reformer*, 10 July 1898, p. 10.

48. *The Hindu*, 25 October 1920.

49. *Minutes of the Third Madras Youth Conference* (1928), p. 247, G-39, AICC Papers, NML. The League of Youth was broadly concerned with the eradication of poverty and concentrated its efforts on the promotion of temperance, sanitation and disease prevention.

50. A. Muni, *My Open Letter to His Excellency the Governor of Madras* (Madras: n.p., 1926), IOR.

51. Ibid.

52. See G.O. No. 1900, Revenue Department, 7 October 1930, TNA, for an overview of the considerations that motivated the election day closure of toddy and liquor shops.

53. Extract from the Official Report of the Madras Legislative Council Debates, 12 December 1926, Economic and Overseas Department (E&O) Department, p. 445.

54. *Indian Review*, March 1905, p. 170.

55. Ibid.

56. Antoinette Burton, *Dwelling in the Archive: Women Writing House, Home, and History in Late Colonial India* (New York: Oxford University Press), pp. 15–17. See also Suruchi Thapar, 'Women as Activists; Women as Symbols: A Study of the Indian Nationalist Movement', *Feminist Review* 44 (1993), pp. 81–96.

57. Ian Tyrrell, *Woman's World/Woman's Empire: The Woman's Christian Temperance Union in International Perspective, 1880–1930* (Chapel Hill and London: University of North Carolina Press, 1991), pp. 55–60.

58. Jan Waterson, *Women and Alcohol in Social Context: Mother's Ruin Revisited* (New York: Palgrave, 2000), p. 7. See also Michael O. West,

'Liquor and Libido: Joint Drinking and the Politics of Sexual Control in Colonial Zimbabwe, 1920s–1950s', *Journal of Social History* 30 (1997), pp. 645–667; and Lori Rotskoff, *Love on the Rocks: Men, Women, and Alcohol in Post-World War II America* (Chapel Hill: University of North Carolina Press, 2002), pp. 27–33.

59. Catherine Gilbert Murdock, *Domesticating Drink: Women, Men and Alcohol in America, 1870–1940* (Baltimore and London: Johns Hopkins University Press, 2001), p. 43.

60. Mukerjie, *Report on the System of Abkari Administration*, p. 6.

61. Ibid.

62. *Sasilekha*, 2 March 1906, p. 66, Native Newspaper Reports (1907), TNA.

63. *Report of the Indian Excise Committee*, 1905–1906 (Bombay: Government Press, 1906), p. 108.

64. *Collected Works of Mahatma Gandhi*, vol. 15, p. 75, quoted in Nalini Natarajan, *Atlantic Gandhi: The Mahatma Overseas* (New Delhi: Sage Publications, 2013), p. 118. Thapar, 'Women as Activists; Women as Symbols', pp. 81–96. See also M. Sundara Raj, *Prostitution in Madras: A Study in Historical Perspective* (Madras: Konark Publishers, 1993), p. 9, for perspectives on the convergences that presented between drinking and sex work.

65. Moffat, *The Drink Traffic in the Madras Presidency*, p. 12.

66. *Swarajya*, 22 May 1926, NNPR (April-June 1926), pp. 662–663.

67. *Madras Excise Revenue*, 1925–1926 (Madras: Government Press, 1926), p. 25.

68. G. H. Gregson, *Drinking and the Drink Traffic in India* (London: n.p., 1887), p. 4, IOR. See also Henry William Blair, *The Temperance Movement or the Conflict between Man and Alcohol* (Boston: William E. Smythe Company, 1888), p. 260, IOR.

69. See, for instance, *A Pamphlet Attacking the Evils of Intemperance* (Madras: Christian Literature Society for India, 1923); *Simple Stories Illustrating Evils from Toddy Drinking* (Madras: Minerva Press, 1927); *Baalar Sugaathaara Vithigalum Paattugalum* (Rules and Songs of Hygiene for Children) (Madras: Christian Literature Society for India, 1932), IOR. See also D. J. Melchizedek, *The Temperance Mission: An Outline of the History of the 'Temperance Mission'* (Madras: n.p., 1898), p. 25.

70. Ethel Landon, *Alcohol: A Menace to India* (Madras: Christian Literature Society for India, 1918), pp. 6–7, IOR.

71. Ibid.

72. Y.G. Bonnell, *Kudumpa Madhuvilakku Saastiram*, pp. 34–35, IOR.

73. *Karnataka Prakasika*, 22 February 1892, NNPR (January–March 1892), p. 127. See also G.O. No. 952 and 953, Revenue Department, 30 April 1928, TNA, for an overview of the considerations that influenced the official classification of beverages like Hall's Wine as medicated wine.

74. C. Rajagopalachari, *Kal Oliga!* (May Toddy Be Destroyed!) (Madras: Kamala Publishers, 1943), pp. 34–35. See also C. Rajagopalachari, *Indian Prohibition Manual* (Madras: Indian National Congress Prohibition Committee, 1931), p. 24, TNA.

75. Douglas E Haynes, *The Emergence of Brand-Name Capitalism in Late Colonial India: Advertising and the Making of Modern Conjugality* (New York: Bloomsbury, 2022), pp. 68–72.

76. Swaminatha Desigar, speech at the Kanchipuram Conference, June 1926, quoted in *Ananda Vikatan*, 1 July 1926, p. 62.

77. Venkatachalapathy, *In Those days There Was No Coffee*, p. 16.

78. *Times of India*, 19 October 1931.

79. V. Kalyanasundaran, *Seerthirutham Allathu Ilamai Virunthu* (Reform or the Celebration of Youth) (Madras: Balan Publishing House, 1930), p. 1.

80. V. Lakshmi, 'Role of Women in Freedom Struggle with Special Reference to Tamil Nadu (1885–1947)', unpublished master's thesis, Queen Mary's College, 2003. *Devadasi*s were temple prostitutes.

81. Padmini Sengupta, *Sarojini Naidu: A Biography* (Bombay: Asia Publishing House, 1966), p. 19.

82. *Times of India*, 3 July 1928.

83. Resolutions of the Sixth All-India Women's Conference in *Indian Ladies' Magazine* (January 1932), MSS EUR F/191/192, All-India Women's Conference Papers, pp. 296–297, IOR.

84. G.O. No. 2062, Revenue Department (Mis.), 17 August 1938, p. 2, TNA.

85. Speeches and Writings, vol. 2, pt 2, pp. 116–154, 'Speech on Legislative Council Budget', date unknown, p. 1, S. Muthulakshmi Reddi Papers, NML.

86. Lakshmi, 'Role of Women in Freedom Struggle', p. 210.

87. *Manchester Guardian*, 22 June 1931, quoted in Ambika Prasad Sharma, *Prelude to Indian Federalism: A Study of Division of Powers Under the Acts of 1919 and 1935* (London: Sterling Publishers, 1976).

88. *Sutantira Sangu*, 3 January 1932, NNPR (January–March), p. 77.

89. *Chandramarutham*, 12 January 1932, NNPR (January–March 1932), p. 128.

90. *Alma-E*, Madras, 3 May 1930, NNPR (May–June 1930), p. 716.

91. Samita Sen, *Women and Labour in Late Colonial India: The Bengal Jute Industry* (Cambridge: Cambridge University Press, 1999), pp. 12–15. I refer here to Sen's argument that women were an internally highly differentiated category whose motivations frequently did not align with that of state officials or social elites.

92. *Times of India*, 17 April 1939, p. 11.

93. *Madras Excise Revenue*, 1931–1932 (Madras: Government Press, 1932), p. 19.

94. *Swadesamitran*, 12 March 1934, NNPR (January–March 1934), p. 142.

95. Gramsci, *Prison Notebooks*, pp. 448–450. See also T. J. Jackson Lears, 'The Concept of Cultural Hegemony: Problems and Possibilities', *American Historical Review* 90, no. 3 (June 1985), pp. 567–593.

96. See, for instance, Stuart Blackburn, *Print, Folklore and Nationalism in Colonial South India* (Delhi and Bangalore: Permanent Black, 2003), pp. 7–10, for a discussion of how the rise of print journalism in the Tamil districts coincided with the rise of literacy in the Tamil districts. Rising rates of literacy, urbanisation and the rising tide of nationalist mobilisation provided the impetus for several new newspapers to emerge over the course of the twentieth century. The colonial government considered newspapers like *Desabhaktan* and *New India* to be so radical and influential that it responded to them with press censorship.

97. *Mathrubhumi* was founded and managed by V. P. K. Menon whilst the *Swadesamitran* was owned by Subramania Iyer.

98. Ibid., pp. 125–127.

99. *Swadesamitran*, 13 March 1889, NNPR (January–March 1889), p. 127.

100. *The Hindu*, 15 February 1908, NNPR (January–March 1908), p. 89.

101. *Krishna Patrika*, 12 February 1927, quoted in G. Somasekhara, *Telugu Press and Indian Freedom Movement* (Raleigh: Lulu Publication, 2018), p. 65.

102. *Sutantira Sangu*, 26 January 1930, NNPR (January–March 1930), p. 54.

103. See, for instance, Julia Skelly, *Addiction and British Visual Culture, 1751–1919: Wasted Looks* (London: Routledge, 2017), pp. 28–31.

104. The Kannada saying in question is quoted in Lakshmi Sreenivas, *House Full: Indian Cinema and the Active Audience* (Chicago: University of Chicago Press, 2016), p. 184. The Telugu expression is quoted in P. Yenadi Raju, *Rayalaseema During Colonial Times: A Study in Indian Nationalism* (New Delhi: Northern Book, 2003), p. 127. The film *Gruhalakshmi* released in 1938.

105. Subramania Bharati, 'The Glory of Freedom' (date unknown), translated from Tamil and quoted in S. Ramakrishnan, *Bharati: Patriot, Poet, Prophet* (Madras: New Century Printers, 1982), p. 42.

106. See, for instance, T. P. Manikka Chettiyar of Kunnaram Patti, in *Ananda Vikatan*, 9 July 1926, p. 2; *Ananda Vikatan*, 16 November 1931, p. 736; and *Sutantira Sangu*, 3 January 1932, NNPR (January–March), p. 77.

107. Piramanayagam Gomathinayagam, *The Role of Tamil Poets in Freedom Struggle* (Chennai: Mukil Publishers, 1989), pp. 46, 50, 55.

108. Penta Sivunnaidu, *Proscribed Telugu Literature and National Movement in Andhra, 1920–1947* (Chennai: Reliance Publishing, 2002), p. 147.

109. 'Kalki' Krishnamurthy, 'Banker Vinayaka Rao', in *Tamil Short Stories by Kalki* (Chennai: Manonmani Publishers, 2014), pp. 391–402. The story's original date of publication is unclear, although it is likely that it was written in the mid-1930s.

110. Sandria Freitag, *Culture and Power in Benaras: Community, Performance, and Environment, 1800–1980* (Berkeley: University of California Press, 1989), p. 152.

111. *Ananda Vikatan*, 16 November 1931, p. 736.

112. Selvaraj Velayutham, *Tamil Cinema: The Cultural Politics of India's Other Film Industry* (London: Routledge, 2008), p. 118. See also S. V. Srinivas, *Politics as Performance: A Social History of the Telugu Cinema* (London: Permanent Black, 2013), pp. 251–253; and Bindu Menon, 'Coming into Cinema: Critical Cosmopolitanisms of Malayalam Cinema (1930–1955)', in *A Companion to Indian Cinema*, ed. Neepa Majumdar and Ranjani Majumdar, pp. 412–432 (London: Wiley Blackwell, 2022), especially p. 414.

113. Theodore Bhaskaran, *The Eye of the Serpent: An Introduction to Tamil Cinema* (Chennai: East West Books, 1996), p. 70.

4

The Prose of
Subaltern Alcoholism

Profiling as Policy

At the height of the Non-Cooperation movement in 1921, supporters of the Congress harassed six men – all of them labourers – trying to enter a toddy shop in Vellandivalasu, Salem district. The violence was enough to deter four of the men, who promptly turned away from the premises. However, Innasi Muthu and Sowariappan were determined to have their drink that day. Leaving the establishment later, Sowariappan was 'garlanded and beaten with a shoe, and Innasi Muthu was garlanded and slapped on the cheeks'.[1] The latter was reportedly so furious that he would have whipped out a knife in self-defence but for the number of assailants. Filtered through the perspective of colonial officials, this account noted that Innasi Muthu and Sowariappan were Dalit Christians and sympathised with the drinking public for the caste violence they had had to endure owing to Congress nationalism.[2]

Excise records surfaced a distinctive administrative term towards the end of the nineteenth century: 'the drinking public'. Akin to 'the criminal tribes', the term circulated through repeated usage, so much so that official correspondences often did not elaborate any further on the subject.[3] As we have seen, drinkers came from every strata of society and drinking in public triggered a great deal of alarm. However, the drinking public meant something entirely different and very particular. Erected at the intersection of caste, class and gender identities, it referred to working-class men drawn from the lowest caste communities. In the Presidency of Fort St George, it also included tribal communities from the Nilgiris whom the state defined by their economic role as servants of the resident European community.

The administrative category profiled drinkers whom the state identified as harbouring addictive tendencies. State authorities typecast entire communities as addicts. They thus not only ascribed a decided fixedness to the behaviour they referenced, but also – in the process – raised target populations for subsequent policymaking.

Of course, official discourse was always called to the aid of the state. In his seminal essay *The Prose of Counter-Insurgency*, Ranajit Guha argues that official discourse of so-called subaltern behaviour was not just produced by those who were directly employed by the government but also by those in the non-official sector who were 'symbiotically related to the Raj', a list encompassing a broad cross-section of society including Europeans and Indians. Moreover, even when such discourse marshalled so-called facts from the subaltern side, it did so 'only as part of an argument prompted by administrative concern'; 'the production and circulation' of such discourse were always 'necessarily contingent on reasons of the State'.[4] The discourse of subaltern drinking maintained that working-class drinkers needed access to some alcohol for their productivity and overall welfare – in other words, for their own good. Regardless of whether the colonial state devised structures and institutions of control or sought to condition subaltern behaviour through subtler modes of intervention, colonial alcohol policy repeatedly sought to prove the skewed, self-serving wisdom of its discursive underpinnings.

The term 'the drinking public' thus developed as an outcrop of the prose of subaltern drinking; it reflected cross-cutting colonial ways of knowing the subject population and the categories undergirding them that colonial rule had fostered. Labour historians have shown that state intervention constituted labour as a distinct, homogenous category defined by gender and caste.[5] Alcoholic drinking was mapped onto colonial categorisations of the working classes to produce this category. By the end of the nineteenth century, excise officials recommended that the government ought to consider Dalits as important consumers of alcohol rather than as the most marginalised individuals in society. This recommendation marked a radical departure from the stance adopted by colonial officials like James Henry Apperley Tremenheere, Chingleput's acting collector, whose report on the socioeconomic conditions of that district's Dalits subsequently paved the way for a landmark reform bill. Tremenheere had emphasised that while they were sometimes paid more than usual, Paraiyars spent their earnings on alcohol only because 'the state allowed an excess of public houses to exist'.[6]

The Board of Revenue disagreed with Tremenheere's assessment. In the view of its officials, the situation was not so dire as to conclude that drinking was impoverishing the Depressed Classes. They looked to crime rates instead as the foremost indicator of poverty. Quite unlike the situation in Britain, they pointed out that there was no obvious correlation between alcoholic drinking and crime in Chingleput. It followed that as there was no visible increase in crime rates in the district that could be directly traced to drinking, colonial alcohol policy could not be held responsible for Dalit poverty. All the same, however, excise officials agreed with Tremenheere that alcoholic drinking was widespread among the Depressed Classes. The notion that individuals from this segment of society were inveterate drinkers with money to spare was echoed in several other official correspondences as well. 'When there are large public works going on, such as those at the Madras Harbour,' noted a temperance pamphlet, 'the coolies get high wages, with the result that the consumption of toddy and arrack in the district ... shows a very decided increase.'[7] Likewise, in 1916, Tanjore's collector had argued that the Depressed Classes should be encouraged to invest their disposable income in land before they drank it all away.[8] 'The drinking public' was thus as much an economic category as an administrative one.

Excise officials often referenced the category in order to legitimise highly selective and discriminatory types of intervention. In this line of reasoning, the state ought to intervene not to prohibit alcohol, which would be counterproductive as it would only push the drinking public to find more deleterious sources of intoxication. Instead, it should intervene to regulate access to alcohol, paying heed to both the quantity and quality of the alcohol that the drinking public could access, thus boosting industrial productivity and public welfare. The revenue aspect was never far from the objective of initiating reform for the drinking public.[9]

Owing to the influence of subaltern studies, the focus of labour history shifted in the 1980s and 1990s from examining trade unionism to studying the politics embedded in the very lives of workers.[10] Whilst it became evident that the state could not be excised from the equation, scholars started to propose alternative approaches for thinking about the dynamics of the relationship that presented between labour and governmental intervention. This oeuvre yielded four major interventions that are germane to our present discussion on prohibitioning and the labouring poor.

First, state repression of behaviour that was deemed subversive produced certain conditions that subaltern drinkers, along with labour overseers and industrialists, were constantly responding to in the late colonial context.[11] Second, governmental intervention in the areas of industrial activity and temperance produced legislation that had a direct, if contradictory, bearing on how industries approached labour wellbeing and productivity.[12] Third, labour recreation and sociability became a key focus of scholarship as the erstwhile focus on the politics of unionised male labour in large-scale industrial settings – mills, factories, looms and the like – gave way to scholarly interest in everyday labour interactions in abutting spaces like working-class neighbourhoods.[13] Finally, notwithstanding the state's attempts to collapse them into a flattened category, the working classes were highly diverse in their motivations and actions, comprised constantly shifting employer relationships, and engaged with policy measures in ways that foremost prioritised their respective interests.[14]

Deliberation on what a coherent and sustainable alcohol policy for labourers should look like hinged on all these factors, although their net impact on alcohol policy far exceeded the sum of all the parts involved. As regulating subaltern alcohol use was part of an overarching engagement with temperance involving diverse segments of society, the different priorities that motivated them also left an indelible imprint on alcohol policy for this demographic. The tension between processes constituting Congress state formation, on the one hand, and colonial governmentality, on the other, inflected the debate. The argument that the state should take the foremost responsibility for introducing legal institutions and frameworks to regulate drinking coexisted with the notion that it should encourage subaltern drinkers to self-regulate. Alternating forms of governmentality thus continued to leave their imprint on alcohol policy. The colonial state's greatly diminished power, particularly by the interwar period, was responsible for this situation. While the nationalist leadership advocated for the maximum state in curbing drinking, the approaches of the colonial state, various segments of society and subaltern drinkers themselves defy any such generalisation. Instead, they frequently shifted between calling for direct intervention and indirect conditioning through policy. The considerations, measures and responses that arose in consequence were inconsistent, contradictory and fraught with tension, thus necessitating sustained prohibitioning. The cumulative impact of these processes on subsequent iterations of alcohol policy was tremendous, to say the least.

Access, Visibility and Working-Class Drinking

During his visit to Madras city in the 1920s, 'Pussyfoot' Johnson had recommended the judicious surveillance of plebeian liquor shops. He pointed out that working-class drinking establishments needed to be visible at all times, an opinion that excise officials shared. In order to police what it categorised as drunk and disorderly behaviour, the colonial government formally adopted the policy of locating toddy and arrack shops, the working-class establishments that it saw as the root cause of the problem, in public thoroughfares. Indeed, one of the stated aims of colonial alcohol policy in the Madras Presidency was the discouragement of 'drinking by persons who were amenable to public opinion' by making toddy and arrack shop interiors 'visible from the street'.[15] Excise officials endorsed the view that liquor shops should be located in public places so that individuals entering these establishments did not escape observation. Such surveillance, they claimed, would eventually condition and socialise the drinking public into responsible drinking behaviours. The Board of Revenue even proposed the establishment of 'model' toddy and arrack shops that would serve as visible examples of expected sanitary standards in working-class grog shops, although the government ultimately dropped the scheme owing to the unsavoury implications of 'promoting' a house of vice on government expenditure.[16]

Public opinion concurred with the state on the importance of ensuring the visibility of working-class liquor shops, at least in principle. *The Hindu* newspaper surmised that 'in this Presidency at any rate, the lover of liquor who has not yet lost his sense of shame, would think twice before entering a shop in a public place, while he would without hesitation go several hundred yards out of his way to get his drink surreptitiously'.[17] In practice, however, achieving the generalised surveillance of working-class liquor shops also became the subject of prohibitioning as it was anything but uncomplicated. The visibility and proximity of these shops to civic spaces proved deeply unsettling for well-heeled segments of society who raised demands for shop relocations and closures; 'subjection to the panoptical gaze' could frequently only be achieved at the expense of offending upper-caste sensibilities.

However, even in instances where public opinion evidently supported the policy, the excise establishment found ways to reject demands that did not align with its foremost priority of maximising revenue. In 1925, several European residents petitioned the government in Ootacamund against the planned relocation of a beer shop as it was 'not in a visible place and will give easy opportunity for Badagas and other prohibited people to drink'.[18] The local collector replied that the objection was baseless as the entrance was on the main thoroughfare, from which it would be 'the easiest thing in the world' to see whether any Badaga went inside.[19]

Far from being a monolithic entity, the colonial state encompassed various government departments. The authorities involved in policymaking for the working classes frequently came to the table with vastly differing interests and agendas, in the process developing policies that were riddled with inconsistencies, as Aditya Sarkar's work has shown.[20] Where alcohol policy was concerned, the situation was further complicated by prohibition activism. In the Presidency of Fort St George, the colonial government viewed alcoholic drinking as 'a sign of a settled, healthy [hence productive] and economically stable agrarian work force'.[21] In this line of reasoning, excise officials interpreted alcohol consumption in lower-caste families as simultaneously being inevitable and as an index of prosperity. Yet ensuring productivity and heeding civil society demands for public order meant that regulatory systems needed to be introduced and strengthened to ensure that the 'drinking public's' supposedly natural propensity for drinking did not get out of hand.

We see contradictory measures at work in that the imperative of ensuring the visibility of drinking establishments did not always align with the official priority of maintaining a minimum distance between the industrial workplace and liquor shops. Indeed, the issue of minimum distance, the amount of alcohol that labourers ought to have access to, the days when they could be allowed to drink and the times of the day deemed suitable for drinking were all matters that were debated in the provincial legislatures. Prohibitioning for the drinking public involved excise and other government officials, representatives of the public who demanded the right to determine the location of liquor shops, mill and factory owners, and labour overseers, the last of whom apparently represented drinkers themselves. Their respective priorities and agendas shaped the contours of actual policy measures in far-reaching ways. Achieving optimal productivity was a key consideration in the deliberations that ensued, as did the objective of maximising revenue. Technical considerations pertaining to the shelf-lives of alcohol moderated the zeal with which regulatory legislation was proposed. Alcohol policy thus brought forth measures that, while ostensibly concerned with subaltern drinking and drinkers, frequently hinged on extraneous considerations.

It would not be too much of a stretch to assume that excise officials based their recommendations for Indian society on similar debates and developments in the metropole as 'colonial state practice and European legal discourse contributed to and drew upon each other'.[22] E. P. Thompson's work demonstrates that policymakers interpreted access to beer among the English working classes as proof of labour welfare and prosperity, in spite of the enormous costs of living they faced in early-nineteenth-century London.[23] A related consideration was the 'time-thrift' consideration that undergirded industrial production. Workers needed to function as disciplined units of production that could yield a desired output within a stipulated amount of time. There was little tolerance for individual idiosyncrasies, which could disrupt production as the labourer's body was only 'a useful force if it [was] both a productive body and a subjected body'.[24] Laziness needed to be weeded out. The same was true of intoxication, which threatened to incite excitability in labourers, who were expected instead to be industrious, ambitious, thrifty and sober. In the Indian context, considerations of productivity informed alcohol policy in several far-reaching ways.

A key consideration influencing licensing decisions related to the minimum distance to be maintained between industrial complexes and liquor shops. To be sure, there was widespread public consensus that city liquor shops needed to be located far away from factories. The *Andhraprakasika* newspaper set out that if the number of toddy and country liquor shops was reduced and shops were distanced from industrial workplaces, 'the habit of drinking will diminish to a great extent, as people may not like to go long distances in the sun or rain'.[25] As the goal of achieving lowered rates of drinking could not be entrusted with the drinking public or toddy and arrack shop renters, temperance activists, industrialists and government officials agreed that 'temperance parameters', or liquor-free belts of land, would be secured around industrial centres. Moreover, they agreed that liquor shops should be located at least 400 metres away from factories. Again, however, this was easier said than done. Although some big mills and factories like Binny's established these parameters, they could not ensure that liquor shops remained closed on Sundays and after-work hours.[26]

Moreover, the consideration that the area around industrial workplaces should be kept liquor-free did not always prevent the establishment of new toddy shops in precisely those areas. Aided by the Madras Corporation's boycott of its meetings in 1924, the Excise Advisory Committee approved the opening of an arrack shop near the Uppilipalayam mills in Madras city, much to the corporation's dismay.[27]

Rajnarayan Chandavarkar and others have turned their attention to tracing the role of historical contingencies in mediating the interactions that played out between labourers and authority figures in specific industries.[28] Far from suggesting a vertical exercise of power, these works demonstrate for us the consensus-building processes that ensued as agents of the state negotiated with the various interest groups that together made up the industrial complex – amongst them workers themselves, labour overseers, and factory and mill owners.

In this regard, policymaking for the working classes was largely influenced by the experience of the Great Depression. Beginning in the late 1920s, a rapidly worsening economic situation brought forth a greater degree of public interest in and engagement with labour conditions. Owing to greater public scrutiny of matters concerning labourers, the colonial government tasked provincial governments to devote more time and resources to regulating industry, thus contributing to the increasing bureaucratisation of labour management.[29] A direct consequence of these developments was the appointment of a Royal Commission on Labour, whose voluminous report on labour conditions provided the direction for subsequent government policy.

In 1929, the Royal Commission on Labour raised the concern that excessive drinking was contributing to reduced productivity and labour welfare in urban areas. It made three broad recommendations to tackle the problem.[30] First, it emphasised that the facilities for obtaining drink should be restricted in cities and industrial centres. Second, it recommended that the state should consider allowing the sales of bottled toddy instead of only permitting on-site consumption. Third, the commission proposed that business hours in toddy and arrack shops should be limited to certain times of the day, and 'in no case include any part of the forenoon'.[31]

The recommendations show us that calls for direct state intervention – with, for instance, the emphasis on restricting facilities where alcohol could be procured – sat alongside the legitimation of policy measures constituting more liberal forms of governmentality, through the advocacy for bottled toddy, for instance. Both approaches, however, ultimately sought to serve the state. Where the second recommendation was concerned, the reasoning was that bottling toddy would enable the alcohol's consumption in smaller quantities at home than in the social setting of the toddy shop, where subaltern drinkers were apparently prone to drinking more in the company of their friends. Strategies for labour management thus extended beyond the workplace and were brought to bear on labourers' 'free' time and earnings, with agents and allies of the state alike thus claiming the state's right to intervene in non-elite drinking behaviours. Equally, however, the rationale given was that temperance measures ought to be directed towards helping subaltern drinkers govern and regulate their own drinking.[32]

At any rate, excise officials accepted – in principle – the first two recommendations raised by the Royal Commission on Labour, but rejected the last one. They pointed out that toddy shops needed to be kept open in the forenoon to receive the morning shipment of liquor; failure to do so would result in over-fermentation and thus heavy losses to shop renters.[33]

Moreover, nearly all the collectors and deputy commissioners of excise in the province opposed the forenoon shop closures that the commission proposed, on the grounds that labourers started work earlier than the shops' opening hours. They argued that closure up to midday, along with the recommendation of bottling toddy, would constitute an 'unwarranted curtailment of the liberty of the casual consumer'.[34] In practical terms, there was little to distinguish between the hardened drinker whose access to toddy needed to be restricted and the casual drinker whose rights as a consumer ought to be upheld. The real reason behind this resistance was more the consideration that renters would use the restrictions as grounds for reducing their bids for the shops, thus lowering profits. Bottling toddy, excise officials warned, would have the unintended effect of encouraging drinkers to indulge their addiction at home, free from the censuring gaze of the public.[35] The recommendation to close shops in the forenoon, however, received unanimous support in the legislatures as it meant that workers would not be absconding from work to drink. The requirement to close shops in the forenoon was thus entered into licences when toddy and arrack shops were put up for auction in the 1930s, although concerns still lingered about its enforcement. To quote an elected member in the Madras Legislative Council, shop renters were known to 'close the front doors and open the back doors' to thirsty labourers.[36]

Factory and mill owners tried to find solutions for insobriety and the problems it posed for productivity by closing toddy and arrack shops on paydays. The rationale was that labourers' increased purchasing power on those days would tempt them to drink to excess. However, this approach surfaced several problems. Industrialists and members of the public raised demands in 1938 for the payday closure of toddy and liquor shops in the province's mill areas, particularly in the industrial centres of Madurai, Coimbatore and Madras. A similar policy had been recently implemented in Bombay. Moreover, two arrack shops and five toddy shops in the vicinity of Madras city mills were already being closed on paydays during certain stipulated hours. It would not have been unprecedented to extend the policy. However, the Board of Revenue responded that the proposal was untenable. It emphasised that alcohol consumption in Madras, Coimbatore and Madurai was not 'excessive on pay days or on the successive days, and in some cases, the consumption on these days [was] even less than on other days'.[37]

Excise officials also raised the related concern that the production of date palm toddy – the most common toddy variety in Bombay – could be temporarily halted, whereas coconut and palmyra toddy production could not be stopped on an ad hoc basis without incurring heavy losses from the spoilage of palm spathes. As the plantations that supplied town shops in the province were located near densely populated areas and the toddy needed to be tapped everyday to prevent spathe spoilage, they feared that halting the supply to toddy shops would trigger illicit sales, the prevention of which would require additional staff.[38] Eventually, the board rejected the proposal on the grounds that all the toddy and liquor shops in all three centres – Madras, Coimbatore and Madurai – would need to be closed to achieve the intended objective of lowering rates of consumption.

Wage labourers, colonial officials pointed out, drank more on Saturdays than on other days. They apparently were also more likely to 'present their offerings to their gods and goddesses ... join in songs and dances, and all get more or less drunk' during festival days.[39] Public opinion thus often demanded a ban on liquor sales on all Hindu and Muslim fair and festival days, catalysed by developments elsewhere in India. Muharram celebrations in Patna in 1928 had raised concerns in the Presidency of Fort St George about alcohol's potential to incite communal riots.[40] Yet, while the state recognised the importance of liquor shop closures in principle, the closures themselves ultimately depended on local collectors' assessments of the situation. In Kovilpatti village, Tinnevelly, the local Excise Advisory Committee recommended the closure of toddy and arrack shops on two important days of the Tamil Chittirai festival. However, the assistant commissioner of excise ultimately overturned the recommendation due to the apparent risk involved in forcing drinkers to turn to more noxious sources of intoxication.[41]

The decision to close liquor shops also rested on a delicate balance of priorities: between preventing crime on the one hand and upholding the interests of local liquor barons on the other. In 1939, the Karur Municipality Council requested the closure of three toddy and two arrack shops operating within the municipal limits of Karur town, Trichinopoly, during the celebration of the local Mariamman and Muharram festivals. The petition elaborated that the annual Mariamman festival attracted large crowds, largely consisting of Adi Dravidas, who, according to official discourse, were prone to drunk and disorderly behaviour in that setting.[42] The council requested the closure to ensure that 'avoidable nuisances were prevented and possible clashes [were] avoided'.[43] Trichinopoly's collector, on the other hand, opposed the closure on the basis of law and order: the police officers in that district reportedly did not foresee any trouble in keeping the toddy and arrack shops open during the festivals. The colonial state and elements of society alike thus used the prose of subaltern drinking to predict problems well before they occurred and proposed self-serving solutions to mitigate them. What was taken for granted on both sides was the notion that subaltern drinkers lacked control over their drinking behaviours. Their assumed propensity for criminality ultimately served the state. Not only did it inform societal demands for greater governmental intervention, but it also supported the government's reassurance to the public that the institutions and structures it had put in place were more than adequate for tackling potential future problems.

The circumstances arising from rural poverty dovetailed with the concern of policing crime to prompt the closure of toddy and arrack shops. In his work on the state's efforts to ameliorate the effects of famine in late-nineteenth-century-southern India, William Digby noted that famine camps attracted villagers from the surrounding countryside who had money to spend on neither food nor shelter, but who nevertheless revelled in the pleasures of toddy.[44] In 1938, the Servants of India Society appealed for the closure 'especially [of] toddy shops', in areas affected by famine.[45] Famine labourers apparently could not resist the temptation to frequent liquor shops located near their camps, with the consequence that 'the few pice they earn[ed] was often wasted on drink'.[46] Indeed, colonial officials complained that the government-appointed Health Unit's relief efforts were being thwarted by the sheer degree of working-class drunkenness. To this end, the petition recommended the enforcement of shop closures during famine situations or, at the very least, the imposition of a five-mile dry belt around famine work camps.

Excise officials, however, responded by emphasising that illicit tapping and distillation would increase manifold with the closure of shops, the prevention of which would require additional staff and hence increased administrative costs. In a related case, a local collector argued that as the offensive arrack shop was already at a distance from the petitioners' villages, a further removal could provide an incentive for labourers, some of whom were apparently from the criminal tribes, to go 'long distances in search of arrack and then come back late at night in a mood to commit crimes'.[47] In both cases, official assessments of the desirability of liquor shop closures were based more on the priority of streamlining governance than on the promotion of labour welfare.

The state's commitment to regulating the country liquor industry prompted wider debate on the feasibility of government-run toddy and arrack shops. District-level administrators proposed that such a course of action was aligned with the colonial state's pro-temperance stance: it would enable better quality control over the liquor that was supplied, which, in normal course, varied from district to district and even between shops operating within the same district. Of course, they had vested interests in proposing that the government should take over the day-to-day running of toddy and arrack shops, which would free up the time and resources that were otherwise being expended managing liquor businesses, not to say anything of the operational aspects involved in governing the country liquor industry. The incidence of working-class drunkenness in Madurai prompted the district collector to recommend that government-run toddy shops in certain townships could provide food and non-alcoholic drink to help 'reform' the tastes of the labourers who frequented toddy shops.[48] Members of the Madras Legislative Council also raised the policy's feasibility during the budget debates of 1934.[49] The call for measures constituting governmentality thus dovetailed with an emphasis on state power through institutions and structures, and their ability to effect lasting change. However, the Board of Revenue stressed that the prospect of government-run toddy shops was highly impractical as it would only be achieved at the expense of the state; it would require the government to manage the entire process of toddy production and distribution, which in turn entailed steep operational costs.[50]

Although ubiquitous in much of the province, toddy was not the alcohol of choice for the drinking public of the Nilgiris. Beer took toddy's place in the highlands. Just as official discourse emphasised hard drinking as a badge of dishonour marking the Depressed Classes elsewhere in the province, it ascribed to the hill tribes of the Nilgiris a purported notoriety for alcoholism. An anthropological study noted that the Kotas ate carrion with the same relish with which they drank beer and strong spirits.[51] The prose of subaltern alcoholism thus intersected with, and reinforced, an overarching discourse of tribal degeneration.[52] Two factors supported the state's surveillance networks and, hence, discourse of subaltern drinking that thus became reified through sheer reproduction and circulation: the increased facility for drinking enabled by market Tuesdays and the location of taverns along the main thoroughfare frequented by Europeans.[53] During shandy day, colonial officials observed:

> Domestic servants belonging to the plains, who are ever under the temptation to fortify themselves with strong waters against the unaccustomed cold and wet of the hill climate, take advantage of the fact; the cartmen who have travelled up with merchandise from the low country, tired and ill-clad as they are, fall in with greater readiness, up from the low country, while the Badagas and other inhabitants of the hills who have brought in vegetables and other produce to the market are unusually flush of cash then and indulge in a luxury which is unattainable in their distant villages or on the other six days of the week.[54]

Like the colonial state, the nationalist leadership took it for granted that the working classes could not be trusted to guard against the temptations of the bottle. Congress leaders not only shared the colonial state's working assumptions on the issue of subaltern drinking, but also sought to extend and strengthen a model of governance derived from them. M. K. Gandhi remarked that 'the one thing most deplorable next to untouchability [was] the drink curse', thus establishing a watertight association between caste, class and alcoholism. This may be further seen in a *Harijan* editorial, which set out that

> [i]n India, the toddy shop may well be called 'The Poor Man's Club'. The well-to-do folks have Willingdon Clubs and Gymkhanas of diverse description, to fulfil their instinct of sociability and to give them recreation even when they do not need it. So does the poor man have the toddy shop for the same purpose. There he finds a relaxation after a long day in the dust and roar of the factory such as the crowded and slouchy rooms he calls home will not furnish. Here he can escape the crying children and get the companionship of men interested in the same things ... The toddy shop is a democratic institution, open freely

to everyone, disregarding caste and creed. For when you reach there, all are pruned to a common level from where you rise above human sentiments into an ethereal state of existence.[55]

In both colonial and nationalist approaches to alcohol policy, drinking constituted a fundamental rule of subaltern difference: proof simultaneously of the subaltern drinker's inability to resist drinking to excess and, hence, proof of the need for effective governance. The Congress, however, differed on the point that it opted for the maximum state model through prohibition in its approach to subaltern drinking. It nevertheless became critical for the organisation to try and replace the institutions and practices supporting drinking among the working classes with sustainable, non-addicting beverages rooted in Indian culture by way of conditioning society into eventually accepting prohibition.

While colonial officials generally acknowledged the importance of encouraging temperance in the working classes, they disagreed with the Congress leadership on the latter's insistence that prohibition was the ideal solution for the problem. In fact, Indian labour overseers and industrialists also tended to echo the government's insistence on regulation over prohibition as the ideal approach to the drinking public. Herein lay the fundamental contradiction underpinning alcohol policy prior to the Madras Prohibition Act's introduction: alongside the imposition of restrictions on the working classes' access to alcohol, the assumption that labourers had to be provided with some kind of alcohol for their own good dominated much of policymaking.[56]

Indian industrialists and labour overseers agreed with colonial officials on the point that the provision of a regulated quantity and type of alcohol was not only desirable but also essential to ensuing continued productivity and labour welfare. Educated opinion that represented labourers' interests in the provincial legislatures often reiterated the staid argument that access to toddy should be encouraged and ensured as the subaltern drinker was better off with a regulated supply of the alcohol than being denied it altogether.[57] While welcoming proposals banning other, especially distilled, classes of alcohol, they warned against attempting the same for toddy on the grounds that the latter was the most benign choice available to the drinking public. Like the colonial state, they welcomed separating toddy from arrack and foreign liquor for legislative purposes. The reasoning that fermented and distilled classes of alcohol should be treated differently was informed by the same considerations that had prompted the administrative separation in the nineteenth century. However, in the context of the gathering storm of prohibition politics, this insistence meant that toddy's place in society became particularly polarising.

This is borne out in a series of debates that played out in the provincial legislatures. Diwan Bahadur M. Ramachandra Rao had moved the first Temperance Bill endorsing eventual prohibition in the legislative council in 1921. The Bill, however, sought only to prohibit arrack, while supporting the continued production and consumption of toddy.[58] In 1924, an Excise Advisory Committee appointed by the government put forth its views on the feasibility of total prohibition. The committee consisted of three European missionaries; two Indian social workers; a lawyer; a government servant, whose work apparently acquainted him with 'the illiterate classes'; two members of the excise staff; an Indian contractor, who employed large numbers of labourers; a witness representing a European firm of distillers; a member of the legislative council representing the Depressed Classes; and a professor of economics. The labour contractor Rao M. C. Madurai Pillai argued that unless labourers took toddy every evening, it would be 'physically impossible' for them to do any work the next day.[59] In 1929, an elected member of the legislative council, S. Muthiah Mudaliyar, advanced a similar sentiment when he recommended that toddy should be left out of a proposed list of liquor shop closures near factories and mills, as 'toddy is a drink that should be available to [labourers] in the place of alcohol. Toddy is not as injurious as alcohol. A man could live on toddy for days together. Even infants are, when no milk is available, fed on toddy.'[60] The effect of prohibitioning was such that, while most shades of elite Indian opinion welcomed prohibition, the measures they proposed to implement it were based on the same assumptions, presuppositions and prejudices – the prose of subaltern drinking – that undergirded colonial alcohol policy.

To Drink or Not to Drink: The Drinking Public's Responses

Notwithstanding the colonial state's insistence of drinking as a sign of Dalit prosperity, ethnographic studies and labour family budgets demonstrate that raising taxes had the effect of plunging labourers into serious debt. Chronic indebtedness emerges from these studies as the foremost reason why working-class drinkers frequented a particular toddy shop over extended periods of time. In a discussion of the economic conditions confronting 800 textile mill workers, Congressman and trade union leader B. Shiva Rao observed that all but thirteen were heavily in debt. He noted that the workers were paying as much as 150 per cent interest on their debt. The contributory factors ranged from sickness in the family to rising expenditure on drinks and drugs, although the latter was of outsize importance.[61] Similarly, a report on the family budgets of industrial workers in Madras city found alcoholism to be the root cause of the labourers' indebtedness. Whilst *beedi* workers and tailors apparently spent a relatively small proportion of their daily income on alcohol, harbour coolies and handcartmen reportedly spent as much as 30 per cent of their family expenditure on liquor and tobacco.[62]

Statistics aside, 'the history of the history-less', to quote Sabyasachi Bhattacharya, can also be written privileging alternative records of the past like poems, plays and the like as sources of labour history.[63] From these sources, the agency of subaltern drinkers emerges as of vital importance in influencing changes – subtle though they may have been – in subsequent policy measures. A Tamil folk song captured toddy's place in the social world of the labouring classes thus:

> The toddy I trust; the toddy that knows my pulse,
> The toddy that saw my brother, grandfather and ancestors,
> The toddy that saw generations,
> Mischievous toddy, will I see you today?
> You boil like rice in the vessel,
> And like gold, you enrich and embolden!
> The labourers all say their toddy supply has stopped
> Ragupathy shop toddy pokes all night
> Round junction shop toddy incites craziness!
> The Paraiyans' slum shop toddy inspires song and dance
> The wretched cemetery toddy renders one topsy turvy.[64]

Such accounts show that while the state sought to standardise and rationalise excise administration, there were clear limitations to how far it could actually succeed in this endeavour. Subaltern drinkers discerned different types of toddy, which they associated with different establishments, in the process raising their own knowledge networks. This situation meant that the authorities were forced to revise their approach to the drinking public at various points in time.

Although prohibition discourse took it for granted that there was no need to consult subaltern drinkers for their opinions on alcohol policy on the grounds that their actions spoke for them, subaltern drinkers resisted being 'acted upon by an immutable culture or by the strategies of management'.[65] Instead, owing to constantly shifting social relationships, they offered up highly diverse responses, often engaging with management policies in ways that foremost prioritised their respective needs and interests. The subaltern studies corpus has positioned marginalised groups' subversive actions and behaviours as expressions of their resistance against elite hegemony, exercised as it was through policy initiatives.[66] Prohibition histories have similarly surfaced insights about bootlegging and illicit distillation, which figure in the literature as manifestations of drinkers' agency against a top-down policy imposition.[67] Crime assumes prominence in both these bodies of scholarship as the foremost index of the people's resistance to the state.

Gayatri Chakravorty Spivak's essay, which has variously been read as both confirming and challenging the premise that she sets out to interrogate – that the subaltern can indeed speak – is pertinent here. According to her critique, it would be futile to expect the existence of a truly autonomous domain of subaltern politics as the category of 'subaltern' is in itself an elitist construct.[68] The colonial state's approach to the drinking public had far-reaching repercussions for alcohol policy and the responses it elicited. Although the issue of working-class drinking may not have originated from elite politics, the choices that subaltern drinkers had in such matters as the type, quantity, venue and timing of drinking were certainly influenced by the vagaries of elite politics in the decades leading up to prohibition.[69] In fact, even providing working-class drinkers with a semblance of choice became a consideration in alcohol policy, as we have seen. Subaltern interactions with alcohol policy thus operated within the state's administrative frameworks, policies and legislation, regardless of whether they took the form of compliance, negotiation or resistance.

This is because the prose of subaltern drinking was pervasive, becoming foundational to a self-serving state machinery that sought to exclude the working classes from the decision-making process, whilst rewarding 'respectable' members of society for speaking on their behalf. To engage in any action that violated policies raised on this discourse and its undergirding assumptions was to become an enemy of the state. Subaltern acts of 'defiance' warranted their being identified, surveilled and punished by agents of the state. Elite groups used any exercise of agency by subaltern drinkers that defied the state's diktat's – whether colonial or nationalist – as justification for the further exercise of state power. For prohibition's supporters, subaltern agency – cast as crime in the official perspective – became further justification for the policy.

However, attempts to govern subaltern drinking in the 1920s and 1930s show that state power could also only operate within the limits of subaltern cooperation with alcohol policy. As the motivations and behaviours of the drinking public frequently frustrated policymakers – with alcohol policy becoming a feedback mechanism – they revised measures to better reflect ground realities. The coercive powers of the state, as they were expressed through alcohol policy, interacted with subaltern responses to influence prohibitioning right through the Madras Prohibition Act's introduction, and beyond. While subaltern drinking proved the logic of prohibition, it also helped to ensure that policy measures arising from that stance were necessarily limited.

Subaltern drinkers experienced various kinds of hardship owing to state intervention, which prompted a variety of coping strategies on their part. The piecemeal closure of toddy and arrack shops gave rise to the increased consumption of foreign liquor, thus imposing a serious financial burden on working-class drinkers in some districts. An arrack ban in Tenkasi contributed to the increased consumption of foreign liquor there, while the closure of country liquor shops in Ootacamund on Saturdays prompted coolie labourers to buy bottles of beer, which they stored and drank at home.[70] The ad hoc closure of toddy and arrack shops proved equally problematic. Closures on Sundays often resulted in increased sales that took place on Saturdays, as drinkers indulged in 'a double ration on Saturdays to last them over the weekend'.[71]

The incidence of working-class drinkers switching to other types of alcohol or drinking on other days of the week, both of which ultimately still fed state coffers, did not therefore elicit the kind of state attention that other types of subaltern innovation did. The authorities viewed activities that brought about increased costs of administration, or that lowered profits from sales or taxation, as crime.[72] The problem of moonshine liquor ticked both boxes. In the interwar period, Madras city became the site of an alarming increase in the manufacture of a rice liquor that could be easily brewed at home. Known locally as *sonti soru*, it had in fact been legally sold through a system of licences in the nineteenth century. However, the government had banned the liquor as early as 1897 on the grounds that drinkers should be drinking 'the more wholesome fermented alcohol', that was toddy.[73] Ironically, however, steep toddy prices and the paucity of plebeian liquor shops within municipal limits drove *sonti soru*'s production to the northernmost limits of the city. By the late 1920s, its manufacture in the city's northern slums posed such a serious threat to toddy revenue that it warranted the government's immediate attention. The commissioner of excise reported that

> the tactics adopted by the offenders in manufacturing it made detection extremely difficult. The rice required is boiled inside the houses and mixed with 'Sonti' and put in pots which are buried two to three feet deep in open places, such as the seashore, burial grounds etc. It is then left undisturbed for about 24 hours and after fermentation is removed in the dark. When the Excise staff approach the scene of sale, the crowd melt away and it is not possible to find out to whom the pots belong. The only thing possible in most cases is to unearth the pots and destroy the stuff.[74]

The costs involved in policing what amounted to an elusive moonshine industry and the urgency of curbing *sonti soru*'s appeal as a rival to toddy were not lost on the state, which was thus forced to consider legalising the alcohol all over again.[75] Clearly, therefore, the state was not all-powerful in its dealings with subaltern drinkers.

At the level of the district, the government experimented with partial prohibitions since the early 1920s. These policy measures were deliberately limited in their scope as they sought to test the waters before prohibition's actual introduction. When arrack shops were closed for good in Tanjore, Ramanathapuram, Tirunelveli and Salem, rates of illicit distillation soared, thus prompting their subsequent reopening. Although the closure of arrack shops in Tanjore did not cause an upsurge of serious criminal activity in that district, working-class drinkers responded by turning to illicitly distilled arrack in the Tiruvadanai and Paramakudi *taluk*s of Ramnad. This prompted the state to moderate the policy by allowing arrack shops straddling the border with Travancore to sell a regulated quantity of the liquor to drinkers.[76] It also necessitated increased policing efforts and, hence, costs of administration, as nine serious cases of smuggling of Travancore arrack were detected in a single year in just the district of Tenkasi.[77]

The problems presented by partial experiments with prohibition in the 1920s worsened in the 1930s. In fact, the reason why they remained partial was because policymakers were forced to accommodate the responses of working-class drinkers. The illicit distillation of arrack was especially pronounced in the Tamil countryside, as entire villages were identified as hotbeds of *abkari* crime. In 1932, a group of illicit distillers in Aiyampalayam village, Puduchatram range, caught excise officials' attention as they were plying their business with the covert support of the local village *munsif* (headman). The *munsif* apparently made a tidy fortune from the trade in contraband alcohol.[78] Embarrassingly, illicit distillation flourished in Rajaji's stronghold of Tiruchengode as well, so much so that all the arrack shops that were closed in that district had to be reopened within a year.[79] Meanwhile, restrictions placed on liquor production became the basis of another set of innovations. When officials moved to clamp down on illicit tapping in Tinnevelly and parts of Ramnad, the admixture of sweet and fermented toddy presented an opportunity for the enterprising to continue to cater to subaltern drinkers.[80] While these acts of subaltern agency played into the colonial state's hand by supporting the reopening of liquor shops, they simultaneously also prompted demands from the pro-prohibition camp for the government to abandon its limited stance of regulation for prohibition instead.

Modern transportation facilities also complicated efforts to establish 'dry' areas flanking decidedly 'wet' districts. The motor bus traffic enabled liquor to be transported to dry areas during partial experiments with prohibition.[81] The smuggling of alcohol from surrounding areas into Coimbatore and Attur, designated dry districts during a partial experiment with prohibition, was so rampant as to prompt official surveys about the feasibility of enforcement.[82] Some districts became breeding grounds for illicit tapping and distillation as they were too large for effective enforcement. Salem and Sankari fell into this category and it was reported that 'crime of all kinds [was] exceedingly common in the *taluks*'.[83] Illicit liquor running in motor buses became so common that the transportation of spirituous beverages from one district to another through Salem was expressly forbidden; special surveillance units were established to monitor buses that plied routes between towns in Salem district.[84]

Although tea and coffee were promoted as substitutes for alcohol, they never quite succeeded in changing the preferences of the vast majority of drinkers. The Indian Tea Association had been established in 1881 with the aim of encouraging tea drinking among Indians. The association stepped up its marketing efforts, including distributing tea for free among Indian drinkers, who were used to imbibing arrack and toddy, at the peak of the

anti-alcohol movement in the interwar period. The state also took upon itself
the task of promoting coffee in India. In the Presidency of Fort St George,
the Tamil intelligentsia came to see it as an instrument of Western cultural
imperialism that was chipping away at the very foundations of Indian family
life, beginning with women. Their objections notwithstanding, A. R.
Venkatachalapathy reminds us that the drink had 'captured the imagination
and diet of the middle class' in the Tamil country by the beginning of the
twentieth century.[85]

While the tea scheme was attempted in earnest between 1916 and 1919
with the opening of around thirty new tea shops, it quickly became evident
that they had failed miserably in 'reforming' the tastes of individuals who
preferred stronger drinks. In 1917, the excise establishment reported that

> there [was] no indication that any of them effected a reduction of
> drunkenness, while all but about three appear to have been conducted
> at a loss. At the same time, the objection is taken to the scheme by
> some educated Indians that, if tea and coffee are not liable to injure the
> drinker as spirit does, they are equally effectual in reducing the share of
> his wages that is available for food.[86]

By 1919, the Board of Revenue declared that the tea-for-alcohol scheme
had died 'a natural death'.[87] It was clear to most observers that the policy of
substituting toddy with tea was at best a case of wishful thinking. Remarking
that the consumption of tea had remained unaltered while that of toddy had
actually increased, the *Swadesamitran* argued that

> one madly after drink will drink at any cost … A rule that liquor or
> toddy can only be sold for a few hours in the evening will certainly
> diminish the quantity sold. If instead of doing so, curious posters are
> posted everywhere suggesting the use of tea, it will in no way benefit the
> poor but only form an advertisement for tea.[88]

The *Ananda Vikatan* drew attention to the futility of the tea endeavour in a
commentary that quipped, tongue-in-cheek:

> It seems our countrymen must keep drinking something or the other.
> The Indian Tea Cess Committee has great concern for poor Indians.
> Alas! It cannot bear to see Indians, especially those living in villages,

suffering on account of their refusal to take up tea drinking. Hence, the Committee is determined to cultivate this habit amongst Indians. It seems that a forty-member committee, appointed to carry out propaganda work, provides villagers with sample tea-leaf packets, cups of tea, and also teaches them the proper way of brewing the beverage - all free of charge.[89]

Although the state continued to experiment with counter-inducements as part and parcel of its alcohol policy, country liquor retained its unrivalled importance in subaltern lives and livelihoods.

The most noteworthy partial prohibition in the province was attempted in the Nilgiris. Alarming rates of public drunkenness in previous decades and the relentless efforts of the Nilgiris Temperance Association convinced the local Excise Advisory Committee to approve a complete ban on alcohol in Ootacamund, Coonoor and Kotagiri districts in the mid-1930s.[90] Prohibition's enforcement in the Nilgiris markedly differed from similar efforts elsewhere in the province as it focused on surveilling individual drinkers rather than drinking establishments. This was due to the specific intersections that class and race presented in that district. Whereas toddy and arrack shops had been subject to systematic processes of surveillance elsewhere in the province, arrack shops and beer taverns were the main working-class watering holes in the Nilgiris.

The resident European community, however, also frequented taverns. The deputy commissioner of excise thus opposed the closure of these establishments citing 'a large consuming public other than the hill tribes' who would suffer due to the proposed restrictions on shops.[91] Instead, he proposed a blanket liquor ban on the basis of ethnicity. He recommended that access to alcohol should be prohibited to members of the Badaga, Toda, Kota, Irula and Kurumba tribes except on production of medical certificates, the onus of which was on shopkeepers to verify. Although it thus became theoretically illegal for tribesmen and women to possess alcohol, it was quite another matter to enforce penalties charging them with illicit possession and consumption. The Badagas and other tribesmen proved remarkably adept at sidestepping lax liquor regulations, a fact that became amply evident within the very first year of the prohibition policy's introduction. While some of the more 'timid' communities, to quote colonial contempt, switched to drugs instead of persisting with arrack or beer, a few members of the Kota tribe sought exemption from prohibition.[92] Still others proved resourceful in procuring their alcohol through Tamil or Cannarese coolie middlemen whom they hired 'on commission basis' for the purpose.[93] Enterprising tea shopkeepers, ironically, became middlemen for Badagas looking to buy their arrack or beer despite the state's diktats.[94] When elected members raised the issue of punitive legislation for repeat offenders in the legislative council in 1933, the government demanded information as to whether the hill tribes themselves supported the measure. In response, the hill tribe communities presented several petitions to the government, recording their opposition not only to the proposed penalties but, more fundamentally, to prohibition as a policy stance itself.[95]

Alongside these developments, toddy consumption increased in the district due to the paucity of the more preferred arrack and beer. Between 1932 and 1933, the Koya tribals tapped an estimated 46,310 trees for toddy. Individuals from the community thus responded to the prohibition by exploiting the pre-existing concession of tapping two trees per individual without charge.[96] The situation caused a great deal of unhappiness to the other hill tribes. In 1938, several wealthy Badagas and members of the planting community appealed to the government that prohibition ought to be enforced for the 'primitive tribes alone' and discontinued for the Badagas, who were apparently more civilised, and hence could be trusted to exercise self-restraint.[97] The district collector supported their appeal. On its part, the excise establishment recommended allowing the hill tribes to consume beer 'in order to convert their taste from arrack, which was relatively harmful', instead of persisting with prohibition.[98]

Partial experiments with prohibition in the Madras Presidency reflect the consensus that prevailed in official circles that access to some type of alcohol would need to be allowed, particularly in designated 'toddy-drinking areas'. In keeping with the debates that the regulation of alcohol brought forth in industrial centres, this alcohol would be the relatively benign toddy. The necessity of enabling choice to the drinking public, albeit with inherent restrictions, was even more pronounced where the Nilgiris was concerned. As a satisfactory solution to problematic drinking behaviours could not be found, it was eventually deemed desirable to allow hill tribesmen and women with access to beer as the least harmful alternative. However, drinkers' responses to alcohol policy diverged considerably from official expectations and calculations, prompting the authorities to resort to remedial action and even policy reversals.

An internally differentiated category, 'the drinking public' thus presented the state with varied responses to alcohol policy. Some subaltern drinkers referenced the same arguments that had been raised by Indian elites. One such argument was the insistence that they needed alcoholic drink to be content and productive. Indeed, individuals belonging to the lower castes also manipulated the logic of caste to justify their demands for continued access to alcohol. In contrast to the ignorance or criminality of the working classes that state officials expected, these petitions evidenced a commitment to civil methods of protest. A letter of protest against prohibition, which was published in the *Times of India*, argued:

> When they declare that the whole of India is for prohibition, they only mean their communities - the vegetarian, non-drinking classes who form not even 1/20th of the population of India ... Sir, we the labouring classes, belonging to the Harijan, Sudra, Rajput and such flesh-eating communities have been used to liquor for over 5,000 years ... we are still vigorous, strong, healthy and in every way fit to take our place alongside other communities to do our duty by the nation ... we are better able to take up arms in defence of the country, should occasion arise, than the non-drinking classes of India ... Drink in excess is bad for health, in the same way as milk in excess is poison, as a Tamil proverb says.[99]

Moreover, alongside petitions that demanded the relocation or closure of toddy and arrack shops, working-class drinkers appealed to the government to retain these drinking establishments in their original locations near their homes and workplaces. One such petition was received from manual labourers drawn from the ranks of the Adi Dravidar, Chakkiliyar, Pallar, Naicker, Dalit, Ubbravar, Valluvar, Oddar and Chetty Balija caste communities. The thirty petitioners, comprising fishermen, weavers, oil mongers, masons, blacksmiths, rickshaw men, cart pullers and coolies from Madras city, pointed out that the toddy shops of Pycroft Road, Triplicane, had in recent years been closed one after another and expressed concern that the one remaining shop in the vicinity was also facing imminent closure.[100] Their petition further elaborated:

> This is the only shop located in a central place to suit our conveniences ... This shop is very useful to those of us who are coolies in the market and Rice Bazaars near by. After having worked all day long we get awfully tired in the evening and by drinking toddy we recoup our energy for the next day's work ... Arrack never suits us and creates Dysentery. We are

very thankful to the Government for all the benefits we have had from
their hands but our only request to Government is to pass favourable
orders for locating a Toddy shop in this useful centre.[101]

The petitioners thus echoed the official stance that toddy was indispensable to
the health and vitality of the working classes. Their appeal, however, was met
with little sympathy – except, rather predictably – by the commissioner of
excise. Reiterating his conviction that the interests of the drinking public and
liquor businesses should be represented on the Licensing Board, a proposal
that had previously been submitted to the government for consideration, the
commissioner emphasised that 'given the existing habits of the working and
drinking classes, it is idle to suppose that abstinence can be imposed upon
them by the mere closure of shops; the result can only be, and has been,
to cause overcrowding of the shops that remained, and to stimulate illicit
practices'.[102]

*   *   *

This chapter has shown that colonial conceptualisations of 'the drinking
public' had far-reaching implications for alcohol policy. It fortified a
self-serving colonial machinery that premised policymaking on skewed
understandings of working-class drinking cultures in ways that ultimately
furthered the state's interests. Although 'the drinking public' emerged as an
administrative category that profiled working-class drinkers, endowing a
certain fixedness to their habits and supposed propensities, they were far from
being a homogenous category. Even as their circumstances and motivations
differed, colonial alcohol policy interacted with ground realities to produce
outcomes that simultaneously justified the need for prohibition, whilst
limiting its subsequent trajectories in significant ways.

Notes

1. G.O. No. 2020 (Mis.), 9 September 1921. The incident was recorded as
   having taken place on 24 June 1921.
2. Ibid.
3. See, for instance, Mukerjie, *A Report on Toddy Taxation*, p. 53; G.O. No.
   488, Revenue Department (Mis.), 8 March 1925, extract from proceedings

of a meeting of the Ootacamund Municipal Council held on 26 December 1925, p. 3, TNA; and G.O. No. 1290, Revenue Department (Mis.), 15 August 1925, p. 1, TNA. For perspectives on the construction of criminal tribes, see Anand A. Yang, *Crime and Criminality in British India* (Tucson: University of Arizona Press, 1985); see also Henry Schwarz, *Constructing the Criminal Tribe in Colonial India: Acting Like a Thief* (West Sussex: Wiley Blackwell, 2010).

4. Ranajit Guha, 'The Prose of Counter-Insurgency', in *Culture/Power/ History: A Reader in Contemporary Social Theory*, ed. Nicholas B. Dirks, Geoffrey H. Eley and Sherry B. Ortner, pp. 336–371 (Princeton: Princeton University Press, 1994).

5. Leela Fernandes, *Producing Workers: The Politics of Gender, Class and Culture in the Calcutta Jute Mills* (Philadelphia: University of Pennsylvania Press, 1997). For perspectives on gender issues in the state's approach to labour, see, for instance, Samita Sen, *Women and Labour in Late Colonial India: The Bengal Jute Industry* (Cambridge: Cambridge University Press, 1999); see also Nirmala Banerjee, 'Working Women in Colonial Bengal: Modernisation and Marginalisation', in *Recasting Women: Essays in Colonial History*, ed. Kumkum Sangari and Sudhesh Vaid, pp. 269–301 (Calcutta: Kali for Women, 1990).

6. 'Note on the Pariahs, Tremenheere', G.O. No. 1010, 1010A, Board of Revenue, 30 September 1892. Tremenheere's report recommended that the state should allocate lands to Dalits to help them overcome the marginalisation they faced.

7. Moffat, *The Drink Traffic in the Madras Presidency*, p. 11.

8. R. B. Wood (1916), quoted in Viswanath, *The Pariah Problem*, p. 173.

9. Nikhil Menon, 'Battling the Bottle, Experiments in Regulating Drink in Late Colonial Madras', *Indian Economic and Social History Review* 52, no. 1 (2015), pp. 29–51.

10. For perspectives on the politics of trade unionism, see, for instance, A. S. Mathur and J. S. Mathur, *Trade Union Movement in India* (Allahabad: Chaitanya Publishing House, 1957); V. B. Karnik, *Indian Trade Unions: A Survey* (Bombay: Allied Publishers, 1960); G. K. Sharma, *Labour Movement in India: Its Past and Present* (Jullundur: University Publishers, 1963); S. C. Jha, *The Indian Trade Union Movement* (Calcutta: K.L. Firma Mukhopadhyay, 1970); C. Revri, *The Indian Trade Union Movement 1880– 1947* (Delhi: Orient Longman, 1972); and Sukomal Sen, *Working Class of India: History of Emergence and Movement, 1830–1970* (Calcutta: K.P. Bagchi

& Co., 1977). For major works on labour from the Subaltern Studies corpus of scholarship, see Dipesh Chakrabarty, *Rethinking Working Class History: Bengal 1890–1940* (Princeton: Princeton University Press, 1989); see also Dipesh Chakrabarty, 'Conditions for Knowledge of Working-Class Conditions: Employers, Government and the Jute of Calcutta, 1890–1940', in *Subaltern Studies II: Writings on South Asian History and Society,* ed. Ranajit Guha, pp. 259–310 (New Delhi: Oxford University Press, 1983); and Dipesh Chakrabarty, 'Trade Unions in a Hierarchical Culture: The Jute Workers of Calcutta, 1920–50', in *Subaltern Studies III: Writings on South Asian History,* ed. Ranajit Guha, pp. 116–152 (New Delhi: Oxford University Press, 1984).

11. Rajnarayan Chandavarkar, *The Origins of Industrial Capitalism in India: Business Strategies and the Working Classes in Bombay 1900–1940* (Cambridge: Cambridge University Press, 1994). See also Dilip Simeon, *The Politics of Labour under Late Colonialism: Workers, Trade Unions and the State in Chota Nagpur, 1928–1939* (Delhi: Manohar, 1995); Parimal Ghosh, *Colonialism, Class, and a History of the Calcutta Jute Hands, 1880–1930* (Hyderabad: Orient Blackswan, 2000); and Priyanka Srivastava, *The Well-Being of the Labor Force in Colonial Bombay: Discourses and Practices* (London: Palgrave Macmillan, 2017), for a discussion of wellbeing as a focal point in deliberations over labour policy that involved a broad cross-section of colonial society.

12. Aditya Sarkar, *Trouble at the Mill: Factory Law and the Emergence of the Labour Question in Late Nineteenth-Century Bombay* (Oxford: Oxford University Press, 2018), pp. 129–131.

13. Janaki Nair, *Miners and Millhands: Work, Culture and Politics in Princely Mysore* (Delhi: Sage Publications, 1998); Menon, 'Battling the Bottle'; Nitin Varma, *Coolies of Capitalism: Assam Tea and the Making of Coolie Labour* (Berlin; Boston: De Gruyter, 2016).

14. Prasannan Parthasarathi, 'Indian Labor History', *International Labor and Working-Class History* 82 (fortieth anniversary issue) (Fall 2012), pp. 127–135.

15. *Madras Excise Revenue, 1916–1917* (Madras: Government Press, 1917), p. 12.

16. G.O. No. 51 Revenue Department (Mis.), 18 April 1925, TNA.

17. *The Hindu,* 1 March 1906.

18. G.O. No. 488, Revenue Department (Mis.), 8 March 1925, extract from proceedings of a meeting of the Ootacamund Municipal Council held on 26 December 1925, p. 3, TNA.

19. Copy of letter no. R.C. 525/25/B-2 from Collector of Nilgiris addressed to Madras Commissioner for Excise, 3 March 1925.

20. Sarkar, *Trouble at the Mill*, pp. 89–92. Sarkar's work shifted the focus of scholarship beyond the scope of the Factory Acts of the 1880s to examining the labour legislation that was introduced over the course of the early to mid-twentieth century.

21. Eugene Irschick, *Dialogue and History: Constructing South India, 1795–1895* (Berkeley: University of California Press, 1994), pp. 153–154. Irschick has written about the 1880s and 1890s in the Madras Presidency as a time of tension. It was on the one hand 'a utopian movement' in the history of colonial India as it was characterised by British and Indian efforts to understand why the poor were getting poorer, although it was also a time when the colonial government was concerned about how the labour of itinerant individuals could be harnessed to sustain productivity in society.

22. Bhattacharya, 'Colonial State and Practice', p. 5.

23. E. P. Thomson, *The Making of the English Working Class* (2nd edition) (London: Pelican, 1968), p. 316.

24. Ibid. See also Sidney Pollard, 'Factory Discipline in the Industrial Revolution', *Economic History Review* 16, no. 2 (1963), pp. 254–271, pp. 256–258.

25. *Andhrapatrika*, 18 February 1921, NNPR (January–March 1921), p. 263.

26. F. De Souza, *The House of Binny* (Madras: Associated Printers, 1970), p. 35.

27. See G.O. No. 629, Revenue Department (Mis.), 30 April 1925, p. 2, TNA.

28. Chandavarkar, *The Origins of Industrial Capitalism in India*, pp. 101–104. I refer to Chandavarkar's discussion about the equation that presented between jobbers and labourers in the cotton textile industry. See also Simeon, *The Politics of Labour under Late Colonialism*, pp. 64–73.

29. Sabyasachi Bhattacharya, 'Introduction', *International Review of Social History* 51 (supp. 14: Coolies, Capital, and Colonialism – Studies in Indian Labour History) (2006), pp. 7–19.

30. G.O. No. 12, Revenue Department (Mis.), 4 November 1932, TNA.

31. Ibid.

32. Nair, *Miners and Millhands*, pp. 98–101; Menon, 'Battling the Bottle', pp. 29–51. See also Varma, *Coolies of Capitalism*, pp. 89–93.

33. G.O. No. 12, Revenue Department (Mis.), 4 November 1932, TNA.

34. Ibid.

35. Ibid.

36. Extract from the Madras Legislative Council Debates, 27 September 1929, p. 389. Resolution regarding the closure of liquor shops on holidays and days of election; transferred to Secretary, E & O Dept., 12 December 1929, IOR.

37. G.O. No. 399, Revenue Department (Mis.), 14 February 1939, p. 9, TNA.

38. G.O. No. 1577, Revenue Department (Mis.), 21 February 1939, p. 1, TNA.

39. Moffat, *The Drink Traffic in the Madras Presidency*, p. 12.

40. E & O Department, 143/1929, 24 August 1928, p. 1, IOR.

41. D. No. 1694, Excise Department (Board of Revenue), 6 August 1938, p. 1. Letter from Collector of Tinnevelly to Madras Board of Revenue (Excise), TNA.

42. G.O. No. 2129, Revenue Department, 25 April 1939, letter from Sri Rao Bahadur K. Raman Nayar, Collector of Trichinopoly to Assistant Secretary to the Board of Revenue (Excise), TNA.

43. Ibid.

44. William Digby, *The Famine Campaign in Southern India (Madras and Bombay Presidencies and Province of Mysore) 1876–1878*, vol. 1 (London: Longman, Greens & Co., 1878), p. 211.

45. G.O. No. 1577, Revenue Department (Mis.), p. 1, TNA.

46. Ibid.

47. G.O. No. 640, Revenue Department (Mis.), 17 February 1941, copy of letter from Collector of Chingleput, No. 2413/41-B1, Public Works Department, 4 April 1941, TNA.

48. G.O. No. 1737, Revenue Department (Mis.). 25 August 1939, p. 1, TNA.

49. Budget Debates, 1934-1935/1936, Proceedings of the Legislative Council of the Government of Madras (1936), p. 837.

50. G.O. No. 1737, Revenue Department (Mis.). 25 August 1939, p. 2, TNA.

51. Edgar Thurston, *Anthropology of the Todas and Kotas of the Nilgiri Hills: And of the Brahmans, Kammalans, Pallis, and Pariahs of Madras City* (Madras: Madras Government Museum, 1896), pp. 182–187.

52. See, for instance, Dirks, *Castes of Mind*, pp. 174–177; and Kavita Philip, *Civilising Natures: Race, Resources and Modernity in Colonial South India* (New Delhi: Orient Longman, 2003), pp. 148–149.

53. Francis, *District Gazetteer of the Nilgiris*, pp. 287–288.

54. Ibid.

55. *Harijan*, 18 September 1937.

56. Darinee Alagirisamy, 'Toddy, Race and Urban Space in Colonial Singapore, 1900–1959', *Modern Asian Studies* 53, no. 5 (September 2019), pp. 1675–1699. I refer here to my argument that this self-serving logic also informed colonial alcohol policy for the south Indian diaspora elsewhere in the empire, like Singapore.

57. *Report of the Excise Advisory Committee Appointed by the Government of Madras* (Madras: Government Press, 1924), IOR.

58. Baliga, *Compendium on Temperance*, p. 53.

59. *Report of the Excise Advisory Committee*.

60. Extract from the Madras Legislative Council Debates, 27 September 1929, resolution regarding the closure of liquor shops on holidays and days of election; transferred to Secretary, E & O Department, p. 389, IOR.

61. B. Shiva Rao, *The Industrial Worker in India* (London: George Allen & Unwin, 1939), p. 135.

62. *Report on an Enquiry into the Family Budgets of Industrial Workers in Madras City* (Madras: Government Press, 1938), p. 51.

63. See, for instance, Chandavarkar, *The Origins of Industrial Capitalism in India*, pp. 94–100. See also Chitra Joshi, *Lost Worlds: Labour and its Forgotten Histories* (New Delhi: Anthem Press, 2003).

64. *Kallukkadai Ennum Kudiyar Sintu* (Toddy Shop or Drinkers' Song) (Madras: Sundravilasa Achu, 1901), Roja Muthiah Library, Chennai (RML).

65. Parthasarathi, 'Indian Labor History'.

66. See, for instance, Guha, 'On Some Aspects of the Historiography of Colonial India', p. 40.

67. Jeffers and Kyvig, *Repealing National Prohibition*, pp. 121–123; Andersen, *Politics of Prohibition*, pp. 137–145; Burns, *The Spirits of America*, pp. 54–55; Beyer, *Temperance and Prohibition*, pp. 87–88.

68. Spivak, 'Can the Subaltern Speak?'

69. Guha, 'On Some Aspects of the Historiography of Colonial India', p. 40.

70. G.O. No. 116, Revenue Department, 22 January 1926, p. 3, TNA. See also Baliga, *Compendium on Temperance*, p. 15.

71. *Madras Excise Revenue, 1931–1932*, p. 16.

72. Slater, *Southern India*, p. 182.

73. *East India: Accounts and Estimates, 1907–1908*, Parliamentary Papers, House of Commons (London, 1907), p. 53, BL.

74. G.O No. 2386, Revenue Department, 10 October 1928, TNA.

75. Ibid.

76. *Madras Excise Revenue, 1930–1931*, p. 18.

77. Ibid.

78. G.O. No. 177, Revenue Department, 25 January 1932, TNA.

79. G.O. No. 1857, Revenue Department, 6 September 1932, TNA. The shop had been closed in October 1931 and had to be reopened in August 1932.

80. *Madras Excise Revenue, 1935–1936*, p. 11.

81. G.O. No. 2675, Revenue Department, 17 December 1931, p. 1, TNA. G.O. No. 51, Revenue Department (Mis.), 9 January 1930, p. 1, TNA.

82. G.O. No. 552, Revenue Department (Separate Revenue), 23 March 1926, CR No. 8491, TNA.

83. Ibid. *Taluk* refers to district.

84. G.O. No. 1905, Revenue Department (Confl.), 18 September 1937, TNA.

85. Venkatachalapathy, *In Those Days There Was No Coffee*, p. 27.

86. *Madras Excise Revenue, 1916–1917*, app. 2, p. 15.

87. G.O. No. 884, Revenue Department (Separate Revenue), 20 October 1916, TNA.

88. *Swadesamitran*, 21 November 1918, NNPR (September–December 1918), pp. 1695–1696.

89. *Ananda Vikatan*, 17 September 1931, p. 639.

90. Excise Department, D. No. 1237 Abk 40 (Excise), 11 June 1940, p. 2, TNA.

91. Ibid.

92. *Madras Excise Revenue, 1930–1931*, p. 18.

93. *Madras Excise Revenue, 1932–1933*, p. 16.

94. G.O. No. 1063, Revenue Department (Mis.), 12 January 1933, pp. 4–5, TNA.

95. Ibid. The consensus in opinion was obtained through informal surveys involving eighty-six tribesmen.

96. *Madras Excise Revenue, 1932–1933*, p. 4.

97. Excise Department, D. No. 1237 Abk/40 (Excise), 11 June 1940, p. 2.

98. Ibid.

99. Letter from V. Pandurang, from Goa, *Times of India*, 11 July 1939.

100. G.O. No. 1290, Revenue Department (Mis), 15 August 1925, p.18, TNA. Revenue Department officials translated the petition from the Tamil language, in which it was written.
101. Ibid.
102. G.O. No. 1290, Revenue Department (Mis.), 15 August 1925; CR No. 7304 Abk., 10 August 1925, TNA.

5

Liquor Businesses and
the Business of Prohibition

Three-Way Tango: Politics of Liquor Production

Any account of prohibitioning in the decades leading up to the Madras
Prohibition Act would necessarily be incomplete without addressing the
politics of alcohol production. Colonial officials and nationalist elites were
interacting as much with one another and diverse segments of society as
with liquor business interests to devise policies aimed at regulating drinking.
The cumulative impact of the ensuing developments had a tremendous
impact on prohibitioning by influencing the momentum towards the policy's
introduction in 1937.

During the period in question, liquor businesses had to contend with
mounting social pressure against their trade on the one hand and political
manoeuvring by both the colonial government and the Congress leadership
on the other. Whilst prohibition discourse cast drinkers as victims who
could eventually be redeemed of their affliction and transformed into
upstanding citizens, it painted the producers, distributors and retailers of
alcohol unforgivingly and with a large brush stroke as traitors of the nation.
'A number of Indian merchants, be it said to their shame,' charged a letter
that was published in *The Hindu*, 'have taken up the merchandise of liquor
to ruin their countrymen.'[1] The most spectacular anti-alcohol protests were,
unsurprisingly, directed at toddy and arrack shop contractors.

The constraints imposed on liquor business interests by, first, the colonial
establishment and, subsequently, the nationalist leadership were part of an
overarching political contest to dictate the terms of liquor production. If the
colonial government was concerned that the emergence of liquor monopolies
would result in lowered revenue yields for the state, the nationalist leadership
sought the right to altogether remove liquor production from the workings

of the national economy. However, this was easier said than done. For the Congress leadership, the decades leading up to prohibition necessitated sourcing viable solutions for the economic problems that prohibition threatened to unleash. As it prepared to take up the reins of governance, the nationalist organisation increasingly found itself having to think like the government, which was reflected in its efforts to find new uses for the country liquor industry.

The coercive arm of the state came down upon alcohol industries in response to the gathering storm of prohibition protest in the interwar period. However, as they were not created equally to begin with, the state was selective and discriminatory in its legislative treatment of the various industries. By and large, the foreign liquor industry had a greater say in liquor legislation and was afforded concessions that its country liquor counterparts were systematically denied.

Relatedly, liquor businesses had a diverse range of interests, which had a significant bearing on the dynamics of the representation they sought as the provinces made rapid progress towards prohibition. The interrelationship of interests among liquor producers, the colonial government and, finally, the nationalists militate against a straightforward narrative of the politics of prohibition from the production side of the equation.

Liquor businesses engaged with prohibition at the points wherein the policy intersected with the economy on the one hand and with law on the other. Sabyasachi Bhattacharya coined the term 'discriminatory interventionism' to show that colonial laissez-faire policies found their limits in political self-interest.[2] The combination of pro- and anti-interventionist measures insofar as they served the Raj and the resultant flexibility of government policy are discernible in the state's approach to liquor businesses. More than most other aspects of prohibition politics, the state's management of its relationship with liquor businesses brought forth a careful balancing act between revenue maximisation and regulation. Whilst the auction system that was in place for toddy and arrack shop rentals ostensibly operated in response to free market conditions, the colonial government reserved the right to intervene in it for the purpose of securing its goals.

Indeed, even as the meaning of alcohol underwent tremendous transformation in the interwar period, which wrought the coming together of prohibition politics and nationalist mobilisation, the state tried to reassert control over the situation by engineering new solutions. Along with the tea campaign, it tried to promote power alcohol, although 'a coherent industrial policy for alcohol did not emerge' owing to the state's 'half-hearted industrial policy and the ambiguous character that alcohol itself had'.[3] This lack of clarity was complicated by two factors: the actions of liquor businesses, which threw a spanner into the programs of the state, and the fact that provincial governments had to scramble for revenue generation following the Montague–Chelmsford Reforms, which transferred excise administration to the provinces, as we have seen.

Precisely because discriminatory interventionism was thus driven by 'political considerations, with the state aiming to alter relationships of power between specific sets of economic actors', there was 'a persistent tension' between the most prudent course of action for the state and the consequences of those actions for other stakeholders.[4] The disputes that thus ensued were frequently negotiated at more local levels of administration, like the offices of provincial administration. Conflicts of interest relating to liquor legislation pitted the colonial government against the Congress leadership, segments of Indian society and liquor businesses. These disputes primarily unfolded in the provincial legislatures, which became spaces to build consensus over what a fair and effective alcohol policy should look like. As can be imagined, the search for an alcohol policy that was both 'fair' and 'effective' – both of which positions already subsumed within them diverse perspectives and conflicting interests – led to more prohibitioning.

In contrast to the dichotomy that the literature presents between the colonial and nationalist leaderships on the subject of their attitudes towards liquor businesses, sustained consensus-building efforts leading up to prohibition show that official approaches did not differ all that much.[5] When the Congress realised the costs of prohibition, it moderated its approach to liquor producers considerably, from a stance of complete intolerance in the 1920s to one of limited tolerance instead in the 1930s.

Finally, liquor businesses themselves played a tremendous role in prohibitioning. The 'liquor lobby' in late colonial India comprised diverse socio-economic profiles and business interests. Subsumed within the category were wealthy business communities, brewery operators and corporations that dealt in imported and Indian-made foreign liquor. Although not as visible as the contractors who took out licences or the renters to whom they subleased the shops, *mirasidar*s and landlords also had a stake in prohibition politics as it developed. These individuals made a tidy profit by leasing out the lands on which the coconut and palm trees used in country liquor production stood. At the same time, the liquor lobby included middling and small liquor businesses involved in vending country liquor. Toddy tappers, for instance, occupied a rung below contractors and renters in the supply chain. Although the measures introduced by the colonial government to centralise excise administration directly affected contractors and renters, rather than tappers, the latter often bore the brunt of prohibition politics as they lacked the financial means or political clout to weather the storm.

Liquor contractors wielded considerable clout in many cases. When a public plea was made for the piecemeal closure of toddy and liquor shops during festive periods in Trichinopoly district, a toddy contractor based there opposed it as it would bring heavy losses to contractors.[6] As a community, the contractors, he argued, were not prepared to withstand the proposed changes as the possibility of closures had not been entered into their licences. As the state was motivated by the imperative of revenue maximisation, it sided with the liquor businesses against public opinion to reject the appeal for the shop closures in this instance.

In the Madras Presidency, the toddy-drawing castes were generally rather prosperous and ranked high in literacy. The tensions that arose between the Nadars' rising wealth levels and the lowly position they occupied in the caste hierarchy have received much scholarly attention. Admittedly, segments of these communities renounced the trade in favour of more socially acceptable work, particularly in the context of prohibition politics.[7] Relatedly, while those who were involved with alcohol production generally belonged to the lower castes, it was not uncommon to see high-caste individuals prospering as toddy contractors in parts of the province. This was particularly so in districts like Krishna, where a local newspaper reported that the Brahmins were 'regrettably stooping to bid', thereby bringing about 'a strain' on their caste.[8] Nor was it uncommon to see divergent attitudes to the trade in alcohol even within communities that were associated with it. In northern Malabar, Mappila Muslims successfully challenged the dominance that the Tiyya tapping community had established over the toddy trade. Elsewhere in Malabar, however, the Mappilas were ardent advocates of prohibition. Members of the community even crossed swords with the Tiyyas over the picketing of toddy and liquor shops, particularly during the Non-Cooperation movement, which coincided with the Mappila rebellion.[9]

Indeed, the relationship that surfaced between communities that were engaged in liquor-related economic activity and prohibition was anything but straightforward. As we have seen, the Bhandaris of western India dealt a severe blow to the state by collectively refusing to supply toddy following the Bombay Abkari Act of 1878.[10] As past scholarship has shown, some of the first attempts at non-cooperation were in fact initiated by disgruntled liquor barons who saw in nationalist mass mobilisation the opportunity to resist state intervention in their livelihood. 'Publican allied with pussyfoot to promote temperance campaigns', spurred more by the motives of gaining political leverage and keeping auction prices lowered, than patriotic fervour.[11] The Congress's campaign against alcohol proved advantageous to liquor barons who exploited the situation to obtain their contracts at a bargain. At the same time, it was not uncommon for toddy-tapping communities like the Nadars to take out toddy shop licences so that they could be self-sufficient in alcohol.[12]

Demands by liquor businesses for representation and redress against the losses that prohibition-related developments inflicted on them forced the authorities to devise stop-gap solutions, which in turn affected the contours of prohibition policy as the latter took shape. The state's intervention in this aspect of regulating alcohol production took several forms, including introducing legislation that prevented vendors from combining the legal sales of toddy and arrack. The official rationale for such policy revisions was that liquor businesses could be regulated most effectively when they were subjected to market forces. The real reason, however, was that they sought to prevent the development of liquor monopolies, a situation that the state especially feared as it would mean diminished revenue and hence power.

Various segments of Indian society demanded that the auction system should be replaced with a system of fixed annual fees so as to 'obviate the reckless competition among shopkeepers'.[13] The colonial government, however, refused to budge from its stance. If the right to vend alcohol was not sold by auction, it maintained, there would be no checks and balances on the contractor who would then sell the liquor cheap. The colonial government cloaked its laissez-faire approach in a familiar paternalist rhetoric. In this line of reasoning, it was only ethical that 'the state should compel (the seller) to put into the public purse any portion of that value which [was] in excess of a fair profit'.[14] Collusion amongst contractors would not only result in increased prices of toddy and arrack, it could also in turn trigger an undesirable spike in illicit liquor supply, both of which outcomes would be detrimental to drinkers.

Besides guarding against the emergence of monopolies through the sales of shops in groups, rather than individually, the commissioner of excise also recommended that one or more 'key' shops ought to be reserved and operated under direct government management in key urban centres to regulate liquor prices. However, he warned that it was equally important to resort to this measure, which would undoubtedly invite the ire of toddy and arrack contractors, only at the discretion of local collectors when the latter deemed it an absolutely indispensable course of action to safeguard the state's interests. Indeed, one of the foremost considerations that influenced state intervention in alcohol production was the knowledge that toddy and arrack shop contractors together made up 'a very influential body'.[15] The state thus struck a careful balancing act between embracing laissez-faire and intervention.

Although the state reserved the right to lay down the law, it also made arbitrary policy revisions in response to contingencies. We see this in its management of the auction system, which frequently prompted state intervention in the name of course correction. Toddy and arrack shops put up for auction were suddenly withdrawn at the excise commissioner's discretion when collusion between bidders was even suspected. Needless to say, this caused great frustration and, frequently, loss to liquor businesses. Between 1928 and 1929, the excise establishment attributed the fall in sales of the right to vend toddy to strong collusion amongst bidders, which prompted it to close eleven shops as a pre-emptive measure.[16] The move was met with stiff resistance by toddy and arrack contractors, one of whom was V. Vydialingam Pillai. Pillai wanted to rent a shop on Elephant Gate Street, Madras city. In his petition to the excise minister, he complained about the removal of the shop on the orders of the collector of Madras. Even though Pillai's bid of 6,010 rupees had been the highest for the year in question, the shop that he had bid for had been arbitrarily offered by a system of tender instead. Pillai noted that it was 'extraordinary' for such a revision to be made without precedent or prior notice, and that too for a single shop. He appealed that had the information about the number of shops to be put up for auction been clearly communicated beforehand, he would have bid for another shop. Instead, 'the law of government had been seriously and prejudicially affected' by its capriciousness.[17] In response, the excise commissioner echoed the official stance that 'in special cases where a sale by auction had proved infructuous on account of strong combination among the bidders', the tender system would be implemented instead, as it had been in this situation.[18]

Notwithstanding its stated commitment to preventing liquor monopolies, the state not only allowed them to exist, but it also demonstrated great flexibility in situations where broader strategic interests and considerations were at stake. Although the right to vend toddy and arrack was mostly contested by Indian contractors, as these were designated as Indian industries, definitions changed with political expediency. One of the effects of the close relationship the state struck with urban business interests, 'whether metropolitan or expatriate', was that it supported a relatively favourable tax structure for the imported and Indian-made foreign liquor industries.[19] We see this in the government's approval of Messrs Parry & Company's application to hold exclusive rights over the distribution of Malabar arrack. In the 1920s and 1930s, the oldest agency house in the province controlled the distribution of the arrack, which it sold as a mixer to foreign liquor sellers.[20] Malabar arrack was classified as foreign liquor to circumvent the legal restriction preventing contractors from establishing monopolies over country liquor. For all intents and purposes a special concession, this situation prompted the *Kerala Patrika*'s comment that 'the inclusion under the foreign liquors of the locally distilled arrack from coconut toddy [was] intended to benefit' that business interest.[21] It is more accurate to say that the arrangement was mutually beneficial. While the partnership enabled Parry & Company to edge out local business rivals to dominate a lucrative Indian industry, it ensured for the colonial government a reliable supply of liquor and jaggery at prices that it could manipulate.

Likewise, when it appeared that the supply of arrack to the shops might be threatened in the early 1920s owing to the increased cost of its primary ingredients, molasses and jaggery, the colonial government intervened in the industry by extending a compensation of 4.44 lakh rupees to arrack distillers. 'There was a real danger,' excise officials emphasised, 'of several of them going bankrupt and the supply of arrack to the shops ceasing – a contingency that might have had serious economic and political implications.'[22] While the colonial government's interest in liquor businesses could thus either spell profit or loss for contractors, state intervention itself was thus premised on highly pragmatic calculations. The government directly intervened to support liquor businesses when its priorities and prerogatives, with revenue maximisation topping the list, appeared to even be threatened. The Congress leadership would adopt a similar approach to liquor businesses when fiscal considerations soon arose as a crucial consideration in prohibition's implementation.

Liquor Businesses during the Non-Cooperation and Civil Disobedience Movements

As wealthy liquor business interests wielded tremendous power and influence, the Congress realised that striking out at them was beneficial at two levels. On a symbolic level, liquor and foreign cloth represented an assault on the

Indian national body. On a pragmatic level, preventing liquor businesses from conducting their business would deal a severe blow to the colonial treasury, bringing the mighty Raj to its knees. To this end, liquor shop picketing took pride of place in nationalist mass mobilisation efforts during the Non-Cooperation and Civil Disobedience movements. In the Presidency of Fort St George, it was especially important in contributing to the Non-Cooperation movement's success, whose effects were most pronounced in coastal Andhra and the interior parts of the Tamil districts.[23] Of these, the hardship that liquor businesses suffered as a result of nationalist agitation was most pronounced in the Telugu districts.

Like the colonial government, the Congress was unsympathetic to the country liquor industry's troubles, at least until the mid-1930s. Notwithstanding their place within the local economy, culture and society, Indian nationalism demonised toddy and arrack as constituting a foreign assault on the Indian body. In fact, nationalist ire was particularly focused on the country liquor industry owing to its associations with the Indian underclasses as it yielded a disproportionately large amount of excise revenue.[24] Rajaji wrote that it was a patriotic duty to help Dalits 'towards getting a square meal and feeding their women and children by shutting up the toddy and arrack shops'.[25] The Mahatma himself endorsed violence against the palm industry when he declared that he would – if he could – 'close without compensation all the liquor shops' and 'destroy all the toddy palms'.[26] In Madras city and the adjoining countryside, volunteers were issued with instructions to picket toddy and arrack shops.[27] Destroying the country liquor industry became key to redeeming the Indian underclasses in the calculations of Congress leaders, which resulted in widespread ecological devastation. Entire coconut and palm plantations were cut down and set aflame owing to nationalist mass mobilisation. Whilst contractors hesitated to put up bids for toddy and arrack shops, the number of foreign liquor shop licences that were issued actually increased in the early 1920s. The discrepancy between the foreign liquor and country liquor industries prompted the *Desabhaktan* newspaper to report that 'the reason assigned for this in the Government report itself is that "dances" are on the increase ... even in the matter of the pernicious practice of drinking, we are continuing to the foreigners' profit'.[28]

The violence continued with the Civil Disobedience movement, albeit to a lesser extent. Between 1931 and 1932, the consumption of country liquor in the province fell sharply by 19 per cent from 1,210,221 proof gallons to 980, 633 proof gallons, although the fall in consumption owed more to the Great Depression than mass mobilisation.[29] The Civil Disobedience movement generally failed to take off in the Tamil districts, where picketing had to depend on sporadic outbursts of police violence for its popularity and Congress volunteers were issued with instructions to provoke the authorities to achieve this outcome.[30]

During the Non-Cooperation movement, violence and counter-violence became commonplace at toddy and arrack shops as well as the auctions that were held to lease them out. Extensions of caste violence, the most egregious crimes were committed on the bodies and homes of those who were physically present at the shops. Caste violence has historically been normalised, through both banal aspects of everyday life and more spectacular acts, the latter perpetrated by groups that have justified their deeds with reference to seemingly noble causes – anti-alcoholism, in this case.[31] It was thus that an angry mob torched a toddy shop watchman and his wife in Tuticorin.[32] Congress party cadres were quick to condemn such expressions of unspeakable brutality, which therefore remained relatively rare.

Other forms of violence, however, continued unabated. Congress workers and their followers alike justified them as much by invoking patriotic duty as through reference to religion and culture. In Uthukuli, the Kongu Vellalar Sangam warned toddy shop contractors that they would not only be risking social boycott but also have the spathes on their trees cut if they showed up to bid at auctions. Contractors were threatened that they would not be allowed access to trees from which they could obtain toddy; potters would refuse to sell vessels to them; they would lose their initial investments with the destruction of their spathes and toddy pots.[33] In Tirupattur, Congress volunteers dressed like holy men to warn the public against plying the liquor trade. In Erode, graphic posters taunted passersby with the message that it would be more honourable to earn money by prostituting one's female kin than leasing trees for toddy tapping.[34]

Often, just the threat of non-cooperation was enough to deter business. In the village of Koothiarkundu, Madurai, where the effects of the liquor boycott were most strongly felt, subsequent prohibition propaganda was so strong that toddy shops remained closed for extended periods of time. Stiff social pressure was also brought to bear on toddy shop renters with the reversal of caste roles and conventions. In Nellore and Guntur, Brahmins reportedly fell at the feet of tappers and renters, which apparently shocked some amongst the latter into renouncing their trade.[35] Whilst more likely a rumour rather than fact, we know that rumours often held more power than fact in the context of nationalist mass mobilisation.[36] Regardless of whether the rumours in question contributed to M. K. Gandhi's emergence as the 'Mahatma', a miracle-working, almost mystical figure, or embarrassed individuals from non-Brahmin communities into kicking the habit of drinking by inverting the logic of caste, they acquired the force of truth in a situation wherein established meanings were rapidly coming undone and new ones were being forged. At the same time, picketing also provided an avenue for villagers to 'pay off old grudges'.[37] Political protest thus intersected at several points with the politics of caste hatred and local, district-level animosities.

Due to the strength of the backlash, successful bidders at toddy and arrack shop auctions had little recourse but to seek personal protection from the state, in the form of the local police and excise departments. In Tiruchengode, bidders took refuge in the sub-inspector's house after the auction. This situation prompted concern amongst excise officials that the campaign could have 'engendered in the minds of more timid renters (the majority) the idea that Government are either unable or unwilling to protect them in the exercise of their lawful trade'.[38] Toddy shopkeepers also voluntarily closed their shops to perform their nationalistic fervour. 'Though some of the toddy-sellers are prepared to pay monthly instalments if necessary, while keeping their shops closed,' the *Andhrapatrika* observed, 'the authorities [were] giving them trouble', by pressuring them to reopen for business.[39]

Having said this, liquor business interests were not always hapless victims of their circumstances. Instead, they engaged with the dynamics of nationalist mass mobilisation in different ways. Toddy and arrack shop renters had to devise innovative ways to resist the nationalist onslaught. In Tiruppur, 'an equally strong campaign in favour of drinking toddy [was] being openly conducted' by toddy renters and drinkers, who 'joined together and danced in front of Congress volunteers', whom they doused with toddy.[40] Moreover, just as liquor dealers' resentment had been an important contributory factor for the Congress's anti-liquor campaign to begin with, the restrictions wrought by nationalist mass mobilisation rendered toddy and arrack more lucrative than ever before as these drinks were now in short supply.[41] Hence, during the Civil Disobedience movement, bidders 'took advantage of the threatened picketing and kindred evils' to get their shops for very low bids.[42] The situation became so serious in fact that many shops were leased by a system of private tender.

Tuticorin was among the districts where toddy and arrack shop sales actually increased at the height of the Civil Disobedience movement.[43] In fact, it was among the districts with the highest revenue yield. Here, we see the politics of liquor businesses intermeshing with 'dry' and 'wet' zones of another kind, with important consequences. David Washbrook, Christoper Baker and others have argued that the ecology of various regions had direct and serious implications for their respective political economies. As the agrarian structure of zones that were organised along dry cultivation became increasingly stratified, the political systems therein became dominated by a 'rural magnate elite'.[44] Growing market opportunities helped to further entrench the wealth of groups that were already rich and powerful in the dry zone, which included the Ceded Districts and most of the hinterland Tamil districts. Through the extension of credit lending and trade, elites in these areas were able to further consolidate their economic power by diversifying into other areas of economic activity without encountering serious challenges from the outside world. As many among them wielded considerable clout in the local liquor industry, they were able to withstand the gathering storm of prohibition politics.

Moreover, the interwar period saw attempts by toddy-tapping communities to not only reject the liquor trade but also reconcile that rejection with expressions of loyalty to the colonial establishment. In the spirit of community self-strengthening, there were calls within the Nadar community to eschew their habit of toddy drinking 'without entertaining the false fear that their conduct might be construed to be non-cooperation and to take to military service for their future avocation which will indicate their loyalty'. [45] However, most were unwilling to stop plying the only trade they knew and that, in fact, became a lucrative source of income given the context of the 1920s and 1930s.

The line between picketer and renter was not as clear-cut as the nationalist movement made it out to be either. This becomes evident when we consider incidents like the riot that broke out at a toddy shop in Edappadi, Salem, in September 1921. The case involved a group of men whom the Congress leadership referred to as non-cooperators. Excise officials and the police, however, called them dacoits who beat up the shop renters at one of the toddy shops. They claimed that two Congress volunteers jointly rented the arrack shop in the same town, which had suspiciously not been boycotted. According to them, it was 'evident that the aim of these so-called non-cooperators [was] a purely selfish one of putting down sales in the toddy shop so that there may be a corresponding increase in the arrack shop'.[46]

There was an inherent pragmatism in the Congress's strategy relating to liquor shop picketing that would also be seen in its approach to prohibition subsequently. Significantly, the picketing of toddy and liquor shops was never seriously attempted in the provincial capital itself owing to the 'fear of lathi charges'.[47] The governor of Madras reported to the viceroy that Madras city was 'remarkably quiet' during the non-cooperation years, concluding that people had 'realised the senselessness' of picketing.[48] The enthusiasm for the Congress's liquor boycott campaign that was evident in other parts of the province was clearly not experienced in the provincial capital. Nevertheless, nationalist mass mobilisation had had the effect of prompting Indian society to rethink the very legality of the liquor trade, its aim to begin with.

The Prohibition of Liquor Businesses and the Business of Prohibition

The heavy social cost of the nationalists' mass mobilisation gradually became evident over the course of the 1930s. Small and middling liquor businesses disproportionately suffered the adverse effects of the anti-liquor campaign that paved the way for prohibition. The progress towards prohibition meant that the Congress leadership needed to seriously reckon with the fact that alcohol, particularly country liquor, had put down deep roots in the local economy. Although excess distilled liquor could be converted into power alcohol, toddy presented a much bigger problem.[49] Prohibition was poised to cause the decimation of the local industry, unleash mass unemployment that was inflected along caste lines and trigger serious fiscal deficits that would require alternative sources of revenue to offset.

Moreover, various segments of society resisted the colonial state's laissez-faire approach to the management of alcohol production with demands for a degree of protection to be extended to the country liquor industry. This influenced the development of a protectionist discourse that dovetailed with social anxiety that foreign liquor was rapidly gaining in popularity. Shortly before prohibition's introduction, the concern was raised in the provincial legislatures that prohibition would only 'increase the import of foreign liquor and completely destroy the indigenous industries'.[50] The nationalist leadership was all too acutely aware that prohibition's economic problems would quickly precipitate a political crisis, which it particularly sought to avoid in the 1930s.

All these developments interacted with the change in the Congress's stance from a former reliance on agitational politics to constitutionalism. Together, they influenced the party leadership's push to rehabilitate the country liquor industry in the mid-1930s. Whilst stemming from pragmatic considerations, ideology supplied the language and ethos for these efforts. The Congress leadership needed to find urgent solutions to tackle the problems that toddy presented, as it considered prohibition from the point of view of governance. From the time it suspended the Civil Disobedience movement, the nationalist organisation was focused on establishing new utilities for palmyra and coconut trees. Country liquor would be reconstituted as the indigenous juice and sugar industries instead. The Congress looked to the very industry that it had previously tried to dismantle to provide India with a viable alternative to not just toddy but also to tea and coffee as temperance beverages. The answer lay in promoting the fresh, unfermented counterpart of toddy known as *neera*, or *padaneer*, in Tamil.

In order to encourage people to drink *neera* rather than toddy, tea or coffee, the Congress and its supporters forged complex linkages between the global and the local: they drew liberally on Western medical discourses to rehabilitate the coconut and palmyra industries. The *neera* campaign also sheds light on the modernising ambitions of the nationalist leadership for it is the story of how Gandhi and the Congress tried to transform a fragmented rural industry into India's first national drink industry. Although not quite as spectacular as its toddy and liquor shop picketing efforts of previous years, the *neera* campaign was just as crucial an aspect of the Congress's prohibition efforts in the immediate context of the policy's introduction.

There were several reasons why *neera* appeared to offer the perfect solution for the toddy problem. The first was the Congress leadership's conviction that *neera* had beneficial nutritional properties that qualified it as a valuable fooddrink. 'Pure neera,' Gandhi emphasised, 'is food even as sugar is. Toddy, even sweet, is not in the same sense and to the same extent as neera.'[51] In endorsing it as an ideal source of nourishment for the Indian masses, Gandhi provided a detailed breakdown of *neera*'s nutritional and medicinal properties, including how the drink compared with sugar cane juice in its protein and carbohydrate content. He cited the Nutrition Research Laboratory of India as the source of this information, thus emphasising that *neera* consumption was backed by solid scientific research.[52] By thus emphasising its food value, the nationalists simultaneously sought to carve out a niche for *neera* as a temperance drink and dismantle toddy's popularity.

Neera's nutritional value went hand in hand with its symbolic significance as well. In the Congress leadership's elite worldview, *neera* and toddy stood for two fundamentally different things. *Neera* was fresh and pure, whereas toddy reached its state after fermentation, technically a process of spoilage. Slotted thus into the familiar discourse of the pure and the profane, *neera* and toddy had immense symbolic value. They could equally represent colonial exploitation and nationalist redemption.

In fact, one of the reasons why *neera* became so important to the nationalists as prohibition drew near was because the state regarded it, like toddy, as a taxable commodity. It was critical, therefore, to resist state intervention in the industry to reclaim *neera* as a *swadeshi* beverage. Where *neera* won out over tea and coffee, Congress leaders argued that it was not only non-intoxicating and non-stimulating but also unmistakably Indian in origin. They pointed out that it was 'a popular beverage in some parts of our country since times immemorial', thus emphasising its cultural significance.[53] Equally, such assertions constituted an attempt to dislodge toddy from its place in society.

The *neera* campaign was foremost Gandhi's pet project. Although it stemmed from his vision of self-sufficient village republics, the project evolved into something far more ambitious. *Neera*'s promotion as a nutritious drink had a long history of resistance to the state in Gujarat that Gandhi tapped into. In the late nineteenth century, the social reformer Behramji Merwanji Malabari had written that *neera* was more food than drink and described it as 'the people's elixir'. He posed a question that would inform the nationalists' *neera* campaign subsequently: 'Why should Government starve the populace of their innocent enjoyment and thus drive them to strong drink?'[54] Malabari and reformers of his ilk were joined by temperance leaders of international repute. William Caine had similarly criticised the state's policy of taxing *neera* as 'the toddy palm yields a liquid which for ages has formed one of the staple articles of food for the poorer classes in India. Whilst fresh it is perfectly innocuous and wholesome.'[55] Whereas Caine had thus noted the degree to which *neera* was entwined with the lifestyle of the Indian working classes, the report of the Indian Excise Committee noted that 'unfermented toddy is largely drunk medicinally by well-to-do people who resort to Surat for that purpose'.[56] The state thus made clear that there was no ethical dilemma involved in taxing *neera*. It was being consumed not as food but as supplement. Moreover, it served the wealthy and not the poor. *Neera* had thus become a site of contestation and, hence, consensus-building, even prior to prohibition's introduction. When Gandhi emphasised *neera*'s suitability as India's national drink subsequently, it is plausible that he was responding to the state's prior attempts at bringing it under its control and the resistance those measures had produced in his own province.

The nationalist leadership also saw in *neera* the potential to become the new locus of working-class sociability. Gandhi was convinced that toddy and gambling were so irresistible to the poor that he often demanded that labourers should not be paid more than what they absolutely needed to survive. As the toddy shop had an unrivalled place in the social world of Indian male labourers, he was adamant that they should have access to places where they would be able to obtain 'innocent drinks and equally innocent amusements'.[57] Just as the state experimented with temperance canteens and tea stalls to combat drunkenness, the Congress leadership emphasised the urgency of replacing toddy shops with sober spaces that would appeal to the poor in the 1930s. Gandhi and the Congress sought to counteract the appeal of toddy shops as well as tea stalls and coffeehouses with '*neera* bars' they planned to establish all over the country. These spaces, where subaltern Indians could gather and enjoy their *neera* together, they thought, could potentially rival toddy shops in popularity and influence. Sevagram ashram, which became Gandhi's headquarters beginning in 1936, was the laboratory for the *neera* bar. Here, workers received training from Shri Gajanan Naik in producing *neera* from palm trees following the Bengali method, at that time the most effective method of tapping the trees.[58] It was also at Sevagram ashram that the drink was served every morning as a breakfast item.

Inasmuch as the Congress championed *neera* instead of toddy, it also presented the Indian public with comparisons between *neera* and tea. Drawing upon experiments with *neera* in his ashram, Gandhi insisted that 'if one drinks a glass of *neera* in the morning instead of tea etc., he should not need anything else for breakfast'.[59] The nationalist opposition to 'non-national' drinks did not, however, go unchallenged. In response to a campaign that had forced the closure of tea shops in Ahmedabad, an article in the *Indian Social Reformer* pointed out that

> tea, apart from its non-national fashion, is surely not as innocuous as water or buttermilk, but it is more harmful than liquor, and one cannot help feeling that the 'Pussyfoots' of Ahmedabad in going at tea-shops

in preference to liquor shops betrayed more of a blind zeal than of a reasoned social sense.[60]

Efforts to market *neera* as India's first authentically Indian temperance drink were most pronounced in Madras and Bombay. The choice to unfurl the *neera* scheme in the two provinces was deliberate. First, toddy drinking was part of the local cultural fabric of both. Second, and relatedly, both provinces were home to communities that had traditionally earned their living as toddy tappers. As with the Shanars, Nadars, Idigas and Tiyyas of the Madras Presidency, Bombay's Bhandaris were devastated by prohibition's introduction in the late 1930s. A solution had to be found for the mass unemployment that prohibition would invariably visit upon these communities. The *neera* campaign's success would prove prohibition's viability; it would generate employment opportunities that would mitigate the mass displacement that prohibition would cause. Gandhi insisted that 'if the palms that are used for making toddy are used for making jaggery, India will never lack sugar and the poor will be able to get good jaggery'.[61] In this exercise of nationalist governmentality, toddy tappers were thus themselves held responsible for their post-prohibition fate, specially, through their willingness to embrace *neera*.

Although the history of *gur* in India predates colonial rule, Gandhi's advocacy of *neera* as a source for its production was in response to the indiscriminate colonial policy of importing cheap refined sugar, with which the indigenous sugar industry simply could not compete. To this end, Gandhi argued that 'palm jaggery can be converted into molasses and refined sugar. But the jaggery is much more useful than refined sugar.'[62] Indeed, Gandhi's emphasis on *neera* and *gur* needs to be understood in light of his argument that villages had to be equipped to function, as far as possible, as self-sufficient republics. Encouraging *neera* at a time when the Congress was being held accountable for prohibition's introduction meant that tappers could theoretically be redirected to extract the fresh sap of the palm tree where they had previously collected its fermented version.

It is not too difficult to see the reason for the Congress leadership's optimism. After all, the skills required for both were fundamentally the same – the only difference being, again theoretically, that *neera* required the application of a suitable amount of *chunam*, or lime, on the inside of the collection pot to ensure that fermentation did not take place. In the nationalist leadership's calculations, encouraging tappers to divert their labour into producing *neera* would encourage self-sufficiency in two ways: it would provide India with a steady supply of a wholesome health-drink as well as a cheap source of sugar. In this, the Congress leadership's embrace of governmentality was strikingly similar to that demonstrated by the colonial state.

However, even the best laid plans can – and, often, do – go awry. This became especially evident as the Congress leadership stepped up its *neera* campaign following prohibition's introduction.

*   *   *

The Congress leadership's approach to drinkers bore striking similarities with the high-handed policy stance of the colonial leadership. The solutions that the Congress proposed to the problem of drink – particularly country liquor – betrayed an inherent pragmatism in the 1930s that was not all that different from colonial governmentality. This is borne out in the colonial state's tea and the nationalist state's *neera* campaigns, respectively.

The Congress leadership was acutely aware, even prior to prohibition's introduction, that the policy would pose major problems for governance. The enforcement of liquor legislation in the provinces had already revealed potential setbacks and hurdles. The most serious of these were fiscal in nature as alcohol had worked deep inroads into provincial economies. As the Congress leadership calculated that economic problems would quickly spiral into a political crisis, it sought to find solutions ahead of prohibition's introduction. It thus tried to reconcile the ideals that had buoyed the anti-liquor campaign of previous decades with the constitutionalism that increasingly characterised its political strategy in the 1930s. This change in stance predicted the delicate balancing act that prohibition in Madras would subsequently become.

Notes

1. *The Hindu*, 28 January 1922.
2. Bhattacharya, *Financial Foundations of the British Raj*, pp. 107–108. See also Tirthankar Roy, *Economic History of India, 1857–1947* (Oxford: Oxford University Press, 2011); and Tirthankar Roy, *How British Rule Changed India's Economy: The Paradox of the Raj* (London: Palgrave Macmillan, 2019).

3. Nandini Bhattacharya, 'The Problem of Alcohol in Colonial India (c. 1907–1942)', *Studies in History* 33, no. 2 (2017), pp. 187–212.

4. Tirthankar Roy and Anand V. Swamy, *Law and the Economy in Colonial India* (Chicago: University of Chicago Press, 2016), pp. 5–6.

5. I refer to Chandra, Mukherjee, Mukherjee, Mahajan and Panikkar, *India's Struggle for Independence*, pp. 73–74, 263; and Judith M. Brown, *Gandhi's Rise to Power: Indian Politics, 1915–1922* (Cambridge: Cambridge University Press, 1972), pp. 315–317. These works suggest that whilst the colonial government sought the growth and development of alcohol industries, the nationalist leadership was singularly intolerant toward liquor businesses.

6. G.O. No. 2129, Revenue Department, 25 April 1939, letter from Sri Rao Bahadur K. Raman Nayar, Collector of Trichinopoly to Assistant Secretary to the Board of Revenue (Excise), TNA.

7. Hardgrave, *Nadars of Tamilnad*, p. 107. See also Sarah Dickey, 'Permeable Homes: Domestic Service, Household Space, and the Vulnerability of Class Boundaries in Urban India', *American Ethnologist* 27, no. 2 (May, 2000), pp. 462–489; and Sarah Dickey, 'Conundrums of Caste, History, and Truth: Hindu Nadar Identities in Urban South India', in *The Anthropology of Power, Agency, and Morality: The Enduring Legacy of F. G. Bailey*, ed. Victor C. de Munck and Elisa J. Sobo, pp. 132–148 (Manchester: Manchester University Press, 2022).

8. *Kistnapatrika*, 13 August 1921, NNPR (July–September 1921), p. 1002.

9. Mappila Muslims are thought to have descended from Arab traders as well as converted from, and intermarried with, castes like the Tiyyas.

10. Schrad, *Smashing the Liquor Machine*, pp. 203–204.

11. Baker, 'Non-Cooperation in South India', p. 106. See also Irschick, *Tamil Revivalism*, pp. 32–33; and De, *A People's Constitution*, p. 64. In Baker's discussion, 'pussyfoot' refers not to Pussyfoot Johnson, the individual, but temperance reformers more generally.

12. Mukerjie, *A Report on Toddy Taxation*, p. 57. See also *Times of India*, 22 May 1913.

13. G.O. No. 3010, Revenue Department, 5 October 1912, TNA. This quote is from a letter received from nominated member of the Madras Legislative Council, Kameswara Rao Nayudu.

14. Ibid.

15. L/P&J 3633/37, Governor's Situation Report, 5 August 1937, IOR; see also G.O. No. 417, Revenue Department (Confl.), 24 February 1936, TNA.

16. G.O. No. 576, Revenue Department, 20 March 1929, TNA.

17. G.O. No. 532, Revenue Department, 9 March 1928, TNA.

18. Ibid. Response from Board of Revenue, No. 572 D/28-1, 5 March 1928.

19. Rajnarayan Chandavarkar, *History, Culture, and the Indian City: Essays by Rajnarayan Chandavarkar* (Cambridge: Cambridge University Press, 2009), p. 97. See also Colvard, 'A World without Drink', pp. 19–20, for a discussion of the impact of colonial tax policy on the foreign liquor and country liquor industries.

20. *Administration Report of the Madras Board of Revenue, 1914–1915* (Madras: Superintendent of Government Press, 1916), p. 16.

21. *Kerala Patrika*, 28 May 1907, NNPR (April–June 1907), p. 192.

22. *Madras Excise Revenue, 1920–1921*, p. 1.

23. Sarkar, *Modern India*, p. 214.

24. Eugene Irschick, 'Gandhian Non-Violent Protest: Rituals of Avoidance or Rituals of Confrontation?', *Economic and Political Weekly* 21 (1986), pp. 1276–1285.

25. Kalidas, *Writings of C. Rajagopalachari*, p. 154.

26. *Young India*, 25 June 1931.

27. V. Ramakrishna, *Social Reform in Andhra, 1848–1919* (Hyderabad: Vikas, 1983), pp. 147–150.

28. *Desabhaktan*, 5 February 1921, NNPR (January–March 1921), p. 183.

29. *Madras Excise Revenue, 1931–1932*, pp. 2–3. See also Judith M. Brown, *Gandhi and Civil Disobedience: The Mahatma in Indian Politics, 1928–1934* (Cambridge: Cambridge University Press, 1977), p. 140. Brown argued that the Madras Presidency was so quiet during the Civil Disobedience movement that the ordinances never had to be applied there. David Washbrook, 'Gandhian Politics', *Modern Asian Studies* 7, no. 1 (1973), pp. 107–115. Washbrook's essay critiqued the arguments that Brown presented in her book.

30. Arnold, 'The Politics of Coalescence', p. 265.

31. See, for instance, Hugo Gorringe, 'Banal Violence? The Everyday Underpinnings of Collective Violence', *Identities* 13, no. 2 (2006), pp. 237–260; Hugo Gorringe, 'Which Is Violence? Reflections on Collective Violence and Dalit Movements in South India', *Social Movement Studies* 5, no. 2 (2006), pp. 117–136; and Ania Loomba, 'The Everyday Violence of Caste', *College Literature* 43, no. 1, *Banalization of War* (Winter 2016), pp. 220–225.

32. G.O. No. 1654, Revenue Department (Mis., Confl.), 3 August 1931, TNA.

33. G.O. No. 1982, Revenue Department (Confl.), 3 September 1921, TNA. This information is from a letter dated 16 August 1921, which was received from the Inspector of Erode Circle.

34. G.O. No. 1982, Revenue Department (Mis., Confl.), 3 September 1921, TNA.

35. Ibid.

36. Shahid Amin, 'Gandhi as Mahatma: Gorakhpur District, Eastern UP, 1921', in *Subaltern Studies III: Writings on South Asian History and Society*, ed. Ranajit Guha, pp. 1–61 (New Delhi: Oxford University Press, 1984).

37. G.O. No, 1654, Revenue Department (Confl. Mis.), 3 August 1931, TNA.

38. Ibid.

39. *Andhrapatrika*, 9 November 1921, NNPR (October–December, 1921), p. 1347.

40. *Times of India*, 23 May 1931.

41. Sarkar, *Modern India*, p. 214.

42. *Madras Excise Revenue 1931–1932*, p. 18.

43. *Government on Civil Disobedience Movement, 1930–1931: Report by J. Hussain Khan, District Magistrate, Dated 4 January 1931* (Madras: Superintendent of Government Press, 1931), p. 54.

44. David Washbrook, 'Country Politics: Madras 1880 to 1930s', *Modern Asian Studies* 7, no. 3 (1973), pp. 475–531. See also David Washbrook, *The Emergence of Provincial Politics, The Madras Presidency 1870–1920* (Cambridge: Cambridge University Press, 1976); David Washbrook, 'Economic Development and Social Stratification in Rural Madras: The "Dry Region" 1878–1929', in *The Imperial Impact: Studies in the Economic History of Africa and India*, ed. Clive Dewey and A. G. Hopkins, pp. 68–82 (London: Athlone Press, 1978); Christopher Baker and David Arnold Washbrook, *South India: Political Institutions and Political Change 1880–1940* (Delhi: Macmillan, 1975); Christopher Baker, *The Politics of South India, 1920–1937* (Cambridge: Cambridge University Press, 1976); and Bruce Robert, 'Economic Change and Agrarian Organization in "Dry" South India 1890–1940: A Reinterpretation', *Modern Asian Studies* 17, no. 1 (1983), pp. 59–78. Robert based his discussion on Washbrook's seminal essay.

45. *Nadarkulamitran*, 1 September 1921, NNPR (August–October 1921), p. 1208. See also Hardgrave, *Nadars of Tamilnad*, pp. 126–127. Hardgrave argues that nationalist mass mobilisation prompted the majority of the

Nadar community to transfer their loyalties from the colonial government to the Congress.

46. G.O. No. 2020, Revenue Department, 9 September 1921, TNA.

47. Preliminary Report on Civil Disobedience in Tamil Nadu, 20 June 1930, G-167 to G-189 (1930), p. 6, AICC Papers, NML.

48. Ibid.

49. Bhattacharya, 'The Problem of Alcohol', pp. 187–212.

50. Dr Sir K. V. Reddi Nayudu, Madras Legislative Council Proceedings, vols. 1–2, 29 September 1937, p. 416, TNA.

51. *Harijan*, 15 July 1939. See also Fahey and Manian, 'Poverty and Purification'. Parts of this discussion have been previously published as a journal article. See Darinee Alagirisamy, 'The Problem with Neera: The (Un)Making of a National Drink in Late Colonial India', *Indian Economic and Social History Review* 56, no. 1 (2019), pp. 77–97.

52. Gajanan Naik, *Harijan*, 7 January 1939, quoted in M. K. Gandhi, *Diet and Diet Reform* (Ahmedabad: Navajivan Mudranalaya, 1949), p. 139.

53. Ibid.

54. Malabari, *Gujarat and the Gujaratis*, p. 116. This book was originally published in 1889.

55. John Newton, *W. S. Caine, M. P.: A Biography* (London: Nisbet, 1907), p. 237. Caine was a British politician and temperance reformer.

56. *Report of the Indian Excise Committee*, 1905–1906, p. 59.

57. *Young India*, 25 June 1931. See also Srivastava, *Labor Force in Colonial Bombay*, p. 125.

58. Gajanan Naik was a Gandhian whose association with the Congress started in the 1930s and continued throughout his life. He was appointed 'palm-*gur*' adviser to the Government of India by Rajendra Prasad following independence. Naik went on to establish the All-India Palm-Gur Training Centre, under the auspices of the Khadi and Village Industries Commission, in Dahanu.

59. M. K. Gandhi, *India of My Dreams*, ed. Krishna Kripalani, comp. R. K. Prabhu (Ahmedabad: Navajivan Mudranalaya, 1960), p. 156.

60. *Indian Social Reformer* (1920), p. 66. See also *Times of India*, 23 September 1935.

61. M. K. Gandhi, *Healthy Living According to Gandhi* (New Delhi: Orient Longman, 2014 [1921]), p. 29.

62. Gandhi, *India of My Dreams*, p. 157.

6

Enforcing Prohibition

Prohibitions, Permits, Power

A mill owner in Salem conducted his own social experiment in sobriety in February 1939. He assembled his workers and instructed them to sit and stand several times in rapid succession, noting that they would 'never have been so responsive to orders in the days when they drank'.[1] Salem went dry on 1 October 1937. Chittoor and Cuddapah followed suit a year later, and North Arcot went dry in 1939. Prohibition's introduction occurred at the convergence of state-directed reform, political competition, entrenched social anxieties and waves of resistance to the policy. Official assessments painted a glowing picture of its successes, reflecting the 'idiom of enthusiasm' so characteristic of Congress mass mobilisation.[2] English and vernacular newspapers joined studies commissioned by Rajaji's government in heaping praise on prohibition for apparently improving the lives of former addicts. Much of the extant literature has echoed this bias while dismissing non-elite resistance to prohibition as 'local nuisances' to a policy of great societal importance.[3]

That there would be such a bias is not surprising. Prohibition had been won after a long, hard struggle. By the time the policy was introduced, the priority was proving that it would work. Policymakers found themselves having to justify the sacrifices that had already been made and that were yet to come. Publicly, they feted prohibition. Privately, however, the policy continued to function as prohibitioning between political elites, between the authorities and society, and between different social groups. Prohibition thus developed a double life until the colonial government suspended it in September 1943. We may see its perceptible impact through the legislative amendments these multi-sited negotiations brought about. Prohibition-related crime was no less significant in shaping its subsequent development either.

Prohibition was the first major programme of national social reform that the Congress ministries introduced upon taking power in the provinces. There were two aspects at work here. First, the Congress saw in the policy a prime opportunity to flex its muscles. If prohibition succeeded, as the nationalists were sure it would, it would demonstrate the superiority of the Congress model of governance to the colonial authorities and their regional political rivals. Second, and relatedly, the reins of the state had formerly been entirely in the hands of India's colonisers. The nationalist leadership had taken the lead in criticising state intervention under those circumstances as constituting foreign intrusion into Indian affairs. However, acquiring political power in the aftermath of the Government of India Act of 1935 enabled the nationalist state to rewrite the rules of state-directed social reform. Whilst it was admittedly a limited form of state power, it was power nevertheless. Prohibition thus *had* to succeed.

M. K. Gandhi's southern commander, Rajaji, made a pitch for prohibition as soon as he became chief minister. The leadership positions that he had held at the national, provincial and district levels stood him in good stead in this endeavour. One of the most ardent proponents of dry India and the undisputed father of prohibition in the south, Rajaji had been directly involved in publishing journals and manuals endorsing the policy. These included the English *Prohibition* and the Tamil *Vimochanam* (Deliverance). The Congress stalwart pursued his pet project with his home district foremost in mind. Salem became ground zero for prohibition's introduction in the late 1930s, just as it had been in the 1920s.

Rajaji and the Congress looked to the Volstead Act, which had been suspended four years before prohibition's introduction in India, as the model for the Madras Prohibition Act. Consequently, the latter contained many of the same conditions, provisos and exemptions. Like the Volstead Act, the Madras Prohibition Act banned the production, distribution and sales of spirituous liquors. It also allowed for exemptions on the basis of medicinal, scientific, industrial and religious purposes. Both Acts instituted a system of permits, wherein the manufacture, sale, purchase, transportation, consumption or prescription of any liquor required a permit from the commissioner showing that the permit holder had been granted exemption from prohibition law.

State and federal authorities had been jointly responsible for prohibition's implementation in America, which had ended up greatly complicating it. New Jersey's governor, for instance, had promised that he would keep the state 'as wet as the Atlantic Ocean' and, to this end, had pushed for a policy repeal.[4] Although prohibition was envisioned as a policy of national importance in India, its enforcement fell to the provinces, which in turn was filtered through their constituent districts. Moreover, unlike the Volstead Act, which focused on the public manufacture, distribution and sale of alcohol, the Madras Prohibition Act deliberately targeted consumption as well. It was much more ambitious in its scope in that it also targeted domestic drinking, although it made an exception for bottled foreign liquor.[5] The Madras Prohibition Act allowed a certain class of addicts the right to hold permits under strictly controlled conditions. Contravention of the Act's terms carried a hefty fine, jail term or possibly both for the most recalcitrant of offenders.

Prohibition was also introduced in a particularly charged political context in India. The Government of India Act of 1935 had paved the way for the elections of 1937, which the Congress eventually contested amidst internal disagreements about the course the party should take. The result was a landslide electoral victory that proved especially fortuitous for the nationalist party in the Presidency of Fort St George, which secured it its most impressive win. When the nationalists accepted office after some vacillation, the Madras Congress ministry under Rajaji's chief ministership had the perfect opportunity to implement policies from its constructive programme – policies that had long been in the pipeline. The circumstances that heralded prohibition in the short run thus bestowed upon it an air of eager anticipation. The Congress's position as government in most of the provinces directly shaped its approach to alcohol policy in this context. It meant that the party shifted from a former position of overt resistance to one of limited cooperation instead. As the policy manifestation of that stance, the Madras Prohibition Act was introduced in 1937 within the constitutional framework of the Raj.

As a function of state power, practical aspects of prohibition's implementation pivoted on the relationship that prevailed between colonial and nationalist elites in the late 1930s. Constitutionalism meant that political competition, whilst still present, took different, subtler forms. It also translated into a degree of cooperation that the nationalist state was loathe to admit in public. For the British, 'a Congress in office would be a domesticated animal harnessed to the constitutional cart of which the British still held the reins'.[6] The nationalist state's conviction that public opinion favoured prohibition was matched by the colonial state's confidence that the policy would prove suicidal for the Congress.

Madras governor, John Erskine, was 'pretty sure that the popularity of Congress [was] going to be considerably reduced in this district before many weeks have passed'.[7] Public opinion in London was equally dismissive about prohibition's outlook in India. A particularly colourful commentary on the British Empire predicted that 'Mr. Gandhi can persuade men to go without their trousers, though they would not dream of going without their toddy. They don't want to replace one tyranny by another.'[8] The key consideration for colonial officials was that they would continue to hold the reins of the constitutional cart. For the nationalists, colonial intransigence translated into serious compromises that had to be made before – and so that – prohibition could be introduced at all.

The nationalist government adopted an exceedingly cautious approach: one that conspicuously left Madras city out and focused on just four districts of the province to begin with. Whilst there were plans to extend the policy to six more districts after a year, the extension – which ultimately did not materialise – hinged on prohibition's initial outcomes. The Madras Congress ministry was motivated by two factors in its decision to restrict prohibition's scope. First, limited experiments with prohibition in the 1920s had surfaced serious challenges to enforcement, manifested through skyrocketing rates of illicit distillation and smuggling. The nationalists scarcely wanted a controversy on their hands when they were working hard to prove prohibition's success. Second, they sought to minimise the fallout from the loss of revenue they anticipated with the policy's introduction. When asked why the Madras Prohibition Act of 1937 was introduced in just Salem to begin with, Rajaji said that 'the revenue from Drink ... [had] worked deep into the financial structure of the Province'.[9] Citing enforcement costs and prohibition-related unemployment, he emphasised that a cautious approach would ensure that the policy did not tailspin into a fiscal crisis. Madras city was also excluded from the Act of 1937 for this reason. Even though the capital city had been the epicentre of drink-related anxieties, its thirst for alcohol was too lucrative for the nationalist government to sacrifice at that time. Madras city was not a suitable place for prohibition's introduction, explained Rajaji, as 'being a coastal district, there will be facilities for smuggling in liquor. The bottle is going to be corked, but the cork should be put at the right time.'[10]

Of course, it was a bitter irony of the times that the more powerful the Congress became in the Madras Presidency, the more conservative it was forced to become in its approach to governance.[11] The constraints imposed by colonial authorities and regional political rivals, together with prohibition's painful lessons from previous decades, forced the Congress ministry to moderate its ambitious plans. Even with its conservative approach, however, numerous sticking points soon arose. Rajaji had asked Lord Erskine to endorse prohibition in his public address two months before the policy's introduction. The latter squarely rejected the request. Erskine wrote back stating that not only was he 'violently opposed' to the policy as 'a gross violation of the rights of the individual', but also that supporting prohibition in a public speech in India 'would lead to a great deal of unseemly merriment in political circles in England'.[12]

Although he knew he could not win Erskine over, Rajaji publicly insisted on teetotalism for British officials who were appointed in dry districts. His strategy actually worked where the collector of Salem, A. F. W. Dixon, and his chief prohibition officer were concerned. Neither was a teetotaller in his personal life, although both agreed to abide by the chief minister's request to abstain from liquor for the duration of their service in Salem. Their self-imposed teetotalism aided the nationalists by creating just the 'image that they hoped for: white officials implementing a very un-British policy without fear or favour'.[13] Just as maintaining the knife-edge distinction between drinking and appearing drunk to their Indian subjects had undergirded colonial policy previously, cultivating teetotal British officers as the public face of their pet project became a crucial aspect of the nationalists' prohibition policy. Compelling the British to become teetotallers was a masterstroke that worked to Rajaji's advantage in Salem.

However, it did not work anywhere else. The colonial establishment opposed Rajaji on his expectations of teetotalism for British officials posted in dry districts. The viceroy wrote to the secretary of state noting that 'total abstinence … would become a condition for service of every district officer in Madras. I cannot believe that even a fanatic like Raja will fail to see that this is not practical politics.'[14] The acting viceroy, Lord Brabourne, echoed his views. Brabourne remarked that there was no logical reason to expect young British officers to give up a mild indulgence. Erskine chimed in with the opinion that 'unless a British teetotaller was available in any district to which the Ministry chose to apply provisions of the Prohibition Act, it would be automatically Indianised', which would 'not be in the best interests of the administration of this presidency'.[15]

Shaped as it had been by political competition during its conceptualisation, prohibition's actual implementation thus reflected it as well. In fact, colonial officials not only remained unmoved, but they were also actively committed to putting obstacles in the path of prohibition's success. The resistance he faced eventually forced Rajaji to concede that officials posted in dry districts need not necessarily be teetotallers themselves. As the chief minister was to find out, however, this was not the last or most serious compromise he would have to make.

Instead, prohibition's introduction hinged on a series of confidential agreements that were reached between colonial and nationalist elites. These agreements show that the policy was the product of sustained consensus-building at the highest elite levels of policymaking before it even reached the people. To begin with, the colonial government had made it amply evident that it would tolerate prohibition only insofar as its reach remained limited to Indian society. Indeed, securing 'arrangements for preventing European hardship' had been the foremost consideration for the British prior to 1937. Emphasising the policy's phased introduction, the secretary of state wrote that 'experience will thus show whether the special permit system, together with the concession obtained by Lord Erskine for clubs, provides adequate safeguards for European consumers. If Prohibition were extended to the whole or large part of the Province, the position might be different.'[16]

As with foreign liquor shops, the status of colonial clubs was closed to political interference from the outset. Rajaji conceded more to colonial authorities in this matter than he publicly cared to admit. Addressing the India Office's concern that the first draft of the Madras Prohibition Act contained no provision for clubs, Erskine assured the latter that he had come to a 'satisfactory agreement with the Premier in regard to these institutions'. The position of colonial clubs was 'completely safeguarded', as 'without actually mentioning any race by name', the Act's wording had guaranteed the clubs' continued right to sell liquor, provided the collector thought 'they [were] of a *reputable* character'.[17]

Moreover, the colonial administration was concerned that 'harassment and persecution should be avoided in so far as consumption of liquor by a person in his own home [was] concerned'.[18] To this end, the Madras Prohibition Act made allowances for personal permits that enabled domestic alcohol consumption. Individuals could apply for permits that allowed them to entertain other permit holders over the private, domestic consumption of bottled liquor, although permit holders were only allowed to hold six bottles of whisky or their equivalent at any given time. Permits were issued, subject to official approval, and could be cancelled without any prior notice.

Even subject to these restrictions, archival evidence challenges the notion of the permit system as a policy 'loophole'.[19] Erskine wrote to the viceroy informing him that

> we in Madras have a system whereby permits to possess and consume foreign liquor are granted by Government ... This provision was, as a matter of fact, inserted in the original Bill at my instance in order to protect the rights of Europeans and I have given orders that if any European applies for a permit, he or she is to get one.[20]

Far from being a loophole, therefore, the permit system constituted a deliberate concession by the nationalist government to colonial authorities. It marked a significant departure from Gandhi's earlier recommendation that picketers should not hesitate to 'penetrate into the homes[s] of drinkers'.[21] In practice, Rajaji's confidential agreements with Erskine thus fostered class and race privilege, both in, and significantly *through*, prohibition.

This evidence should not, however, be interpreted as meaning that the nationalist government sold out on prohibition in its pursuit of power. On the contrary, it demonstrates its willingness to make serious compromises in order to introduce the policy at all. Rajaji appears to have harboured hopes that the British could eventually be made to dance to his tunes. This optimism, coupled with the pragmatism that the situation necessitated, translated into a delicate balancing act. Ironically, Erskine's secretary wrote to the Board of Revenue the year after prohibition's introduction. He was requesting liquor permits for the governor, his wife and a party of six members comprising military generals prior to their visit to dry Chittoor. Responding to this situation involving the 'issue of protocol and appearance', Rajaji wrote that while the governor did not require a permit to enjoy his drink, the rest of his party, including his wife, were not above the law.[22] Needless to say, Erskine and his travel party were not amused.

Although official correspondences betrayed concern for the plight of European permit holders, wealthy Indians also applied for personal liquor permits. They were encouraged by the declaration that there was to be 'no discrimination between different communities' in the issuance of permits.[23]

Assurances of impartiality notwithstanding, the rule of colonial difference still applied. All first applications for liquor permits, other than from European gentlemen of status, were directed to the Congress ministry for approval. The system of personal permits, which had previously been used to regulate drinking among tribal communities, was extended to elite segments of Indian society with prohibition, albeit with different results.

In submitting the application of one Santha R. Manicka Mudaliar of Arkonam, the collector verified that the applicant was 'a rich land-holder' who paid land tax of over. 3,000 rupees to the government. He observed that the applicant was habituated to taking brandy to cope with chronic insomnia. An accompanying doctor's letter confirmed Mudaliar's addiction. When another well-heeled applicant from Salem sought the right to hold whisky for purposes of convalescence, Rajaji overruled his request on the basis that he was acquainted with the applicant and hence knew that he would 'not suffer physically by the abstention'.[24] Not one to be easily dissuaded, the applicant repeated his request, supported by not one but two medical certificates from physicians who insisted that whisky was absolutely essential for his health. One of the letters even elaborated that having been accustomed to drinking two ounces of whisky a day for over twenty years, he had 'lost weight, become thin, weak and tremulous' following prohibition's introduction; alcohol had become such 'an essential part of his diet'.[25] Coincidentally, the district medical officer of Salem was granted custodial power to hold two brandy bottles a month for use by hospitalised patients whose alcoholism could be confirmed by doctors.[26]

At any rate, both permit applications were eventually approved on the condition that the applicants would need to pay a special cash security of 500 rupees, which, along with their permits, would be immediately forfeited if they were found to have shared their rations. These were but two of the hundreds of applications that the government received during prohibition's six-year run. Public opinion soon disparaged the personal liquor permit system as a glaring workaround of the policy. An editorial in *Harijan* offered the following defence:

> It has also been suggested that the prohibition introduced by the Madras Government is merely nominal in that it allows the issue of personal permits for the consumption of foreign liquor. The suggestion is a gross exaggeration. Personal permits cannot be claimed as a matter of right. They are granted to a limited number of persons of well-known status

who by habit are accustomed to the use of foreign liquor and cover the possession of only specified quantity of liquor at any time.[27]

The issuance of personal liquor permits rested on applicants' ability to prove their social status *and* degree of alcohol dependency. Scholars have pointed out the glaring double standards that presented in American prohibition, which was 'only enforced among the coloured population'.[28] Although race similarly mattered in determining issues of access to liquor in dry Madras, Indian gentlemen could also lay claim to some liquor within the hierarchical structure of colonial Indian society.

Prohibition was so much a product of political competition that the policy's first amendment also developed as its direct consequence. In the closing months of 1937, Rajaji pushed for a Bill in the legislatures that sought the press censorship of advertisements of medicated wines and the like, except when they were published in specially designated medical journals or were endorsed by the Madras Medical Council. With alcoholic content ranging from 16–20 per cent alcohol, medicated wines like St Raphael's tonic wine, Pancepeptone, Vibrona and Hall's Wine were not only steeply priced, the Congress ministry pointed out, but they also enjoyed wide circulation on account of their exemption from excise laws.

At first glance, the amendment related to the difference between medicinal and medical claims about alcohol. On a deeper level, however, it sought to issue a direct challenge to the colonial government in the area of press censorship. Coming in the heel of a long and protracted struggle over press censorship, the period of provincial autonomy brought forth a fresh controversy. The Congress pledge had charged the British with causing India's economic, political, cultural and spiritual ruination. Treating it as 'a challenge to Government which should be met', the colonial state had proceeded to ban it under the India Press Act in 1937.[29] Amidst this standoff, the Congress calculated that winning the right to censor liquor advertisements would not only constitute a resounding victory for prohibition but also represent Indian victory over the Raj's control of the press.

Predictably, stiff resistance soon followed. Leading the charge on behalf of the resident European community, Sir G. H. Hodgson opposed the Bill. He argued that the Madras Prohibition Act's primary objective had been to prevent the consumption of liquor that the state considered harmful to health and not that which supported health outcomes. Hodgson also rallied dwindling advertising revenues of the province's press as proof of the Bill's undesirability.[30] Ultimately, however, the Congress ministry won out. With the Bill's passing, businesses that advertised liquor in the press were liable to pay a fine of up to 1,000 rupees. The first legislative amendment to the Madras Prohibition Act thus endorsed press censorship of liquor advertisements at a time when personal liquor permits enabled the wealthiest individuals in society to procure alcohol without too much difficulty.

Ground Realities

Whereas alcohol continued to flow freely in the province's clubs even at the height of prohibition, 'for the urban poor, the illicit hooch was not just an alternative, but a release from life itself'.[31] A health officer conducted a medical examination of former 'addicts' in the dry villages of Osur, Perumugai and Munjurpet near Vellore, in which he tracked changes in their weight, reflexes and overall health for a year, beginning with prohibition's introduction. The study emphasised that besides harbouring an 'intensive craving for liquor', the patients were otherwise fine.[32] According to a survey of the policy's health impact in Chittoor, although 'some of the labourers and scavengers fell sick due to the sudden discontinuance of the habit, they could easily adjust themselves to the new environment and surroundings'.[33] The physical effects of forced abstention notwithstanding, this class of drinkers was not considered for personal liquor permits as the individuals concerned could not lay claim to gentlemanly status. State-sponsored studies routinely underplayed prohibition's adverse impact on the well-being of subaltern drinkers.

If Indian nationalism acquired its form and substance from 'that very real tension between force and consent', the lack of consent was why the Madras Prohibition Act relied on police power for enforcement to the extent that it did.[34] The assistant commissioner of excise was redeployed as the prohibition officer. A hundred and sixty-seven extra policemen were deployed in Salem alone. An inspector and three sub-inspectors policed enforcement in the dry districts, collated information about illicit distillers and smugglers, and conveyed it to the government. Sub-inspectors took an 'active part in popularising village sports and teaching villagers indigenous games' to distract them from the paucity of liquor.[35] The Congress ministry issued a prohibition manual to prohibition officers, while liquor vendors in the 'wet' districts were issued strict instructions relating to the geographical limits within which they could ply their business. The nationalist press exhorted every citizen to be a policeman and aid the authorities in preventing liquor smuggling from wet to dry districts.[36] An academic study concluded that the policy required 'utmost tact and doggedness' by the state as it was dealing with 'the unlettered and illiterate masses of the countryside who were ignorant about the material, moral and ethical values involved'.[37]

Prohibition-related crime gave rise to such conclusions. Just because the Congress ministry doubled down on its surveillance efforts did not mean that these efforts necessarily succeeded. Whilst rates of alcohol consumption officially fell in the dry districts, alcohol was procured with ease in practice. In Salem alone, illicit distillation more than doubled from 144 cases between 1938 and 1939 to 296 between 1939 and 1940. By 1943, this figure had risen to a staggering 1,133 cases.[38] A corresponding increase in illicit distillation, smuggling and similar prohibition-related crime was recorded in Chittoor, Cudappah and North Arcot. In November 1937, a toddy renter and his son were found guilty of possessing and offering illicit arrack for sale in Thumbankurichi. The witness arrived with the search party in the village just as the toddy renter was selling the arrack in a shed in his field. Upon spotting the search party, the renter, his son and their customers had attempted to flee the scene, only to be caught red-handed and fined 100 rupees for their crime.[39]

Several similar cases were recorded wherein the sub-inspector received tip-offs about the illicit distillation of arrack and arrived at the scene of the crime, usually the homes of toddy tappers who had been recently laid off work, only to find the arrack and the still, which had been hastily dumped in a nearby well.[40] The prohibition manual described in minute detail the ease with which arrack could be produced in the countryside. The arrack 'wash', inspectors were reminded, could be derived at little cost from 'any sugary matter, such as jaggery' and could be found hidden in wild country, rock crevices, standing crops, manure heaps, hay stacks or river beds.[41] Dixon, Salem's collector, noted in his diary that individuals frequently asked to see toddy tappers' licences and took the opportunity to have 'a swig at their toddy', while 'nervous owners camp[ed] in their topes at night' to ensure that tappers did not break the law.[42] Such accounts simultaneously betray the contempt and helplessness that characterised the authorities' response to subaltern drinkers with prohibition's implementation.

Amidst these circumstances, C. Jagannathachari, an economist, conducted a study of prohibition's effects in Salem. He noted a decrease in rates of indebtedness in Salem village and a corresponding increase in savings and family expenditures. Rejecting the notion that prohibition had engendered widespread economic displacement, Jagannathachari claimed instead that of 'the 39,922 persons formerly dependent on toddy tapping for livelihood, 22,109 [had] taken up agricultural occupations and sweet juice tapping; 1,717 [had] left the district', although he estimated that 2,699 adults were still unemployed. The report concluded that the policy's effects were more favourable in rural Salem than in the town, which had produced 'a higher percentage of addicts, with an annual drink bill of Rs. 88 each, 27 per cent of [their] total income'.[43] Considering the difficulties associated with the detection of prohibition-related crime in rural areas, it is not a stretch to assume that prohibition's success in these parts could have been overstated.

Notwithstanding heightened levels of state surveillance, the policy's phased introduction produced a situation wherein the dry districts were flanked by wet areas from which drinkers could easily obtain their liquor. Two months after the policy's introduction, Dixon met petitioners in the village of Suramangalam, Salem. Although the women were apparently generally 'pleased' with the policy, Dixon noted that the men appeared 'negative' and 'resigned'; they no longer had their familiar, favourite repast to look forward to in the evenings. He also remarked that old pots had been found left attached to trees from the previous year's collection in Mallur. The pots were being used to collect illicit toddy following prohibition's introduction.[44]

P. J. Thomas, an economics professor at the University of Madras, remarked in his report of prohibition's economic impact in Salem that the district's municipal coolies had been visiting the neighbouring 'wet' town of Erode for their toddy and arrack, where it was common for them to spend as much as 5–6 rupees of their meagre earnings on alcoholic drink.[45] Similarly, the people of Kumarapalayam village in Salem took to visiting liquor shops in the town of Bhavani, a mile away. The problem soon reached such alarming levels that Thomas even suggested arrangements with Mysore state, where Bhavani was located, to reduce the incidence of these drink excursions.

The princely states of Hyderabad and Mysore adjoining the Madras Presidency shared neither the Congress ministry's enthusiasm for prohibition nor any obligation to cooperate with the province's reform programmes. Both provided easy access to all kinds of alcohol. The Mysore government duly informed the Madras government that it would not be possible to offer cooperation for the success of prohibition in Salem, Cuddapah and Chittoor. All the shops on the border between the territories had already been auctioned off and cancellation of existing contracts would mean a 'heavy financial sacrifice' for the Mysore government.[46] The Congress ministry responded by reminding the public that it was futile to stop drinkers from sojourning to Mysore; the people should instead see to it that their neighbours did not bring any liquor back with them.[47]

A report prepared by the superintendent of the Excise Intelligence Bureau, A. V. Krishnamurthy, showed that Salem had a thriving underground liquor industry by 1939. Bootlegging was rampant and the district's cloth shop owners apparently privately shared with Krishnamurthy that they could get illicit arrack whenever they wanted. Their quest for alcohol was facilitated by the frequent business trips they took to the wet districts. Sojourns for the express purpose of tapping toddy were equally common, facilitated by the thriving business that was conducted by the seventeen enterprising toddy shops and five arrack shops that operated their business within a five-mile radius of the Salem state border.[48]

Krishnamurthy noted from local interviews that the clientele of these shops had swelled in the dry years. The drink traffic from Salem to Erode was so constant, in fact, that the toddy shops that catered to their needs even provided temporary lodging. The evening train that left Erode for Salem acquired the dubious distinction of being known as the 'Kudikarar Vandi' (Drunkard's Special Train).[49] More permanent migrations to obtain toddy and arrack also took place out of Ayodhyapattanam, a well-known centre of tappers that was located five miles from Salem. A village headman in Salem had informed Krishnamurthy that around five hundred tappers had left the district to non-prohibition areas, including Mysore, in search of a livelihood.[50]

Just as the passage of drinkers and liquor producers from dry into wet districts became exceedingly common, so too did the consumption – often with deadly consequences – of industrial-grade alcohol. A railway constable became suspicious upon seeing two large wooden drums at Madras Central Station in 1942. According to the consignee, the drums contained wood oil, but the constable was having none of it. Upon examining the drums at the Melpatti station, he found that they were filled to the brim with denatured spirit. The consignee was charged with the illicit transportation of close to ten gallons of denatured spirit under the Madras Prohibition Act.[51] Eight bottles of industrial-grade liquor could be obtained for less than a rupee compared to the same quantity of arrack which had previously cost 16 rupees.[52] It was a tragic irony that prohibition thus brought about an increased consumption of denatured spirits in place of the relatively benign toddy and arrack.

The Congress ministry was acutely aware that erstwhile drinkers were increasingly resorting to drinking denatured spirits during prohibition. In 1941, Cuddappah's collector asked for two types of Ayurvedic medicinal preparations containing spirit to be exempted from the Madras Prohibition Act. The collector asked that Arishtas and Asavas be granted exemption as their criminalisation caused 'great hardship and inconvenience to the public who were in need of them on medical grounds'.[53] He added that their steep prices would be a sufficient deterrent to prevent abuse by the drinking public. Advised by Rajaji, excise officials countered that it was not safe to relax control over the preparations in dry districts 'where even denatured spirit was sometimes drunk as a substitute for ordinary liquor'.[54] Although the Congress ministry knew the public health risks that it was taking with prohibition, death by denatured spirit was yet another opportunity cost – admittedly a most deadly one – that it grudgingly accepted in order to realise prohibition. Likewise, the consumption of ganja, lehiams and other medicinal preparations saw a sharp increase in all four dry districts during the prohibition years.[55] Meanwhile, attempts to distract people from alcohol by offering them stimulants instead remained futile. In Salem, the tea campaign failed to take off in spite of the Tea Cess Committee's strategy of offering the beverage free of charge to toddy drinkers.[56]

Protestants, Catholics and Communion Wine

Amidst the difficulties presented by prohibition's enforcement, a serious controversy erupted when the policy ran headlong into religion. As a letter published in the *Madras Mail* put it, 'there is a growing feeling of uneasiness among Christians of South India. The Government's treatment of sacramental wine under prohibition will always remain an open sore. The Government could have easily granted the modest request of Christians without affecting in the least the policy or its enforcement.'[57]

Gandhi had harboured misgivings about where Indian Christians stood on prohibition even prior to its introduction. He had asked C. F. Andrews, a well-known missionary and his dear friend, to enlist the support of the Christian churchmen in India for the policy. Andrews had reached out to his friends in England for support as well. He informed them that the Indian Christian leadership was unanimously in favour of prohibition. To be sure, there were grounds to expect such support. Prohibition had developed as a programme of Protestant Christian reform in the West. Biblical references to wine notwithstanding, Protestant churches were at the forefront of the temperance movement, with several promoting complete abstinence as godliness. Protestants in India also generally supported the policy. Prohibition's experience in the Madras Presidency would prove the policy's Protestant leanings, although the combination of caste and religion would also render it seriously polarising.

The Congress was invested in verifying the Indian Christian stance on prohibition for two reasons. First, it was committed to the principle of religious non-interference, a commitment it shared with the colonial state. Following Queen Victoria's Proclamation of 1858, the Raj had proceeded with marked caution in matters relating to religion. Secularism had subsequently developed as a guiding principle of state power for the Congress leadership as well. By the 1930s, the party's approach to religion and the state reflected the range of positions that its leaders held on these issues. Buttressed by Gandhi's conviction that the good state would intervene to uphold positive religious rights and freedoms, the Congress committed itself to ensuring the equal standing of all religions in the public sphere. The party thus railed against state intervention in matters where such intervention threatened to affect religion and culture. In 1931, Gandhi had objected to the colonial government's tacit support for proselytisation efforts through the humanitarian aid it extended to missionaries.[58] Such state intervention was anti-national in his view as it meant supporting religious conversion at the expense of the Hindus.

Second, Gandhi harboured deep suspicions about Indian Christian loyalties, which then necessitated public proclamations of the community's support for potentially divisive policies like prohibition. The nationalist leadership took it for granted that Hindus and Muslims supported prohibition. Indian Christians, however, were another matter altogether. To the nationalist leadership, it seemed that there was much that the minority religious community shared with the colonisers when it came to religion and culture.[59] This was especially so with the Eucharist, a Christian practice whose equation with religion and culture was fleshed out precisely because it stood in such sharp contrast to upper-caste Hindu and Muslim contempt for alcoholic drinking. The partaking of sacramental bread and wine has tremendous symbolic significance for Christians as it represents both sacrifice and salvation. To the Congress leadership, it appeared that the ritual – premised as it was on the very essence of Christian theology – might just turn Indian Christians against prohibition.

Originally, the Madras Prohibition Act enabled the storage, distribution and consumption of alcohol 'for any religious purpose in accordance with ancient custom' as long as individuals made a formal request for the right to possess liquor. They would need to apply for personal permits, which they would then submit to district magistrates. Magistrates had the power to issue or withdraw licences at their discretion. Requiring Europeans to apply for permits for the right to hold liquor was a calculated power play by the nationalist state.

For the same reason, however, the permit system turned out to be a double-edged sword for the Congress where religious practices were concerned. If subordinating the colonial state to its authority with permits served to demonstrate Congress power, Catholic opposition to the permit system directly undermined the nationalist claim to represent the interests of every community in the country. The permit system touched a raw nerve among south Indian Catholics, who viewed prohibition as the state's intrusion into ecclesiastical authority. With prohibition's introduction, clergymen now had to seek and secure permission for the right to store and distribute alcohol to the congregation. The church's ability to carry out a cherished ritual now depended on the state's permission.

Prohibition thus brought the secular into conflict with the sacred in a very direct and personal manner. The Catholics demanded that sacramental wine should not be treated in the same manner as alcohol that was earmarked for medicinal, scientific or industrial purposes. Instead, they sought the permit system's replacement with a system wherein the province's bishops could procure sacramental wine in casks or bottles and issue it to priests within their jurisdiction for distribution to their congregation as they saw fit. By doing so, the community simultaneously asserted its religious leaders' authority and rejected the state interference that they saw in the policy.

Sacramental wine became politicised in a context wherein political identities had become delineated along caste lines. The Congress's campaign of the early 1930s had 'crystallised ideas of majority and minority' in the process of securing representation for the Depressed Classes. Whilst upper-caste Hindus were the undisputed majority and Muslims the undisputed minority in this equation, the issue of separate electorates had thrown into question the political status of the Depressed Classes. This assumed a pronounced communal angle, particularly in provinces like Madras, where lower-caste communities had converted in large numbers to Christianity. In fact, nearly 40 per cent of the Madras Presidency's Catholics were made up of converts from the Depressed Classes.[60] This situation had fuelled caste-based discriminatory practices within the church, which had in turn raised Dalit Catholic demands for affirmative action.

In a context wherein Christian representational politics was developing in response to the community's acute perception of its minority status, and along clearly delineated denominational lines, Protestant leaders like K. T. Paul and S. K. Datta had sought alignment with the Congress. A devoted Gandhian, Paul had coined the term 'Christian citizenship' in the early 1920s as an expression of Christian responsibility to the Indian nation. He sought to bridge 'the sacred' with 'the secular' by exhorting Christians to become the country's peacemakers between warring communities. He stressed that Christians needed to work to remove 'internal discord and social evils such as alcoholism', educate themselves and embrace Indianisation.[61] Unlike the Catholics who sought close alignment with the Vatican, the Protestant political leadership's Janus-faced orientation to international developments and Indian politics meant that the latter were likely to view supporting prohibition not just as a personal duty but also as a sacred civic obligation.

By the 1930s, there were serious disagreements between the Catholics and the Protestants on issues of political representation. The Round Table Conferences highlighted the inability of the communities' leaderships to come to an agreement on the issue of separate electorates. The Protestants had made the argument that the persistence of caste in the church was a failing of the Catholic ecclesiastical leadership, for which no other political redress was necessary. The Catholics, on the other hand, had raised the demand for separate electorates through leaders like A. T. Pannirselvam. The Poona Pact, which the Second Round Table Conference culminated in, awarded separate electorates to religious minorities but denied them to the Depressed Classes. For Christians as a whole, separate electorates had come at the cost of giving up claims for representation on the grounds of Dalit identity. Gandhi had played a crucial role in determining the Poona Pact's outcome.[62] Coming in its wake, the Congress's seemingly intentional omission of Christians from its cabinet when it swept to power in the southern Indian province in 1937 added insult to injury. The church wine imbroglio developed in this particular milieu. For the Catholics, prohibition was not just state power but also an authoritarian imposition by a leadership that had shown little sensitivity for the community's sentiments in the recent past as well.

Almost as soon as prohibition was introduced, the Congress found itself being inundated with letters from Catholics demanding redress for the hurt they had experienced over the issue of sacramental wine. The situation prompted Gandhi to double down on his consensus-building efforts. He asked Mahadev Desai to write to 'representative Christian friends to ascertain their voice on the question' of sacramental wine.[63] The secretary of the National Christian Council of India, P. O. Philip, chimed in to add that there was no basis to think of prohibition as a violation of religious rights; the use of wine in the Eucharist was 'a foreign national habit'.[64] The *Madras Guardian* reported that there could be no suspicion in regards to Christians' support for prohibition as there was 'no worthier call awaiting Christians'.[65] The general secretary of the Student Christian Movement of India, Burma and Ceylon, Revd A. Ralla Ram, was much more blunt. He remarked that 'the Europeans who came to this country should fall in with our aspirations and I am afraid that if we should respect their feelings in this matter, we shall leave a loophole for many others'.[66] Only 'European' Christians could be expected to raise opposition to prohibition, which, he argued, should be ignored anyway in pursuit of lofty national goals.

At the height of prohibition, Rajaji received a letter from Tanjore's Tamil Evangelical Lutheran Church. It set out that the congregation was using 'only Woodley's non-alcoholic sacramental wine' and recommended that 'even Roman Catholics' could use unfermented grape juice as it was 'not obligatory' to use alcoholic liquors for the mass.[67] Not all Protestant groups agreed with his view. A Chaplain from Ahmednagar insisted that 'every Anglican priest is definitely and authoritatively required to use bread and wine in the Holy Communion … the Anglican Church, as such, would never for one moment consider departing from this custom'.[68] The archbishop of India would remark, rather wryly, that he had on several occasions been called 'a dignitary of the Church of England, a Parsi' and that his 'connexion with liquor interests [had] been subtly suggested'.[69] The archbishop pledged not to use the personal liquor permit that had been issued to him as a member of the European community, on the Congress's request. 'What I cannot admit,' he added, 'is that such a campaign can be based on the doctrine that drink (not drunkenness) is evil.'[70]

Pannirselvam recorded his opposition to prohibition during the Madras Legislative Council assembly debates. 'Seeing how essential this wine is for our worship,' he said, 'it seems to me you are putting a restriction on our right to worship, on our right to practice our religion.'[71] The Mangalorean Catholic legislator J. A. Saldanha concurred with this view. Countering Rajaji's argument that provision had been made for clergymen to obtain sacramental wine through the permit system, he pointed out that 'if one has to obtain a permit or license for getting wine for this purpose, it is not *infra dig*; that is not the point. The point is, there is interference with religious worship.'[72] Christian legislators in the Madras Presidency thus duly reminded the Congress ministry that prohibition violated the party's commitment to secularism.[73]

The Congress's attempts to build consensus on the Indian Christian stance on prohibition had crucial parallels and precedents. Similar struggles over sacramental wine had previously played out in the West as well.[74] In India, however, colonialism and caste inflected prohibition's intersections with religion and culture. Much of the debate was premised on whether the use of wine in the church was a matter of religious obligation or cultural adaptation. The implication was that religion was inviolable, whereas culture could be negotiated; if the use of wine was 'just' cultural, then Indian Christians could reasonably be expected to embrace non-alcoholic substitutes in place of wine. However, the debate arose in the first place because the nationalist state could not make peace with the cultural proximity that presented between Indian Christian religious practice and the colonial state. The prohibition debate thus prompted the mining of church history for 'facts' that the warring sides selectively applied to legitimise their respective claims.

Vexed by criticisms of the Congress ministry's apparent high-handedness in its approach to sacramental wine, Rajaji pointed out that 'there [was] nothing intrinsically in the wine preventing it from being used as anything other than beverage. It may be used now for religious purposes and at the same time for other purposes.'[75] Nevertheless, the issue caused such a furore that Jawaharlal Nehru wrote to Rajaji expressing concern about the lack of sensitivity that the chief minister had demonstrated in his dealings with the minority community. Nehru also wrote to all the other provincial chief ministers advising them to tread extremely cautiously in the matter:

> The question has arisen immediately in Madras where Prohibition is being pushed with vigour. Inadvertently, no special reference was made in the Act that has been passed. Subsequently, in the rules framed by the Provincial Government the power to grant licenses to doctors, chemists, European clubs etc. and 'for ancient religious usage' was given to district magistrates who have also been empowered to withdraw a license without assigning any reason thereof. This seems to be a perfectly legitimate arrangement for all ordinary purposes, but the Catholics

in the South are vigorously agitating against it in so far as they are concerned. There is talk of religion being attacked, of the fundamental Right resolution being ignored and the like. Opponents against the Congress are trying to exploit religious sentiment against the Congress and some even suggest that Catholic members of the Assembly should resign.[76]

Nehru not only advised Rajaji to issue an official statement to appease Catholic sentiment, but also urged the chief minister to personally attend the all-India Catholic Ecclesiastical Congress as a goodwill gesture later that year. However, this was not the last of the disagreements that prohibition would prompt between the leaders.

While Nehru thought that Rajaji should take a more cautious stance in certain matters, he was concerned that his colleague was willing to make too many serious compromises with the British in order to make his pet project of prohibition work. A month before prohibition's introduction in Salem, Rajaji had written to Nehru stating that as Lord Erskine was scheduled to visit Salem in the month when prohibition was to be inaugurated, 'there should be no feeling of friction ... so I have asked our Party not to be aggressive'.[77] Nehru's reply was swift and stern. 'There is one danger,' he wrote, 'in relaxing the rules because we fear complications ... Soon we shall have to face a conflict on the Federation issue. Are we to say then that we must not take an aggressive attitude because this may interfere with our prohibition programme?'[78]

The unexpected 'storm in a teacup', to quote Nehru, ultimately forced Rajaji's hand in sanctioning the Catholics' demand. Section 3 of the Madras Prohibition Act's second amendment in 1938 replaced the word 'permits' with 'authorities' to reflect the status of the religious leaderships that the Act would apply to.

However, the amendment became a case of much too little, much too late. With prohibition's introduction in Bombay and Bihar in 1938, a fresh slew of protests erupted over the place of wine in Christian ritual and of the place of Christian ritual in Indian prohibition. The Nationalist Christian Party of Bombay enthusiastically endorsed prohibition's introduction in the province, citing biblical references endorsing teetotalism. Similarly, the Gujarat and Kathiawar Missionary Conference issued a press statement affirming that most Protestant Christians of the province were fully on board with the Congress campaign.[79] They expressed concern about the 'misleading statements appearing in the Press from time to time regarding the attitude of Christians toward the liquor traffic, and the use of wine for sacramental purposes'.[80] These expressions of Protestant support for prohibition reflect the political pragmatism that a certain kind of Christian leader, who espoused amenable notions of Christian citizenship, would be more acceptable to the nationalist state.[81]

At the same time, Catholics in other parts of the country demanded nothing less than complete exemption from the Act. Taking issue with the Congress leadership's stance on sacramental wine, the Catholic leader and academic B. S. Gilani wrote to Gandhi from Allahabad stating:

> I am afraid your information that in South India the Catholic Bishops are satisfied is not correct. Exemption has been conceded for purposes less sacred than religion with the unfortunate implication that our Bishops cannot be trusted. In Bihar, only recently the Christians who have not joined the Congress obtained an amendment with the help of non-Congress votes. All this creates unnecessary alarm and the implications to a Congressman are humiliating.[82]

Two days later, Gilani wrote to Gandhi again pointing out that the Bihar Prohibition Act had been passed with complete exemption given to Catholics and members of the Church of England 'for purposes of the Mass and Holy Communion'. He added, moreover, that the 'acceptance of this amendment in Behar should be followed by similar response in the other provinces'.[83] When Gandhi and Desai consulted Rajaji for his opinion on the issue, the latter promptly responded that the provisions made under the Madras Act were 'absolutely adequate and honourable ... I wish you find a way not to help Mr. Gilani's agitation further.'[84] Like prohibition, the consensus-building efforts it necessitated had limits at times too.

The sacramental wine debacle proved to be a crucial lesson in governance for the nationalist state. It prompted backlash, the extent of which caught the Congress by surprise. As it developed, it revealed serious differences in priorities within the Congress leadership and highlighted the lack of a uniform stance on prohibition. It also demonstrates for us the very real constraints confronting the nationalist state when it finally had the opportunity to implement its constructive programme. Although the nationalist state sought to build consensus, it was ultimately not in control of the direction the ensuing debates took, much less their outcomes. Grand national programmes of social change were transformed in unexpected ways as they encountered specific provincial circumstances and dynamics. Christian responses to prohibition emphasised caste and religious differences inasmuch as the Congress's approach to the nation focused on blurring them.

Prohibitioning amidst Prohibition

As prohibition was a crucial project of legitimacy for the Congress, the organisation harboured no illusions about the policy's costs. The greatest losses were lost revenue from alcohol sales and taxes and the steep costs involved in enforcement. The nationalist state adopted a three-pronged strategy to cope with the policy's fiscal fallout. The first was prohibition's gradual introduction in a few carefully selected districts. The second was its promotion of *neera*, or sweet toddy, in place of fermented toddy, which categorically failed to take off. The third strategy was increasing taxes on other consumer goods. Pragmatism aside, however, developments that were beyond the Congress's control translated into a situation wherein all three approaches surfaced consequences that haunted the administration and shaped prohibition's subsequent trajectories.

The biggest challenge for the nationalist state was addressing the issue of the local economy's dependency on revenue from alcohol. During his tour of Kerala, large crowds petitioned Rajaji to introduce prohibition there. He pointed out, however, that his government could only proceed by incurring a further loss of 40 lakhs, which would necessitate the closure of Palakkad's Victoria College.[85] In fact, the decision to extend prohibition to Chittoor was also premised on the strategic consideration that the district only returned 'a very small amount of excise revenue'.[86] Erskine's letter to P. J. Crigg, the finance member of the Viceroy's Executive Council, reveals how far Rajaji's government and the British actually concurred on prohibition's timing and scope:

> I would like to tell you very confidentially – and I hope you won't mention this to Rajagopalachari – that we are only going to extend Prohibition in this Presidency to one district next year and even then not until October. The resulting loss of revenue in the next financial year will therefore at the most, be under seven lakhs but at the same time we are going to reintroduce other taxes on agricultural income

and tobacco which will certainly make up the loss on the prohibition experiment.[87]

Prohibition also brought into the equation the Nehruvian model of the state. As ridding the nation of a vital source of revenue would hurt the treasury, the nationalist leadership was all too keenly aware that the policy would require planning. Along with convincing the people of prohibition's necessity, it needed to generate alternative sources of revenue. By way of doing this, the Madras Congress ministry raised the general sales tax and introduced a new tobacco sales tax, which came into effect on 1 August 1939. The new tobacco tax disproportionately affected Muslims, who were involved in large numbers in the tobacco industry as merchants and workers. As a community, the Muslims had welcomed prohibition; the Muslim League had declared its commitment to ensuring the policy's success.[88] However, the tobacco tax turned the tide of Muslim support against the nationalist state as it came in a context of trade union activism and escalating labour grievances. Protests soon broke out in tobacco factories and shops. Muslim businesses that were set to be seriously affected by the losses from the onerous tax held several meetings to debate Congress policy.[89] Colonial officials rejoiced at the 'fortuitous' turn of events as the tobacco tax 'pressed very hard on Muslim merchants', noting that these taxes affected them to 'a proportionately greater extent than the Hindus'.[90]

By June 1939, the increase in the Madras general sales tax and the impending new tobacco sales tax had become 'extremely unpopular measures', as evidenced by the protest letters the colonial government received from merchants' associations all over the province.[91] In Madras city, the situation was exacerbated by opportunistic merchants who lowered their workers' wages to cope with their projected business losses. Whilst most *beedi* factories were forced to increase prices, a Madras factory that refused to do so was forced to shut down. Consequently, a thousand workers were rendered jobless.[92] An estimated 1,300 *beedi* and cigar workers subsequently went on strike. Mostly Muslims, the *beedi* workers sought the help of anti-Hindi protestors in the Madras Presidency. The predominantly Hindu cigar workers, on the other hand, turned to the socialists for support.[93] Prohibition thus had the unintended effect of deepening existing divisions at a time when communal tensions were already at fever pitch in parts of the country. The Congress ministry responded with a personal appeal to the people that 'responsible' democracy entailed 'enduring a certain amount of discipline'.[94]

As it turned out, the hardship that prohibition wrought fostered waves of dissent, not discipline. Opposition to the policy on economic grounds presented the nationalist state with a frontal challenge it could not ignore. During the legislative assembly debates on the budget in 1940, the party's opponents criticised prohibition for having necessitated the barrage of new taxes. Among the critics ranged against the policy were prominent non-Brahmin politicians, like A. T. Pannirselvam, who argued that 'the government had wickedly, unnecessarily, and mischievously given up the drink revenue'.[95] He was joined in his trenchant critique of Brahmin raj under Congress rule by E. V. Ramasamy, known as Periyar, and the Self-Respect movement. Periyar criticised the Congress's prohibition policy as a strategy that sought to further Brahmin interests at the expense of sacrificing Adi Dravida welfare. The *Kudi Arasu* published articles claiming that prohibition's real motive was to stop the provision of free education to the poor on the grounds that the loss of revenue from prohibition would necessitate cuts in the administration of social welfare programmes.[96] For the duration of prohibition's six-year run, Self-Respect conferences in various districts passed resolutions demanding the policy's termination.[97]

Notwithstanding civil society demands for the policy's extension to other parts of the province, George Joseph, an influential Syrian Christian politician from Kerala, opposed the policy as an undemocratic imposition on the people. Although Joseph had been a staunch Gandhian and advocate of prohibition previously, he came to see the Congress ministry's anti-liquor stance as oppressive and high-handed. When prohibition was announced, Joseph denounced it as a gross violation of the rights of 'a large number of people' who did not consider it wrong to use toddy as a drink.[98]

In fact, prohibition's implementation had made it so patently clear that it disproportionately targeted the country liquor industry and the people associated with it that demands soon surfaced to officially limit the policy's working to toddy and arrack. With prohibition's introduction in Bombay, M. D. Bhat, the municipal commissioner, wrote to the secretary to government advising:

> The concrete suggestion that requires serious consideration is that prohibition should apply only to country liquor. The result of it would be that Indians who drink one-third of the foreign liquor drink in Bombay would be allowed to consume what they are accustomed to. The loss to Government would be a revenue of Rs. 112 lakhs. If the revenue of Rs.

24 lakhs from foreign liquor obtained by the Government of Bombay was raised by the Government of Bombay to about five times the present rate, it would be able to recoup the loss they would make in their revenue on country liquor. Foreign liquor would then be completely out of the reach of the poorest classes and a great deal of the difficulty now encountered by Governments – total prohibition policy could be avoided.[99]

In doing so, Bhat was drawing upon the Madras Presidency's experiences with prohibition. In fact, various stakeholders cited the Madras example as a cautionary tale to learn from. A deputation of liquor and toddy licensees wrote to Gandhi referencing the 'stealthy and cautious' approach of the Madras government and demanded a similarly gradual approach to prohibition's introduction in Bombay as well.[100]

Problems of representation and redress persisted for toddy and liquor shop contractors. Particularly hard hit were liquor businesses that had obtained their licences just prior to prohibition's introduction. The Madras Congress received a series of lawyers' notices complaining that their clients' rights as renters had been severely compromised by prohibition laws, when they had in fact previously been 'solemnly assured by the Government that there was no question of any change of policy in regard to toddy leases in any district other than Salem'.[101] They had rented their shops in Trichy, within a ten-mile radius of Salem, having predicted that prohibition in that district would induce customers to travel to their shops. However, when these customers subsequently tried to take their drinks with them from the shops' premises, they ran into trouble with the prohibition police.[102] With prohibition in full swing, the affected contractors cried foul play and demanded the right to receive full compensation for their losses. According to Arunachala Udayar, who petitioned the government on behalf of six renters,

On August 1937, we the bidders then present asked the Revenue Divisional Officer, if there would be any change or changes in the concessions and customs then available in this district ... I, the petitioner, bid the two shops in auction at a very high rate due to keen competition with complete reliance on the assurances then given by Pending Officer. On 17/10/1937, orders were received from the Inspector of Excise, North Trichinopoly Circle, ordering me to ascertain the number of trees tapped for the five years 1932–1937 and to tap only such number of trees – a restriction which did not obtain sanction in any of the previous years and which was not announced at the time of auction … During my experience for the last thirty years as Toddy Shop contractor of about 4–5 shops at a time, I have had come across no such instances in which original terms and stipulations have been violated by Government itself.[103]

Udayar's petition also claimed an increase in toddy theft from groves by addicts suffering withdrawal symptoms, and he expressed concern that the contractors had to put up with further losses as a result of undue interference from Village Vigilance Committees. The surprise checks that toddy bearers were subjected to as they made their way to storage depots from groves apparently caused long delays in transportation, thus causing the toddy to spoil.[104] Hence, the petitioner requested the transportation of toddy in bottles, a proposal that had previously been raised under different circumstances, and an amendment to prohibition law such that individuals could be allowed to possess liquor outside of licensed shop premises. Unsurprisingly, both his appeals were met with resolute refusal.

The prohibition years wrought sustained efforts by the socialists to mobilise support among toddy tappers at a time when the labour movement was at its peak in the province. During the mid- to late 1930s, the politics of socialist leaders like S. V. Ghate, P. Jeevanandam, and K. Murugesan intersected with prohibition politics. The plight of toddy tappers loomed large. Whilst Madras city toddy tappers had been spared the tragedy of mass unemployment that had befallen their peers in Salem, North Arcot, Chittoor and Cuddapah, they struggled to obtain official recognition of the hardship they had suffered owing to prohibition.

On 14 September 1938, more than a thousand Madras city toddy tappers gathered to present a memorial to the chief minister. They raised two chief demands. First, they sought assurance that the fifteen-mile limit for tapping trees – a rule that had been introduced the previous year – would be maintained without any change. Second, they pressed the government for a minimum guaranteed wage of 14 *anna*s per day and claimed the Workmen's Compensation Act for tappers.[105] Two months later, workers of the Toddy Tappers' Union, along with labourers from the Press Labour Union and the Tramway and Electrical Supply Workers' Association, publicly condemned the *lathi* charge on the workers of Madurai's Mahalakshmi Mills and the arrest of their leaders, Muthuramalinga Thevar and P. Jeevanandam. The growing allegiance between the province's toddy tappers with the socialists was not lost on colonial officials, who responded with marked anxiety. 'The Socialists,' they noted, 'are endeavouring to revive the Toddy Tappers Union after its collapse after the last strike. Meetings have been held with a view to increase the strength of the union.'[106]

Problems with *Neera*

The *neera* campaign added to the troubles of the Congress ministries amidst these developments. The provincial governments doubled down on efforts to make *neera* work following prohibition's introduction. Rajaji's government increased the number of licences that it offered to the cooperative societies of tappers involved in manufacturing jaggery. Tappers now needed to obtain *neera* licences under prohibition law in order to produce jaggery, whereas they had previously manufactured it as a byproduct of fermented toddy. Cooperative societies were formed 'wherever possible', with each tapper given an advance of 10 rupees for jaggery production. Although discussions were held about the practicality of allowing boys, as in pre-prohibition days, to take up *neera* licences, the proposal was ultimately dropped as it would be difficult to charge juveniles with illicit liquor production.[107] Notwithstanding Gandhi's emphasis that the provinces ought to realise 'the economic importance of the four kinds of sugar-yielding palms' and 'do their best to propagate and protect the palms wherever possible', it quickly became evident that *neera* opened up a gaping loophole in prohibition law.[108]

The technology available at that time was not sufficient to prevent *neera*'s transformation into toddy. As prohibition's enforcement made toddy lucrative, there was no incentive to avoid it either. By applying insufficient amounts of lime to their collection pots, tappers easily circumvented prohibition law to produce toddy under the guise of *neera*. The practice soon became commonplace in the dry districts, prompting Rajaji's Congress ministry to extend prohibition law to include *neera* derived from coconut sap. Simultaneously, the *neera* that was obtained from date palm and other varieties of palm sap was brought under tighter regulations with the Madras Neera or Padani Rules of 1939. While the all-India Congress leadership continued to encourage *neera* production, the licences issued for coconut *neera* in the dry districts were rapidly withdrawn. With this drastic change in the government's stance, toddy tappers who had already been displaced by prohibition took a double hit.[109]

These developments caused great frustration and loss to the toddy-tapping communities that suffered the brunt of prohibition's economic effects. Members of the community responded with outrage at this latest instance of governmental intervention in their already restricted trade. A petition from the Madurai Nadar Mahajana Sangam in 1939 declared that it failed to understand 'why the government would insist on putting an end to the manufacture of a healthful and wholesome beverage ... The poor used it both as food and drink, the better classes in rural districts as tea, coffee and cocoa are used in cities and towns.'[110]

The problems that presented with *neera* were all too real, as Gandhi himself rather grudgingly admitted.[111] Compounding the issue were several controversies that erupted when *neera* became a case of delayed toddy, particularly with prohibition's enforcement in Bombay. In June 1939, the *Times of India* published a letter that recalled an interview between Gandhi and representatives of the Bombay Victuallers' Association. When Gandhi had produced his bottle of *neera* to prove to his guests that the drink could be as profitably harvested as toddy, he had been informed that what he had in his possession was, in fact, toddy with an estimated alcoholic content of 5–6 per cent. The letter concluded that 'the bubble of *neera* has thus been exploded and the real truth thus saw the light of day to [Gandhi's] intense surprise, not to say chagrin!'[112] The *neera* had turned into toddy at some point between its collection and Gandhi's demonstration.

One of the greatest sources of opposition from the public to prohibition – and the Congress's *neera* campaign – came from Bombay's Parsis, many of whom had made their fortunes from the liquor business and whose losses arising from the policy were therefore great. In addition to financial losses, the community also had to grapple with loss of life owing to the *neera* campaign. Four Parsis who had consumed it in Sevagram had died from toxicity after drinking over-fermented *neera*. Members of the Parsi community responded with outrage at this latest twist in the prohibition story. They blamed on *neera* the propensity to cause ailments like 'cold, flatulence and diarrhoea' and pointed out that it 'could have fatal consequences'.[113] The Industrial Research Laboratory in Bombay carried out a series of experiments on *neera* with the aim of delaying fermentation, although it could not find any solutions at that time.

Alongside problems caused by the unintended effects of nature in the tropics and intentional demonstrations of human agency, the *neera* campaign opened up another site of contestation between the nationalist and colonial governments. Rajaji sought permission from the central government to spend 1 lakh rupees from the rural development grant on developing the palm jaggery industry. He hoped to generate employment for the tappers who had lost their original source of livelihood. The finance minister responded by highlighting the loss to the government of any policy that would affect the sugar industry. The minister categorically refused to be associated with the policy, which, in his view, was set to become 'a great financial embarrassment to the Provinces'.[114]

Likewise, when Gandhi wrote to the colonial government expressing his intention to collect and sell *neera* to villages in the vicinity of his ashram, an officer denied his request on the grounds that it was impossible to prevent *neera* from turning into toddy. 'The grant of the permission asked for [would] be tantamount,' he wrote, 'to permitting the setting up of unlicensed toddy shops.'[115] Such standoffs in turn brought about a hardening of the Congress's stance. When Nagpur's revenue minister, P. B. Gole, recommended that the ashram's members could continue tapping *neera* for personal consumption as they had before, Desai declined the offer. Instead, he pointed out that as 'the existence of our Congress ministries [was] precarious', any show by the Congress of taking concessions from the British would be interpreted as a sign of weakness, and hence would not be contemplated.[116]

Political competition thus not only brought forth prohibition but also influenced the trajectories of the ameliorative programmes the policy necessitated. Ultimately, although the nationalist state's *neera* scheme failed to take off in the late colonial context, the contestations that it provoked and the infrastructure that it brought forth sowed the seeds for attempts to revive it following the achievement of independence.

'Corking the Bottle': Prohibition's Suspension

The outbreak of the Second World War had a tremendous impact on prohibitioning. The Madras Prohibition Act had originally set out the right of military personnel to possess and consume liquor in dry districts through the issuance of permits. Although the colonial establishment had not been happy with this state of affairs to begin with, the war provided it with the prime opportunity to revive the issue. British troops stationed in India demanded an increase in liquor rations in 1939. The colonial government sanctioned a tremendous increase in the importation of foreign liquor throughout the province, including the dry districts, to meet this demand.[117] The viceroy's office insisted that troops serving in or passing through dry districts should enjoy the same rights and privileges relating to liquor as their compatriots stationed elsewhere in India. It insisted that it was 'very necessary' that the troops, medical staff and other staff attached to them should be free from the restrictions imposed by the Act.[118] These circumstances paved the way for another major amendment in the Act.

It was evident to the British that the popularity of the Congress in the province was precipitously low by 1939. In Erskine's words,

> the most extraordinary thing about Gandhi's fast in Madras was the little attention that the population paid to it. Nobody seemed to mind what happened to the old hypocrite. I put this down to the general dislike of the Congress that has been caused by the onerous taxes they are introducing to pay for prohibition.[119]

Even though the Congress ministries resigned in 1939, the colonial administration continued with prohibition's enforcement for four more years before the policy's suspension. During this time, it relied on the collectors to administer the policy, supported by the police in this endeavour. The administrative and legal frameworks that had been devised previously continued to form the basis for the policy's implementation.

The colonial government continued to play divide and rule among liquor producers in the guise of preventing monopolies. When contractors from North Arcot petitioned for permission to mark trees in excess of the limit of 2,000 trees that had been allowed under prohibition law in the Conjeevaram belt area for shops in Madras city, the government allowed it. An important factor that influenced the decision was the consideration that contractors from the Gramani caste virtually monopolised the use of coconut trees in Madras city. Given this situation, the entry of toddy supplied by the Vellore renters, policymakers pointed out, would constitute 'healthy competition'.[120] Also at stake was the calculation that it would be 'more profitable to take the toddy into Madras for licit sale than to try to smuggle it into North Arcot', where prohibition's enforcement prevented contractors from going about their business as usual.[121] Ultimately, the proposal was accepted, albeit on the condition that the number of trees allowed for tapping would be restricted if any smuggling into North Arcot was even suspected.

There were two reasons for the colonial government's decision to retain the policy in the absence of the Congress's ministries. First, key political personalities were convinced that they could use prohibition to secure Indian cooperation for the war effort. Second, and relatedly, they did not want local unrest on their hands at a time when the state's attention was divided between the war on the one hand and maintaining control over India on the other. It was only when London was duly persuaded that ending prohibition would not seriously ruffle any feathers that it gave the green light to go ahead with the policy's suspension. The viceroy's office noted that the Congress government's ability to ensure the effective enforcement of prohibition had 'rapidly deteriorated' in the years following the policy's introduction.[122] The letter assured that there was 'no need to fear Rajagopalachari's criticism as his stock [was] very low and he [had] admitted on several occasions that owing to the decline of enthusiasm, prohibition [had] not been the success he hoped'.[123] Colonial officials calculated that prohibition's suspension would release scarce funds that could be used to weather the storm ahead. It would divert 'Rs. 65 lakhs to Government instead of to the public', which would help in addressing the food shortages they anticipated.[124] Colonial officials also pointed out that the police forces who had been deployed for prohibition's enforcement could be more efficiently utilised elsewhere. Of course, the Congress ministries' resignation in late 1939 over Britain's decision to commit India to the war effort in Europe also factored into these considerations. These circumstances collectively provided the context for the Act's suspension in 1943.

Notably, correspondence between Madras and London still stressed the importance of keeping up the show of heeding public opinion. The governor-general warned that 'public opinion would certainly regard it as wrong to discontinue the experiment without making future effort to prevent abuses'.[125] Instead, Lord Linlithgow recommended that the administration should look to the revenue reserve fund to meet the increased expenditure involved in enforcing prohibition, rather than take either of the drastic steps of increasing the sales tax or repealing prohibition. He warned that both these courses of action could turn the tide of public opinion against the British at a time when its standing was already dangerously low. Although the colonial administration was unsympathetic towards prohibition, fears of having to manage another public backlash amidst rapidly escalating crises in India and Europe alike had kept it from meddling with the policy until 1943.

However, the context of the 1940s was markedly different from the situation that had presented in 1937. Soaring rates of prohibition-related crime, labour grievances, hardship wrought by the new taxes and trade union activism had all dulled the enthusiasm with which the Indian public had welcomed the new Congress ministry and its pet project of prohibition. Unsurprisingly, the colonial government justified prohibition's suspension in this context with the old argument that it was more desirable that a licit supply of toddy, which in its fresh state apparently had 'a distinct food value', 'should not be denied to the labouring classes'.[126]

The Act was suspended in 1943. Almost immediately, the Congress regained the Muslim League's support in Madras. The Musim League condemned the suspension as British betrayal of the highest degree and launched protest meetings that were jointly organised by the Tamil Nadu Congress. In Madras city, 'there was an attempt at reviving Civil Disobedience by taking advantage of the agitation'.[127] Indeed, the policy's suspension connected a wide coalition of groups, including Congressmen and their followers, socialists, students, toddy tappers and labour organisations who rallied together against the colonial state. Outraged, Rajaji retorted that the problem of illicit liquor had nothing to do with prohibition. Although recent history had proven him wrong on this score, he published another pamphlet wherein he denounced the colonial government's actions as patently self-serving. A small number of people covertly drinking toddy, Rajaji wrote, was preferable to the vast majority getting drunk in broad daylight.[128]

At any rate, the reopening of toddy shops in the dry districts took place without any major incident in 1944. Toddy shop auctions that were held in the four prohibition districts were 'extremely successful, the amount realised in some cases being nearly double than that of the pre-prohibition rentals'.[129] A raised tree tax followed suit and arrack shops were opened a year later in 1945.

* * *

The Madras Prohibition Act of 1937 marked a watershed moment in the history of the Indian state. As a policy that was conceptualised and enforced during a time of political transition, it bore the imprint of the processes that had brought it into existence. The actual experience of governance brought with it several sobering discoveries for the Congress ministries, not least among them the extent of the provinces' reliance on revenue from liquor sales and taxation. The ideals that had paved the way for prohibition's introduction had to be tempered by pragmatism as the nationalist government found itself operating within the limits allowed by the colonial state. This situation had considerably limited the scope of prohibition policy to begin with. The policy was only introduced in four districts, which notably did not include the provincial capital. The system of permits was a deliberate concession by the Congress to the British to ensure the policy's introduction.

Moreover, there were heavy costs involved in enforcing prohibition that necessitated further compromises down the road. It became embroiled in a controversy over minority religious rights, prompting legal revision subsequently. Political opposition to prohibition also intensified with the Act's enforcement. Moreover, it became clear that drinkers turned to illicit hooch and denatured spirits, besides taking long sojourns to adjoining wet districts for their liquor. Yet prohibition's problems were still not enough to dull public enthusiasm for the policy. If anything, its shortcomings often fuelled civil society demands that the state ought to double down in implementing the policy throughout the province. In the short run, the Act inspired and influenced dry experiments in other parts of the country, while prompting amendment after amendment in its province of origin.

In the long run, the Madras Prohibition Act continued to be felt long after the policy's suspension. Policies are routinely suspended or terminated. Ideals, however, refuse to die. Owing to the context that had produced it, prohibition's suspension was but temporary. Upon returning to power, the Congress reintroduced the dry law throughout the province. Prohibition was now reborn as an ideal.

Notes

1. E & O 849/39, 28 February 1939. The source is a handwritten note from the mill owner to the government.
2. Ranajit Guha, 'Discipline and Mobilize', in *Subaltern Studies VII*, ed. Partha Chatterjee and Gyanendra Pandey, pp. 69–120 (Delhi: Oxford University Press, 1992), especially p. 102.
3. See K. Murugiah, 'Enforcement of Prohibition in Salem, 1937', *Indian Streams Research Journal* 2 (2012), pp. 1–4; S. Arunachala Perumal, 'Prohibition Policy under C. Rajagopalachari Ministries: A Study', unpublished MPhil thesis, Madurai Kamaraj University, 1988, pp. 3–5;

K. Ashok Kumar, 'Prohibition of Drinking in Salem District (1937–1943)', unpublished MPhil thesis, University of Madras, 1992, pp. 4–15; and S. Srinivasan, 'Prohibition Policy on Liquor in Madras Presidency from 1937 to 1939', *Golden Research Thoughts* 4 (2015), pp. 1–6.

4. See, for instance, Matthew R. Linderoth, *Prohibition on the North Jersey Shore: Gangsters on Vacation* (New York: Arcadia Publishing, 2010), pp. 87.

5. Madras Government's Order regarding Prohibition, IOR, fortnightly report for the second half of August, Public and Judicial Department, L/PJ/5/197, P & J 4249/1937.

6. Arnold, 'The Politics of Coalescence', p. 281.

7. Governor's Situation Report, 5 August 1937, L/PJ 3633/37, IOR.

8. *Great Britain and the East*, vol. 49 (London: Great Britain and the East Limited, 1937), p. 114.

9. C. Rajagopalachari's speech to the Legislative Assembly of Madras, 1 September 1937, fortnightly report for the second half of August, L/PJ/5/197, IOR.

10. Rajagopalachari's speech quoted in *The Hindu*, 19 June 1939.

11. Arnold, *Congress in Tamilnad*, p. 150.

12. Letter from Erskine to Rajagopalachari, 27 August 1937, Erskine Papers, file nos. 15–23, NML.

13. S. Muthiah, 'Another End to Prohibition', *The Hindu*, http://www.thehindu.com/thehindu/mp/2002/04/08/stories/2002040800140300.htmI (accessed on 12 February 2014). See also Irschick, *Tamil Revivalism*, p. 209.

14. Telegram from Linlithgow to Zetland, 11 July 1938, E & O 5320, IOR.

15. Telegram from Erskine to Brabourne, 7 June 1938, E & O 1938, No. 2-52/38-S (Confl.), IOR.

16. Telegram from Secretary to Government of Madras to Under Secretary of State for India, London, 7 September 1937, p. 2, L/PJ/4249/1937, IOR.

17. Ibid. (emphasis in the original correspondence).

18. Madras Government's Order regarding Prohibition, fortnightly report for the second half of August, p. 109, P & J 4249/1937, L/PJ/5/197, IOR.

19. Colvard, '"Drunkards Beware!' p. 186.

20. Letter from Erskine to Viceroy, 7 June 1938, p. 4. Erskine Papers, files 15–17, NML.

21. C. Rajagopalachari, instructions for picketing; Gandhiji's instructions, (1931), C. Rajagopalachari Papers, 2, NML.

22. G.O. No. 2307, Revenue Department (Mis.), 6 September 1939, NML.

23. Governor's Situation Report, 7 September 1937, p. 1, IOR.
24. G.O. No. 1251, Revenue Department (Mis.), 22 May 1939, handwritten note from C. Rajagopalachari, dated 11 January 1939, TNA.
25. Ibid.; C.R. No. 4612 Abk./39 C.
26. G.O. No. 2564, Revenue Department, 9 December 1937, p. 3, TNA.
27. *Harijan*, 21 May 1938.
28. Fiorello La Guardia quoted in Doug Thorburn, *Drunks, Drugs and Debits: How to Recognise Addicts and Avoid Financial Abuse* (California: Galt Publishing, 2000), p. 293.
29. See, for instance, Devika Sethi, *War over Words: Censorship in India, 1930–1960* (Cambridge: Cambridge University Press, 2019), pp. 39–43.
30. A Bill to Amend the Madras Prohibition Act, 1937, E & O 7354/1938, pp. 4–5, TNA.
31. Chiranjivi J. Nirmal, *Madras Perspectives: Explorations in Social and Cultural History* (Madras: Institute of Indian and International Studies, 1992), p. 66.
32. G.O. No. 602, Revenue Department (Mis.), 14 March 1941, TNA.
33. E. J. M. Sastri, *The Social and Economic Effects of Prohibition in Chittoor District, Madras Presidency* (Madras: Sri Veda Vyasa Press, 1938), pp. 13–14.
34. Guha, 'Discipline and Mobilize', especially p. 102.
35. *The First Year of Congress Rule in Madras* (Madras: Madras Legislative Congress Party, 1938), p. 8.
36. *The Hindu*, 5 October 1938.
37. Perumal, 'Prohibition Policy Under C. Rajagopalachariyar Ministries', p. 21.
38. E & O 5798/1943, From Chief Secretary to Government of Madras to Viceroy, TNA.
39. *Madras High Court: The Public Prosecutor v. Perianna Goundan and Another*, 20 September, 1938(1938)2MLJ813, AIR 1939 MADRAS 53, https://indiankanoon.org/doc/1691025 (accessed on 15 June 2004).
40. See, for instance, *Madras High Court in Re: Vyapuri Kavandan v. Unknown*, 1 March, 1939, (1939)2MLJ109, https://indiankanoon.org/doc/1832385 (accessed on 16 April 2024) and *Madras High Court in the Public Prosecutor v. Poongavana Goundan*, 26 November 1941, (1942)2MLJ37, https://indiankanoon.org/doc/697418 (accessed on 16 April 2024).
41. G.O. No. 1394, Home Department, 13 March 1939, Prohibition Police Manual, pp. 58–62, TNA.
42. G.O. No. 996, Revenue (Confl.), 11 April 1938, pp. 1–2, TNA.

43. C. Jagannathachari, 'Prohibition in Practice: Report on the Working of Prohibition in the Salem District (1939)', in *The Servant of India* (Poona: AB Press, 1939). See also C. Jagannathachari, *A Survey of the Working of Prohibition in Salem District* (Madras: Madras University, 1939), for a longer report on prohibition's impact in Salem.

44. A. F. W. Dixon, personal diary (1938), MSS EUR DIL 11/28, IOR.

45. P. J. Thomas, *Economic Results of Prohibition in the Salem District* (Madras: Madras University, 1939), p. 11.

46. *Daily Mail*, 4 November 1938. Mysore's finance minister's concerns were quoted in the newspaper.

47. Quoted from C. Rajagopalachari's speech during the leader's Chittoor tour in *The Hindu*, 5 October 1938.

48. A. V. Krishnamurthy, Superintendent of Excise Intelligence Bureau, on his observations from his visit to Salem, 17 June 1939, E & O 4368/1939, p. 1, IOR, pp. 3–4.

49. Ibid.

50. Ibid.

51. *Madras High Court in Re: V.A. Gayasudeen v. Unknown*,10 August 1942, (1942)2MLJ547, https://indiankanoon.org/doc/772485 (accessed on 13 May 2024).

52. Thomas, *Economic Results of Prohibition*, p. 11.

53. G.O. No. 559, Revenue Department (Mis.), 10 March 1941, pp. 3–4, TNA.

54. Ibid.

55. Thomas, *Economic Results of Prohibition*, p. 11.

56. Krishnamurthy's Report, 17 June 1939, p. 1, E & O 4368/1939, IOR.

57. *Madras Mail*, 9 April 1938. See also *Harijan*, 19 March 1938.

58. Chandra Mallampalli, *Christians and Public Life in Colonial South India, 1863–1937: Contending with Marginality* (London: Taylor & Francis, 2007), p. 127. For a discussion of the Congress's stance on religion and its place in policymaking, see William Gould, *Hindu Nationalism and the Language of Politics in Late Colonial India* (Cambridge: Cambridge University Press, 2004), pp. 5–7. See also William F. Kuracina, *The State and Governance in India: The Congress Ideal* (London: Routledge, 2010), pp. 47–49.

59. Ibid., pp. 114–118. See also Richard Fox Young (ed.), *India and the Indianness of Christianity: Essays on Understanding Historical, Theological, and Bibliographical – in Honor of Robert Eric Frykenberg* (Michigan: W.M Eerdman's Publishing Co., 2009), pp. 206–209.

60. Mallampalli, *Christians and Public Life*, p. 127.

61. Nandini Chatterjee, *The Making of Indian Secularism: Empire, Law and Christianity, 1830–1960* (London: Palgrave Macmillan, 2011), p. 223.

62. B. R. Ambedkar had made the argument that the Depressed Classes, or Dalits, ought to be treated as a minority political category in its own right. Gandhi had bitterly opposed what he feared as the Hindu community's impending 'vivisection'. Ambedkar had ultimately given up his demand, faced with the threat of Gandhi's fast unto death, whilst the latter held fast to his conviction that untouchability would gradually wither away with the cultivation of self-control.

63. *Harijan*, 11 September 1937.

64. Ibid.

65. *Madras Guardian*, quoted in *Harijan*, 18 September 1937.

66. Ibid.

67. Letter from the Leader of the Tamil Evangelical Lutheran Church in Tanjore to Rajagopalachari, 21 April 1938, C. Rajagopalachari Papers, K. No. 4–5, R4721, NML.

68. *Times of India*, 31 August 1939.

69. *Times of India*, 26 June 1939. Archbishop's comments quoted from 'The Ethics of Prohibition', published in *The Examiner* newspaper.

70. Ibid.

71. Official Report, Madras Legislative Assembly Debates (Madras, 1938), p. 135.

72. Ibid., p. 129.

73. Ibid., p. 135. See also Chatterjee, *Making of Indian Secularism*, p. 6. I refer to Chatterjee's argument that minority religious groups especially clung to the ideal of secularism in presenting their demands.

74. Garrett Peck, *The Prohibition Hangover: Alcohol in America from Demon Rum to Cult Cabernet* (New Jersey; London: Rutgers University Press, 2009), p. 180.

75. Extracts from Debates of Legislative Councils of Province of Madras, Madras Prohibition Act (Second Amendment Bill), 1938, as passed by the Legislative Assembly, 12 December 1938, p. 4.

76. Letter from Nehru, the President of the AICC, to Rajagopalachari, 11 November 1937, AICC Papers, I-26/3269, files no. 2–4, NML.

77. Letter from Rajagopalachari to Nehru, 21 September 1937, AICC Papers, files no. 2–4, NML.

78. Letter from Nehru to Rajagopalachari, 27 September 1937, AICC Papers, files no. 2–4, NML.

79. *Times of India*, 4 October 1939.

80. Ibid.

81. Chatterjee, *Making of Indian Secularism*, p. 220.

82. Letter from B. S. Gilani to Gandhi, 2 June 1938, M. K. Gandhi Papers (Pyarelal Papers), Subject File 190; 1938–1939, Tamil Nadu Congress Committee (TNCC) Correspondence.

83. Ibid.

84. Letter From Rajaji to Mahadev Desai, 10 June 1938, M. K. Gandhi Papers 70 (Pyarelal Papers), Subject File 190; 1938–1939, NML.

85. *Madras Mail*, 20 October 1937.

86. Letter from Erskine to Linlithgow, 19 January 1938, Erskine Papers, files 9–11, MSS EUR 596D, no. 1 of 1938, NML.

87. Letter from Erskine to P. J. Crigg, 17 January 1938, p. 2, Private and Personal, Erskine Papers, NML.

88. J. B. Prashant More, *The Political Evolution of Muslims in Tamil Nadu and Madras, 1930–1947* (Chennai: Orient Longman, 1997), p. 144.

89. Governor's Situation Report, 18 December 1939, p. 2, P & J 30/1940, IOR.

90. Ibid.

91. Governor's Situation Report, 5 June 1939, p. 11, P & J 2893/1939, IOR.

92. Fortnightly report for the first half of April, 26 April 1943, p. 3, P & J 5917 1943, IOR.

93. Fortnightly report for the first half of August 1939, 18 August 1939, p. 1, P & J 4323/1939, IOR.

94. Rajaji quoted in *The Hindu*, 3 July 1939.

95. Debate in the legislative assembly on the budget, quoted in *The Hindu*, 25 February 1940.

96. *Kudi Arasu*, 19 December 1937.

97. See, for instance, *Kudi Arasu*, 21 November 1937; *Kudi Arasu*, 3 June 1940; *Kudi Arasu*, 5 September 1942.

98. George Gheverghese Joseph, *George Joseph, the Life and Times of a Kerala Christian Nationalist* (New Delhi: Orient Longman, 2003), p. 205.

99. Letter from Sd. M.D. Bhat, Municipal Commissioner's Office, Bombay, to H. V. R. Iyengar, Esq., ICS, Secretary to Government of Bombay, 22 June 1939, AICC Papers, file 2, NML.

100. Letter from Manekshaw Sorabhji Shaw c/o Messrs. Monjini Ltd. to Gandhi, 'Prohibition', 2 June 1937, M. K. Gandhi Papers (Pyarelal Papers), Subject File S. No. 236, 1936–1940.

101. G.O. No. 861, Revenue Department (Mis., Confl.), 30 March 1938, TNA.

102. Baliga, *Compendium on Temperance*, p. 30.

103. G.O. No. 861, Revenue Department (Mis., Confl.), 30 March 1938, TNA.

104. Ibid.

105. *The Hindu*, 16 September 1938.

106. Telegram from Erskine to Linlithgow, 6 July 1937, fortnightly report for second half of June 1937, p. 169, P & J 3151/1937, IOR.

107. G.O. 3570, Revenue Department, 19 January 1938, TNA.

108. *Harijan*, 16 July 1938. Gandhi was dismayed when he found that a member of his ashram had chopped down some palm trees in the early 1940s. He wrote: 'The Palm is a poor man's tree. Do I have to explain to you its usefulness … The palm-tree is interwoven with our life.' Gandhi's speech at prayer meeting, 22 October 1941, in *The Collected Works of Mahatma Gandhi*, vol. 75: *October 11, 1941–March 31, 1942* (reprint edition) (New Delhi: Government of India, 2000), p. 119. See also Hardiman, 'From Custom to Crime', for a discussion of how prohibition in Gujarat caused a spike in the illicit production of toddy under the guise of making *neera*.

109. Baliga, *Studies in Madras Administration*, p. 248.

110. *Times of India*, 27 December 1939.

111. Gajanan Naik, *Harijan*, 7 January 1939, quoted in Gandhi, *Diet and Diet Reform*, p. 139. Elsewhere, he recommended that it was best to convert *neera* into palm jaggery as it fermented easily and hence needed to be used on the spot, which was not always possible.

112. *Times of India*, 5 June 1939. The interview actually took place at Birla House, as recounted in Gandhi's writings. However, he left out mentioning the embarrassing discovery that he made that day. See Gandhi, *Collected Works of Mahatma Gandhi*, vol. 75, p. 318.

113. Mark Thomson, *Gandhi and His Ashrams* (Bombay: South Asia Books, 1993), pp. 210–211. See also *Times of India*, 27 December 1939.

114. Letter from Sir P. James Crigg, Finance Minister, Government of India, to C. Rajagopalachari, 28 March 1938, p. 2, C. Rajagopalachari Papers, files No. 5–8, R4722, NML.

115. Letter from C. D. Deshmukh, Secretary to Government, Central Provinces and Berar Secretary, All-India Villages and Industries Association, 8 February 1938, M. K. Gandhi Papers (Pyarelal Papers), Subject File S. No. 236, 1936–1940, NMML.

116. Letter from Mahadev Desai to P. B. Gole, Revenue Minister, Nagpur, 10 March 1938, M. K. Gandhi Papers, Subject File S. No. 236, 1936–1940.

117. Ibid.

118. 'Welfare in India and Southeast Asia', Working Paper (44) 722, December 1944, p. 13, War Cabinet, Cabinet Papers, vol. 5, IOR.

119. Telegram from Erskine to Rodger, 11 March 1939, Erskine Papers, files 18–21, NML.

120. Ibid.

121. G.O. No. 1697, Revenue (Ms.), 26 July 1941, TNA.

122. Telegram from Viceroy to Secretary of State, 7 September 1943, Confidential, E & O 5420/1943, IOR.

123. Ibid.

124. Telegram from Viceroy to Secretary of State, 2 August 1943, E & O 4526/1943, IOR.

125. Telegram from Governor General to Secretary of State, 28 January 1943, E & O 532/1943, IOR.

126. *Hindu Dak*, 17 November 1943.

127. Governor's Situation Report, Pol. 3116/1944, 21 December 1943, IOR.

128. Rajagopalachari, *Kal Oliga!* pp. 82–83.

129. Governor's Situation Report, Pol. 3116/1944, 21 December 1943, IOR.

7

Prohibition in Independent India

Prohibitioning and the Constitution of India

Prohibition was reviewed and re-conceptualised following the achievement of independence, when the foundations of the modern Indian state were formally established. In the long run, the prohibition ideal filtered through new administrative and legal frameworks that nevertheless bore the imprint of both colonialism and the struggle against it. As the independent Indian republic was premised upon the founding principles of secular democracy and federalism, prohibition had to reckon with both debates relating to personal liberties and issues of state autonomy.

Following independence, the national democratic state – having won the mandate of representing national society – sought to intervene in that domain in order to transform it. The processes that had accompanied the birth of the Indian nation had brought forth institutions, structures and practices that enabled policies like prohibition to be operationalised through the workings of the state. However, the problem remained that a national society still had to be fashioned anew from the fluid, overlapping identities that made up the fabric of Indian social life. Amidst such a 'recalcitrant social', which, Prathama Banerjee argues, continued to function as 'a network of multiple nodes of caste, community and regional sovereignties', postcolonial governmentality appeared from the very outset 'a compromised project'.[1]

In this, however, postcolonial governmentality did not constitute as radical a rupture from the colonial past as Banerjee's discussion would suggest. The careful balancing act that the nationalist government attempted to strike between 'mobilising the social and mobilising the political' had already set the tone for things to come before independence was achieved; prohibition's colonial-era origins are a case in point. What we can say with greater certainty is that the postcolonial state alternated between exercising different modes of power in a context wherein new pressures and opportunities for development needed to be reconciled with the ideals of governance that the anti-colonial struggle had crystallised. In fact, these ideals had even brought forth some of the democratic mechanisms and frameworks through which prohibition would subsequently be operationalised. Even as the tensions that presented between representing society on the one hand and transforming it on the other persisted for the Indian state, the gap between the two necessitated the use of such bridging mechanisms that would guide and inform subsequent policymaking.[2]

Reconciling pressures and opportunities for development with the ideals that had buoyed the freedom struggle became particularly crucial as it was bound up with the modern Indian state's project of establishing legitimacy. Having emerged from a moral–modern struggle for legitimacy with the colonial state, the postcolonial state owed it to society to lead it into a better future with moral–modern policies of development. It also had to prove that a policy like prohibition – upon which that vision for a better future had been premised to begin with – would work. While this too is, at one level, comparable to the tussle between the ideals and ground realities that shaped prohibition's trajectories and outcomes in the colonial period, the directions it took after 1947 illustrate for us the flexibility and resilience of the policies that constituted postcolonial state power.

Independence brought with it the realisation that something had to be done – urgently – about the fledgling republic's dependence on alcohol sales and taxation as key sources of revenue. Liquor was so deeply enmeshed in the national economy by the late 1940s that it was as embarrassing ideologically as it was alarming from a public health perspective.[3] However, the first prime minister of independent India, Jawaharlal Nehru, did not share M. K. Gandhi's ideological commitment to prohibition. Although his stance on alcohol policy remained characteristically pragmatic, the tension between the Gandhian legacy of prohibition as a national ideal and the gravity of revenue considerations in the immediate postcolonial context pressed hard on Nehru's administration. These circumstances resulted in a familiar balancing act. The central government accommodated a prohibition department *and* a liquor excise department. It also transferred responsibility for prohibition's future to the Constituent Assembly to determine. The Constitution of India thus emerged as the foremost bridging instrument enabling consensus-building on prohibition's future.

As prohibitioning was funnelled through the Constituent Assembly debates, the consensus that gradually emerged was that the policy would help a newly decolonised India put its house in order. It appeared poised to be the perfect panacea to uplift the millions of Indians who lived, and died, by the bottle. Prohibition promised, simultaneously, to aid in the pressing task of national re-invention as India prepared to take its place in the world as an equal among equals. Gandhians in the assembly emphasised that prohibition was the Mahatma's legacy, which the nation could not allow to be extinguished. The Mahatma's assassination in January 1948 bestowed urgency and emotional intensity to the issue of prohibition's nationwide enforcement. Members like B. G. Kher fell back on the upper-caste argument that prohibition was entirely in keeping with Indian religious traditions and culture, cautioning that a nation dependent on liquor revenue would be a nation consumed by vice. The Madras Prohibition Act of 1937 provided the precedent, template and ideological foundations of the national framework for alcohol policy that emerged in this context.

Prohibitionists drew upon the policy's relatively recent experience in the Madras Presidency in order to justify writing it into the national constitution. Strengthening their case was the fact that the policy had been reintroduced in the entire province in 1948 under O. P. Ramaswamy Reddiyar's premiership. During the debates, Uttar Pradesh's Shibban Lal Saxena, an advocate for prohibition, expressed hope that 'like Madras, all the provinces will enforce it … thus we shall set an example to the whole world in this matter'.[4] Saxena was trying to move an amendment to Article 38, which was concerned with nutrition, standard of living and public health. Like several others in the assembly, Saxena believed that the prohibition of intoxicating drinks and drugs pointed the way forward for all of Article 38's target areas. Madras's minister for prohibition, V. I. Muniswamy Pillai, conceded that although the province had lost nearly 17 crore rupees from prohibition's enforcement, the people of Madras unanimously welcomed the policy. Its success, Pillai claimed, could be most reliably measured through the intangible benefits it had brought to the Depressed Classes. The experience of the state was thus again used to prove prohibition's relevance to the nation.

Yet several prominent voices were raised against prohibition as well. Prohibition's critics asserted the legitimacy of non-elite local cultures and traditions involving alcohol. Jaipal Singh Munda, a member of Jharkhand's Scheduled Tribe Munda community, reminded his peers that even transplanting rice would become impossible in the fledgling republic if the

Santhals were denied access to their rice beer.[5] Munda thus asserted Adivasi culture and traditions, insisting that no prohibition of any kind would be introduced on his community without their consent. Prohibition in Madras had also shown, critics pointed out, that drinkers were a more resourceful lot than the prohibition police. B. H. Khardekar wondered how anyone could consider the Madras example prohibition's success story when people were 'still indulging in drinks' and 'filling the innumerable jails'. He pointedly questioned: '[H]ave you also measured as a result of the squandering of several crores of Rupees, what you have failed to do?'[6] Khardekar's critique included the then unpopular view of prohibition as an attack on civil liberties, which the Catholic and Parsi experiences with the policy had readily exemplified in the late colonial context. The reverberations of prohibitioning thus continued to be felt on postcolonial debates on the policy, thereby influencing its subsequent development as well.

The tensions that the Constituent Assembly debates brought forth were mediated through Article 47. As a Directive Principle of State Policy, the Article set out prohibition as the state's responsibility and obligation, but left out specifying a time frame for its implementation. It implicitly conceded that prohibition's enforcement as a national ideal would need to be reconciled with the ground realities of governance in the states of the republic. Prohibition, which had been an undertaking of provincial governments, now became an undertaking of state governments. Inasmuch as the coming together of ideal and policy had paved the way for the Madras Prohibition Act, the circumstances of the postcolonial context necessitated a delinking between the two. Whilst the Article upheld and enshrined prohibition as an ideal, it left prohibition as a policy open to future mediation and consensus-building. The pragmatic balancing act that had been such a characteristic feature of prohibitioning in the not-too-distant past thus continued into the postcolonial context as well.

Through all this, prohibition retained its crucial place in the workings of the state, both as an expression of its commitment to securing the welfare of its citizenry and as an instrument of its power. By reminding citizens that its stance on intoxicants was unequivocal, the state also issued a clarion call for self-control. 'Dry days', or calendar days when alcohol could not be legally bought or sold, were introduced in several states in the 1950s to honour the struggle for independence. Celebrations of national significance, among them Gandhi's birth anniversary, Republic Day and Independence Day, were designated as dry days. Liquor could not be bought and sold during voting periods either. The modern Indian state thus sought to nurture in its citizens the conviction of teetotalism as a national – rather than as an individual or social – responsibility. In the process, it served to strengthen the culture – and ideal – of prohibition that had been nurtured in the colonial era.

In the 1950s, committees were formed with great gusto to research and advise on the feasibility of nationwide prohibition at the central government level. A Prohibition Enquiry Committee was formed in 1954. A year later, the committee produced a report that outlined an ambitious plan for nationwide prohibition, including a target date for its realisation, an immediate end to public drinking and the establishment of prohibition committees at the local and district levels.[7] Prohibition was also included in the Second Five-Year Plan. A Planning Commission was promptly set up, and its recommendations, which included projections of prohibition's financial repercussions, were included in the plan.

Things started to change in the 1960s. From this point onwards, the pursuit of prohibition at the central and state levels of government gradually began to diverge. This situation owed largely to both the pressures and opportunities that presented for development. The 1960s brought with it a slew of renewed measures to realise prohibition at the national level, although the policy simultaneously became a distant goal as the focus of planning shifted to industrialisation. Having been premised upon the Gandhian vision of self-sufficient village republics, prohibition as an ideal was increasingly relegated to the back burner as the Nehruvian ideal dominated plans for economic development.

Like the two plans before it, the Third Five-Year Plan set out that the Indian nation was committed to the achievement of nationwide prohibition as an indispensable goal and, to this end, encouraged the establishment of voluntary organisations and financial assistance towards its realisation. A task force was set up to gather information for prohibition's eventual enforcement under the leadership of retired judge Justice Tek Chand. The Tek Chand Report, as it came to be called, rallied tomes of statistical data – including referencing what it called the 'relative success' of prohibition in Madras and Gujarat – to advocate for an ambitious programme for nationwide prohibition by 1970.[8] Notwithstanding the study's recommendations for prohibition, state governments' reluctance to extend their cooperation meant that discussions relating to prohibition were shelved. They remained plans for the distant future. Remarkably, however, for all its support for prohibition, the Tek Chand Report was pragmatic in its appraisal of the problems posed by toddy and *neera*. As toddy drinking could not be effectively stopped 'at one stroke', it suggested a lease of life for the alcohol for a decade or so, during which time governments could continue efforts for 'controlling and progressively restricting' consumption.[9]

The most serious push for prohibition by the central government came in 1977. The Janata Party's Morarji Desai, a Gandhian teetotaller who had worked tirelessly to bring about the Bombay Prohibition Act of 1949, stepped in as the country's prime minister when Indira Gandhi's emergency (1975–1977) lost her the elections. Desai spearheaded discussions for nationwide prohibition, representing the new leadership's emphasis on austerity as virtue. However, his decision to introduce the policy first in the national capital also helped to seal the fate of nationwide prohibition.

The experience that most states recorded with prohibition eventually spilled over to moderate the enthusiasm with which the central government pushed the prohibition agenda. The unspoken consensus became evident in the Fourth Five Year-Plan which, conspicuously, did not even mention prohibition. In Delhi, a Directorate of Prohibition was set up to oversee the state's transition to prohibition in 1978, although it was embarrassingly transferred to the Excise Department the following year. Although it was separated from the Excise Department in 1994, the connection between prohibition and the treasury persisted: the principal secretary for finance assumed responsibility for prohibition's future. The search for reconciliation between the pressures of, and opportunities for, development on the one hand and the ideals of the freedom struggle on the other remained skewed in favour of the former. Gandhi's dream of nationwide prohibition remained just that: a dream outlined in Article 47 of the Constitution of India. Yet the Article simultaneously also remained a key legal instrument that influenced subsequent attempts at prohibitioning in the republic's states.

Prohibitioning in the States

Since the 1950s, prohibition – as part of alcohol policy – has been channelled through the workings of Indian federalism, which guarantees a division of powers between central and state governments. This founding principle of the modern Indian nation assured the states a degree of autonomy over their internal affairs in matters relating to local governance. As we have seen, drinking and attempts to prohibit it were both historically entwined with highly localised aspects of governance, which continued into the postcolonial context as well.

Since independence, the states of the republic have exercised full control over all aspects of liquor legislation, excise rates, and alcohol production and sales. Whilst the production of alcoholic drinks has often been carried out under private ownership, state governments have regulated the process through licensing systems. The government issues licences to distributors and retailers in states like Goa and Maharashtra, with manufacturers being free to choose their distributors. Wholesale distribution is done through government corporations in Andhra Pradesh, Chhattisgarh, Odisha (formerly Orissa) and Delhi. Haryana and Punjab operate auction systems in which the state is divided into distinct geographical regions, with each region's liquor vending rights going to the highest bidder. In Rajasthan, Tamil Nadu and Kerala, the wholesale distribution and retail sale of alcoholic drinks are exclusively carried out through government agencies. State-owned corporations monopolise alcohol distribution in Tamil Nadu and Kerala.

Partha Chatterjee's discussion of 'political society' is useful here in thinking about the policy's development in the republics' states, where they were actually implemented. Chatterjee argued that the concept of civil society falls short in explaining democratic processes in a postcolonial society like India, wherein the power structures that had been nurtured during colonialism had largely survived the transition to independence. While the middle classes had taken over the apparatus of the colonial state through a passive revolution, the vast majority of people – subalterns – remained excluded from democratic life as they lacked the resources to participate in it fully. Instead, Chatterjee proposed that we might see the concept of 'political society' as the actual domain in which policy and policymaking take place. Within this schema, wherein civil society and political society are empirical spaces, civil society consists of citizens with legal rights, is composed of the urban middle classes and is the zone of corporate capital. Political society, in contrast, comprises people with no such legal rights, consisting of largely urban but also some rural poor communities. According to Chatterjee, political society is the domain wherein the state engages not with 'the people' as an undifferentiated bloc, but with 'populations' that are specifically constituted around governmental projects like prohibition.[10] Target populations in turn manoeuvre in this domain to 'make their claims on government ... not within the framework of stable constitutionally defined rights and laws, but rather through temporary, contextual and unstable arrangements' that they negotiate with the state.[11]

Several criticisms have since been levelled at the notion of political society. One of the most serious, and helpful for our discussion, is the argument that political society erects a rigid binary between civil society and political society. Those who form civil society often break laws, demand flexibility in rules and come under the purview of governmental programmes as 'target populations', just as members of political society strive to be recognised as equal citizens by the state.[12] Illegal practices thus cannot be taken as the benchmark for the kind of interactions that take place between the state and the urban poor as they equally constitute everyday life among the middle classes. Instead, it is more productive, as Nivedita Menon and others have argued, to see civil society and political society operating not as sharply delineated political spaces but, rather, as modes of political engagement with the state.[13] It is useful also to think, in this regard, of the strategies of political society itself as not static and unchanging, but rather as being dynamic and in accordance with the type of policy in question; if political society comprises target populations that are constituted around different governmental projects, their approaches to the opportunities and constraints presented by different projects of governmentality would necessarily vary in accordance to the project in question as well. The point that Menon makes, which is particularly relevant here, is that any project of radical democratic transformation would have to engage – and, at times, collide – with the ideas, beliefs and practices that this style of engagement enables.[14] Even as the developmental state thus attempts to steer modernisation projects like prohibition through the many contestations that political society surfaces, the strength of those contestations either prompts it to suspend it altogether or modify it significantly to accommodate negotiations on the ground. The true value of political society as a concept then lies in what it can tell us about the trajectories of policy measures constituting postcolonial governmentality.

Indeed, thinking with political society supports an understanding of how various groups have used strategies that have alternated between invoking the discourse of rights in protests reminiscent of civil society on the one hand whilst contravening the law on the other to render prohibition a negotiated settlement. On the one hand, the old balancing act between representing society and leading it acquired new dimensions after 1947 as prohibition was now planned and constitutionalised within a rubric of development. Responding to these circumstances, various groups mobilised themselves alternately within the overlapping domains of the political and the social, as it served their interests. Consequently, prohibition was pulled and stretched in different directions, thus rendering it an ongoing site of prohibitioning.

In the northeast of the country, Manipur, Nagaland and Mizoram all introduced prohibition in the 1990s, a time of great domestic instability characterised by insurgency and lack of development. It was a context wherein increasing numbers of people were turning to alcohol as a coping mechanism, even as state governments were looking to prove their relevance to society. Traditional drinking cultures had endured the transition to independence, leading to all sorts of social protest that state governments drew upon in claiming legitimacy for the policy's introduction.

Passed by the Congress state government in 1989, the Nagaland Liquor Total Prohibition Act (NLTP) banned the sale, consumption and manufacture of alcohol in that state. The regional unit of the Congress in the state, the Nagaland Pradesh Congress Committee (NPCC), justified the policy as being in the best interest of society as it was supported by the Nagaland Baptist Church Council and the Naga Mothers' Association, among others. Since then, however, the policy has run into numerous problems, prompting the criticism that it has 'served only to raise the price of alcohol exorbitantly, impacting those who drink and their families, and benefitting illegal sellers'.[15] Alongside steep costs incurred in enforcement and a pressing lack of personnel and resources required for effective surveillance of prohibition-related crime, liquor continues to pour into the state via the long border that it shares with 'wet' Assam. At the peak of the Covid-19 pandemic, more than a thousand alcohol-related cases were registered within nine months. The authorities seized tens of thousands of bottles of beer and Indian-made foreign liquor (IMFL). Studies have pointed to collusions between bootleggers and the police by way of explaining the proliferation of liquor businesses across the state, often in close proximity to police stations.[16] Notwithstanding these controversies, however, when the incumbent Bharatiya Janata Party (BJP)-led coalition government recently announced its intention to review prohibition in Nagaland, the NPCC opposed the move on the grounds that it was a policy that had the Naga people's unanimous support. The Nagaland Baptist Pastors Union (NBPU) reaffirmed its commitment to prohibition, likewise emphasising the policy's democratic credentials as a mission backed by the church and society.

Similarly, Manipur has had a long history of democratic protest in support of prohibition. Women's groups like Meira Paibi helmed a long-running campaign for prohibition's introduction in the state in the 1970s and 1980s. The militant group, the People's Liberation Army, accused the state government of using intoxication to dull and distract young people from joining armed revolution and, to this end, declared in 1990 that the sale of alcohol and drugs should be banned. Taking its cue from these developments, the Manipur People's Party government introduced prohibition in 1991. However, several villages were notably exempted from the policy. Specifically, the exemption applied to Scheduled Tribe and Scheduled Caste communities who had been traditionally involved in brewing alcohol. These communities were allowed to brew liquor for traditional uses, in keeping with the colonial-era recognition that ancient customs warranted special treatment. Traditional rice beer and, more generally, country liquor thus continued to be widely brewed and consumed throughout the state. In the years since its introduction, Manipur has gained the dubious distinction of becoming India's wettest dry state, with a thriving black market in liquor that has been paved with smuggling, bootlegging and bribery.[17] Here, too, prohibition's political society has struck 'temporary, contextual and unstable arrangements' with state officials.

The incumbent government attempted to lift the policy amidst ethnic conflict in 2023, citing the public health crisis that had been triggered by the consumption of spurious liquor and the health of the economy, which it argued could be improved by selling country liquor to other states. The move was widely condemned. The strongest opposition has come from Meira Paibi – the 'women torchbearers' – who have staged sit-ins and organised protest marches to make their stand against the government. Previous attempts to ease prohibition had proven futile in the state owing to the strength of the backlash. Clearly, the policy thus remains an ongoing site of consensus-building, although Manipur is no longer designated a dry state.

Prohibitioning also continues apace in Mizoram, legally a dry state at the time of this book's writing. The Congress state government introduced prohibition in 1997 in the state following the passing of the Mizoram Liquor Total Prohibition Act (MLTP Act) of 1995. Although several policy restrictions soon followed, the policy itself pulled through until its repeal in 2014, again under the auspices of Congress government. As elsewhere in India, the authorities pointed to the thriving illicit liquor economy, deaths arising from the consumption of spurious liquor and mounting fiscal deficits as reasons for the repeal, which in turn triggered a slew of protests from various segments of society. The Presbyterian Church led the charge, organising large-scale protests against the repeal, which, it argued, would have devastating effects on Mizo society. The public protest that followed prohibition's repeal was so strong that it ultimately cost the Congress the state elections, thus contributing to the Mizo National Front's (MNF) coming to power with the promise of enforcing stricter prohibition laws. Prohibition was thus again introduced in 2019, although the authorities soon relaxed restrictions to allow the sales of wine made from locally grown sales in markets across the state in 2022. The decision to scale back on prohibition notably followed a raid by excise officials to stamp out illicit alcohol that led to the death of a woman who had been involved in the wine business. Netizens took to social media where they linked the woman's death to the raid, which had apparently resulted in the seizure of her merchandise – Mizoram-produced grape wine bottle stores – leaving her penniless. In response, the authorities revised prohibition law to appease public opinion as protests continued against what the people saw as the government's high-handedness.

Governments have likewise tried prohibition on for size in several other Indian states, only to suspend it soon thereafter as better suited for future implementation. Most have opted for regulation over prohibition as there have been compelling economic reasons to do so. Alcohol sales and taxation continue to be indispensable sources of revenue for state governments across the country. In states like Kerala, alcohol sales and taxation remains a major source of revenue generation.[18] In marked contrast, the price of alcohol is significantly lower in union territories like Pondicherry and Diu and Daman, which, being centrally administered, operate under a different tax structure; the excise taxes and duties that prevail in the republic's states do not apply to liquor producers or drinkers in these parts of the country. Both alcohol sales and prohibition in the union territory of Lakshadweep have, however, followed a different trajectory owing to the complex relationship that developed there between religion and politics.[19]

The experience of prohibition in the late 1930s left an indelible imprint on the subsequent development of alcohol policy in the states that were carved out of Madras, Bombay and Bihar Provinces. The Maharashtra Prohibition Act of 1949 was premised upon, and overwrote, prohibition's introduction in Bombay Presidency in 1939; the latter itself had been influenced by the Madras Prohibition Act, as we have seen. Specifically, the system of personal liquor permits was a legacy of colonial-era prohibition, although the Act of 1949 changed the terms and conditions governing them to reflect the changing needs of the times.

As it had in the colonial past, prohibition in Bombay had to continue contending with local drinking cultures. A fishing caste, the Kolis of Bombay supplemented their income with the production of a distinctive country liquor that used an assortment of fruits, salt water and traditional methods of brewing. When, as the chief minister of the state, Morarji Desai enforced prohibition in Bombay state in the 1950s, the Kolis criticised it as an unfair policy imposition by the government. According to them, prohibition was not only poised against country liquor but also contemptuous of the community's right to a traditional – and legitimate – source of livelihood.[20] When the government refused to relent, the Kolis took their liquor business underground. In fact, prohibition spawned a veritable underworld in Bombay between 1949 and 1963, with Varadharajan Mudaliar – better known locally as Vardhabhai – emerging as the most prolific bootlegger of the area. The resultant uptick in crime and practical challenges of enforcement eventually led to the policy's moderation by the familiar system of permits instead. Even as political society thus engaged with prohibition, consensus-building on specific aspects of the policy continued to influence its development at the state level. Permits are still legally required to consume, possess, transport or purchase alcohol in the state of Maharashtra, although they are generally not checked. The permit system as a distinct legacy of the Madras Prohibition Act shows us how governmental institutions and processes operate in tandem with the insistence that individuals need to practice self-control.

Moreover, prohibition's postcolonial development changed with the reorganisation of the states, beginning in 1956. The Maharashtra Prohibition Act of 1949, which outlawed the manufacture, storage, sale and consumption of alcohol, remained enforced in Gujarat even following Bombay state's bifurcation into its constituent states of Gujarat and Bombay in 1960. While the political commitment to prohibition has been strongest in the state where Gandhi's legacy has loomed the largest, this is not to say that Gujarat has been dry in practice. As the state with the longest uninterrupted run with prohibition, Gujarat has also been at the receiving end of the policy's worst effects.[21] The authorities have intermittently reported hooch tragedies resulting in mass casualties. A shocking 132 people were killed in a matter of a few days in Vadodara district in 1989, while 122 people died in a single hooch incident and many more were left hospitalised twenty years later.

This grim situation has spurred the authorities into action from time to time. In 2009, for instance, the state government passed an amendment to prohibition law that doubled down on enforcement. Under the supposedly improved law, individuals found guilty of manufacturing and selling homemade liquor resulting in fatalities would be subject to capital punishment. The Gujarati people, however, thought this too harsh and demanded a repeal. Petitions in the Gujarat High Court sought an end to prohibition on the grounds that it was contemptuous of civil liberties. The authorities, however, did not budge. Instead, prohibition law was made more stringent in 2015 and 2017. Another mass hooch tragedy followed in 2022. Most recently, the state government petitioned the central government to consider allocating compensatory funds so that it could mitigate the approximately INR 12,000 crores from alcohol tax revenue lost annually due to prohibition's enforcement.

While this situation might suggest prohibition's absolute march in the state, exemptions persist, even in seemingly exceptional Gujarat. Tourists and Indians from other states can avail themselves to liquor permits allowing them to consume a stipulated quantity of liquor in private for a period of time. 'Group permits' allow the consumption of liquor in groups, an allowance made to accommodate businesses looking to organise conferences and similar other gatherings. An e-permit system, allowing for convenience of application even before travel to the dry state, has expedited the process of applying for permits in recent years. Designated liquor outlets allow for these accommodations to continue in the state. Moreover, prohibition law does not apply to designated special economic zones, like the Gujarat International Finance Tec-City (GIFT City) in the Gandhinagar district of Ahmedabad. The rationale is that the exemption supports the realisation of 'a global business ecosystem'.[22] Evidently, prohibition can be shelved when it comes at the expense of business. More intriguingly, there are tens of thousands of Gujarati permit holders who are legally entitled to store and imbibe alcohol on medical grounds verified by medical professionals.[23] Another legacy from the Madras Prohibition Act, this system of 'health permits' has intermittently prompted criticism of governmental double standards.

In a historic recent ruling, the Gujarat High Court overturned the state government's objections to its hearing petitions against prohibition. The petitioners' case pivoted on two crucial grounds: the right to privacy, which they claimed prohibition impinged upon, and the manifest arbitrariness of its enforcement. According to their plea, prohibition in the state had erected a 'licence–permit raj' for liquor – a veritable class system discriminating in favour of liquor permit holders, while criminalising other citizens for consuming liquor even within the confines of their own homes.[24] Referencing the *K. S. Puttaswamy v. Union of India* case, in which the Supreme Court of India had enshrined the citizen's right to privacy as an inalienable right, the high court's decision thus brought the Bombay Prohibition Act under judicial scrutiny. At the time of this book's writing, this is an ongoing case – one might add, of consensus-building.

Bihar has had a similarly long – albeit interrupted – history of prohibition dating from 1938, although the state government launched a policy overhaul in 2016. The result of a special cabinet meeting chaired by the chief minister, Nitish Kumar, the Bihar Prohibition and Excise Act replaced previous policy iterations in the state. The Act wrought a blanket ban on the manufacture, bottling, distribution, storage, possession, collection, sale and consumption of alcohol. However, by equipping the state government with discretionary powers to renew existing licences, the Act also made provisions for exemptions and exceptions. The state government has subsequently been criticised for enforcing prohibition in an already impoverished state, one wherein the use of dogs, drones and helicopters have all added exponentially to the costs of enforcing the policy. Several million litres of alcohol have been seized by authorities between 2016 and 2024, although prohibition has been lucrative for neighbouring Nepal with the proliferation of liquor shops on the border that runs between Bihar and Nepal.[25]

In the country's south, when the Madras Presidency gave way to the constituent states of Madras State, Andhra Pradesh, Kerala and Karnataka, the stage was set for prohibitioning to develop along new trajectories. The imprint of anti-colonial protest, however, remained etched on the states' respective approaches towards prohibition. Political personalities who had opposed the colonial state's alcohol policy in their youth often continued to advocate for prohibition subsequently as well. Karnataka's former prime minister Congressman S. Nijalingappa was one such individual. Nijalingappa had launched the Echalu *satyagraha* against wild palm date toddy and arrack during the Civil Disobedience movement. Having helmed the movement for Karnataka's unification, Nijalingappa would go on to lead the movement for a dry state as well. As with the Tamil Nadu Prohibition Act, the Madras Prohibition Act remained the template for the Karnataka Prohibition Act of 1961.

Another crucial colonial-era legacy is that the Congress party has reprised its commitment to prohibition in many parts of the country. Although other political parties have also wielded the prohibition card, the association between the policy and the Congress persists owing to the memory of the anti-colonial struggle, which the party often deliberately invokes in demanding the policy's reintroduction. Such was the story of the Congress's attempts to revive public interest in prohibition in Kerala. In 2014, the then chief minister, Oomen Chandy, announced that the state would implement prohibition in a gradual manner in order to achieve total statewide prohibition by the year 2025. The Catholic Church and the Indian Union Muslim League threw their support behind the Congress in this endeavour. Hundreds of bars were closed and the government declared that it would not renew existing bar licences. The government-owned liquor monopoly – the Kerala State Beverages (M&M) Corporation Limited, or BEVCO in short – was set to support these efforts by pulling the shutters on 10 per cent of the shops it operated every year. Toddy shops, however, were allowed to operate as before, just as alcohol sales continued in five-star hotels.

A familiar controversy brewed in this context. Soon after the government announced its plans to unfurl prohibition, a segment of the Catholic Church sought the right to increase wine production. The church managed its own alcohol plants in the state to manufacture communion wine and referenced the safeguards for the use of alcohol in religious ritual that had been provided by past amendments to prohibition policy. According to the church, the size of its congregation had increased, thus necessitating more wine. However, the timing of the demand, coinciding as it did with prohibition's announcement, raised many eyebrows. Factions of the Hindu right-wing BJP and its affiliated groups opposed the church's demand on the grounds that it was just a ploy to sell the excess wine for profit. The ensuing row triggered a lengthy debate, once again, on the place of wine in Christian ritual. Before the wine issue could be satisfactorily resolved, prohibition itself came to an abrupt end in the state as its fate was intertwined with that of the government that had introduced it. The policy was scrapped following the elections of 2016 when the communist Left Democratic Front (LDF) government defeated the Congress-led United Democratic Front (UDF) coalition. Prohibition was bad for business, pronounced the new chief minister, Pinarayi Vijayan.

Interest in prohibition tends to peak during times of political transition. Political parties turn to the policy as a means of claiming, or reclaiming, moral capital. N. T. Rama Rao's Telugu Desam Party (TDP) won the state elections again in 1994 in the then undivided Andhra State. Before its stunning electoral victory, however, the government had supported the arrack industry's liberal expansion through its aggressive marketing efforts in rural areas. The government's 'Varuna Vahini' scheme, which translates into 'Flood of Liquor', had proven so effective that the revenue from liquor excise contributed to more than 10 per cent of the state's annual budget between 1991 and 1992.[26]

As much as prohibition's relevance as an electoral agenda increases during times of political transition, the loss of excise revenue, dwindling electoral fortunes, high administration costs, public health problems arising from the consumption of illicit hooch and the increased incidence of crime have all influenced state governments' decisions to suspend the policy. In Andhra Pradesh, the prosperity that had previously been made possible by the lucrative liquor trade stood in stark contrast to the fiscal deficits and mass unemployment crisis caused by the closure of breweries following prohibition's introduction. Prohibition's economic cost was so high that it plunged the state into virtual bankruptcy. The government's damage control measures of raising taxes and rice prices did little to reverse the budget deficit, proving hugely unpopular with the electorate instead. Prohibition was replaced by regulation once again in Andhra Pradesh. A similar situation unfolded in Haryana when prohibition was ended in 1998, two years after its enthusiastic introduction in 1996 by the Haryana Vikas Party–BJP coalition government.

One of the most instructive stories of postcolonial prohibitioning may, however, be traced back to Madras State, which was eventually renamed Tamil Nadu. The Act of 1937 governed alcohol policy in Tamil Nadu since 1947, albeit with several major amendments along the way. Prohibition's foundations in the state were strengthened by the Congress's K. Kamaraj as part of an overarching thrust to achieve a welfare state. Kamaraj's credentials as a prohibitionist drawn from the ranks of a toddy-tapping community served to strengthen the policy's moral legitimacy that its advocates claimed.

All this changed in 1971 when M. Karunanidhi's Dravida Munnetra Kazhagam (DMK) government lifted the long-standing ban on alcohol. For the new chief minister, prohibition was a futile endeavour and drain on state finances. He argued that unless prohibition was introduced at the same time throughout the country, the states would never succeed in enforcing the policy as drinkers would have the option to sojourn to neighbouring wet states. Kamaraj, along with parties sympathetic to the DMK like the

Muslim League and the Tamil Arasu Kazhagam, continued to support prohibition – not to mention the disagreement within party ranks, as M. G. Ramachandran (M. G. R.) disapproved of prohibition's suspension.[27] Notwithstanding these tensions, the policy was put to rest and the sale of arrack, toddy and IMFL was permitted. Tellingly, a series of policy flip-flops soon followed. In 1973 toddy shops were closed, followed by arrack shops the following year. The government argued its moves aligned with the goal of improving public health outcomes. Recalling the experience of the Madras Prohibition Act, only permit holders were allowed to purchase IMFL. In 1974 the DMK government introduced total prohibition, this time bringing arrack and IMFL under the purview of the law. The ban, however, triggered the consumption of illicit liquor and methanol, leading to several deaths in the state between 1975 and 1976.

Prohibition became embroiled in the rapidly escalating rivalry between erstwhile friends and former party cadres, Karunanidhi and M. G. R., in precisely this context. As that rivalry came to a head, it prompted the formation of the All-India Anna Dravida Munnetra Kazhagam (AIADMK) under M. G. R.'s leadership in 1972. Notwithstanding M. G. R.'s public polemic against prohibition's suspension by the DMK, the AIADMK government also eventually vacillated between regulation and the dry law. A Gandhian in his youth, much like Nijalingappa, M. G. R. supported the idea and practice of prohibition upon assuming power in 1977. However, the government had changed tack by 1981, when it lifted prohibition. M. G. R. as chief minister introduced liberalised liquor laws that progressively reduced the age at which individuals could obtain liquor permits. More egregiously, the AIADMK government under M. G. R.'s leadership established the government-owned Tamil Nadu State Marketing Corporation (TASMAC) in 1983. TASMAC, the government announced, was the perfect solution for prohibition. Since people were prone to abusing prohibition, and since the state knew best, it would regulate consumption through its liquor monopoly. TASMAC would go on to monopolise the wholesale and retail vending of alcohol sales in the state. Yet the ban was reintroduced on toddy in 1986 on the grounds that the industry was most prone to lapses in regulatory standards and therefore posed the greatest threat to public health. Both DMK and AIADMK governments would subsequently continue to nurture the IMFL industry whilst discriminating against country liquor.

A distinct legacy of the colonial past, prohibition's discriminatory slant thus continues to be felt in the alcohol policies of contemporary state governments. Indian liquor industries are still subjected to differential legislative treatment as they remain cleaved along class and caste lines and contribute unequally to the state's coffers. The formal Indian liquor industry comprises imported liquor, beer, IMFL and country liquor. Of these, imported liquor and IMFL varieties are priced the highest. Whereas the IMFL and beer industries have a distinctly urban flavour and cater to wealthier Indians, country liquor continues to cater to subaltern segments of society. State governments routinely intervene in the country liquor industry citing concerns of adulteration, either due to tampering with the manufacturing process or over-fermentation and toxicity. The tightening of licensing laws and monitoring by excise officials frequently translate into a greater degree of state-led policing of the country liquor industry than of its foreign liquor counterparts. This has elicited a volley of resistance from the communities that have been affected, in turn forcing amendments in subsequent policy. In Madhya Pradesh, excise laws were tightened in 2011, disproportionately affecting several Adivasi communities whose involvement in the production and consumption of *mahua* was subject to criminalisation as a result. They responded with sustained protests and grassroots resistance, leading to a situation wherein officials relaxed enforcement in some districts.[28]

Country liquor also frequently translates into the problem of illicit liquor, which – like the activities characterising political society – operates within the bounds of a flexible legality. It exists beyond the workings of the formal liquor economy, although it remains a challenge formidable enough to merit a category of its own. The industry is distinguishable by its producers' routine evasion of excise duties and licensing protocols. Due to this defining absence of checks and balances, alcoholic content and adulteration levels vary widely between illicit liquor samples, in which industrial methylated spirit frequently surfaces as a deadly additive. Its production centres are also decentralised. Whilst illicit liquor production tends to be particularly rampant in rural India, it also operates out of neighbourhoods and homes that are known among their client circles in towns and cities. As James Manor notes in his discussion of the Bangalore hooch tragedy of 1981, the issue is often not that the state is unaware of the problem. Rather, in a context wherein those who ply the trade secure the tacit cooperation of officials who look the other way, the real problem is that illicit liquor is so enmeshed within local cultures and economies that it cannot be completely eradicated, even if the will to do so is present – which is another matter altogether.[29]

Alcoholisation and Prohibition in Contemporary India

Today, India ranks among the world's largest alcoholic beverage markets.[30] The alcohol tax is a key source of revenue for most states of the republic, accounting for nearly a fifth of their incomes. In fact, it is often second only to the sales tax in importance. Although alcoholic drinking rose steadily in much of the country in the decades following independence, the highest rates of increase were seen following economic liberalisation in the 1990s. Together with globalisation and urbanisation, liberalisation worked to the advantage of the pro-alcohol policies that most state governments adopted in this context. In fact, state governments have often worked hand in glove with liquor barons.[31] Indian alcohol companies have been able to exploit progressively relaxed liquor laws to forge lucrative collaborations with international alcohol brands. Aided by technology transfers and a conducive licensing system, companies like United Breweries Limited manufactured and marketed globally recognised alcoholic beverages targeting the most affluent segments of Indian society. Local companies have cashed in on new drinking subcultures by developing a variety of flavoured alcoholic drinks and multinational corporations have bought out local manufacturers. Owing to the combined impact of these developments, the adult per capita alcohol consumption increased by an astounding 115 per cent between 1980 and 2020.[32] India's alcoholisation, that is, the rapid growth of alcohol industries and the factors supporting such growth, has had tremendous implications.

Indeed, alcohol is not just big business; it is political business in India. This is perhaps most evident when we consider corruption scandals that have laid bare the nexus between alcohol, politics and business in the past few decades. Vijay Mallya, the 'King of Good Times' who reigned over United Breweries Group (UBG), was known as much for the iconic Kingfisher beer as for his connections in high places. Currently a refugee from Indian law settled in the United Kingdom, Mallya had paved his political career with bribes, personal favours and a fleet of private jets, all enabled by UBG's prosperity.[33] Even more recently, the connection between India's liquor economy and politics resurfaced when the formulation of an excise policy sparked a fresh controversy in the national capital. The Delhi government's proposal to revitalise the state's ailing alcohol economy by transferring control over liquor retailing businesses to private firms did not go according to plan when the Central Bureau of Investigation (CBI) accused the incumbent state government of corruption. The rapidly deteriorating situation led to the arrest of the Aam Admi Party (AAP) government's deputy chief minister, Manish Sisodia, on money laundering charges, while the ill-fated new excise policy was scrapped.

To varying degrees, the prohibition ideal continues to coexist with the reality of alcoholisation across the country, with important consequences for the policy's trajectories and scope. While state governments tend to prioritise immediate goals in formulating alcohol policy, as we have seen, societal pressure for prohibition helps to ensure that it remains on the agenda. It was women's mass mobilisation efforts against alcoholic drinking that Rama Rao and the TDP were responding to with their prohibition campaign.[34] The grassroots movement had grown out of obscure origins in Dubaganta village to demand nationwide prohibition. Likewise, the Maharashtra government had been forced to pay attention in 2010 when thousands of women from Shramik Elgar, a grassroots organisation, marched from Chimur to Nagpur to demand prohibition's introduction in the latter. Responding to petitions from the Tamil Maanila Pengal Iyakkam (Tamil State Women's Movement), the state government closed TASMAC shops in several districts in Tamil Nadu. Across the country, women's mobilisation against alcohol and in support of prohibition has had the effect of turning them into vote banks in several states.

Civil society demands for prohibition also routinely exploit the memory of Gandhian *satyagraha* to force state governments into action. In 2017 Kumari Anandhan – a former Congress leader – led a peaceful protest march for complete prohibition in the Hindu pilgrimage destination of Rameswaram in Tamil Nadu. The choice was deliberate, given the historical relationship that persists between religion, morality and prohibition. Hundreds of people joined the march demanding an immediate introduction of the policy. Just two years before Anandhan's march, another Gandhian, Sasi Perumal, had died for prohibition's sake. Perumal had been involved in prohibition activism for several decades. In 2015 he sought the removal of a TASMAC liquor shop that was located near a church and a school. After his hunger strike near a Gandhi statue failed, Perumal decided to stage a protest atop a mobile phone tower. Tragically, Perumal fell whilst climbing down. Thousands of people came to pay their respects as his body was brought back to his home district for cremation. Human chains, sit-ins and mass rallies broke out in solidarity. Police forces were mobilised to deal with potential rioting. Rival political parties criticised the incumbent AIADMK government for its high-handedness and demanded that it introduce the dry law in a phased manner. Prohibition was again on the agenda.

One of the most organised movements of its kind, the Tamil Nadu Toddy Movement (TNTM) launched a campaign against the Tamil Nadu government's toddy ban in 2005. Mass unemployment and displacement had ensued following the ban on toddy tapping. As the newly unemployed tappers could not find alternative jobs, many returned to the only profession they knew of collecting and selling toddy – only illegally now.[35] Since the early 1990s, these dealings have necessitated striking arrangements with the local police, who would also launch raids and crack down on the industry once in a while. A series of scandals soon followed, thus prompting the formation of the TNTM as a means to seek redress for toddy tappers, their families and outlawed profession. The movement has grown steadily since its inception to currently number in the thousands, drawn from various districts, across the state.

The movement has published posters and books replete with quotes from Gandhi, held hunger fasts, issued petitions to the government and courted arrest through passive resistance – strikingly by selling toddy – all of which simultaneously reconstruct the memory of the freedom struggle while subverting it in crucial ways.[36] Toddy, the movement claims, is not only nourishing and wholesome, it is also an inexpensive fuel source and a legitimate source of livelihood. The movement has sought explanation as to why the milder toddy should be banned when a culture of drinking IMFL, with its greater alcoholic content, continues to thrive under TASMAC state patronage. Movements like the TNTM thus not only establish themselves as moral communities but also call out the immorality of the state in the process. During conferences held to assert toddy's legitimacy, many groups of people involved in the movement – including working-class women – have demanded toddy's legalisation owing to its place in their lives, livelihoods and cultures.[37] Several political parties have also chimed in. In 2023 the BJP in Tamil Nadu promised to close the majority of TASMAC shops and reopen toddy shops once it comes to power in the state. Senthamizhan Seeman, the leader of the Naam Tamilar Katchi, a Tamil nationalist political party, recently attended a conference organised by the TNTM in which he demanded that the government decriminalise toddy tapping, withdraw criminal cases registered against tappers and pronounce it a medicinal food-drink. Prohibitioning thus continues in the state.

Notes

1. Prathama Banerjee, 'The Abiding Binary: The Social and the Political in Modern India', in *South Asian Governmentalities: Michel Foucault and the Question of Postcolonial Orderings*, ed. Deana Heath and Stephen Legg, pp. 81–105 (Cambridge: Cambridge University Press, 2018).
2. De, *A People's Constitution*, pp. 15–16.
3. M. Haq, *Drugs in South Asia: From the Opium Trade to the Present Day* (London: Palgrave Macmillan, 2000), pp. 4–5.
4. 7.59.13 Constituent Assembly Debates, 24 November 1948.
5. Ibid.
6. Ibid.
7. *Report of the Prohibition Enquiry Committee, 1954–1955* (New Delhi: Government of India Press, 1955), pp. 47, 61–62.
8. *Report of the Study Team on Prohibition* (New Delhi: Government of India Press, 1966), pp. 211–212.
9. Ibid. p. 414.
10. Whereas Antonio Gramsci saw civil society as ruling through consent and political society as ruling through coercion, Chatterjee proposed an alternative interpretation of political society given its engagement with democratic governance in postcolonial societies like India. Partha Chatterjee, *The Politics of the Governed: Reflections on Popular Politics in Most of the World* (New York: Columbia University Press, 2004), pp. 12–13.
11. Chatterjee, *Lineages of Political Society*, p. 231. See also Partha Chatterjee, 'Democracy and Economic Transformation in India', *Economic and Political Weekly* 43, no. 16 (Apr. 19–25, 2008), pp. 53–62, especially p. 57.
12. Amita Baviskar and Nandini Sundar, 'Democracy versus Economic Transformation', *Economic and Political Weekly* 43, no. 46 (2008), pp. 87–89.
13. Nivedita Menon, 'Introduction', in *Empire and Nation: Selected Essays by Partha Chatterjee*, by Partha Chatterjee, pp. 1–20 (New York: Columbia University Press, 2010). See also Stuart Corbridge, Glyn Williams Stuart, Manoj Srivastava and René Véron, *Seeing the State: Governance and Governmentality in India* (Cambridge; New York: Cambridge University Press, 2005).
14. Menon, 'Introduction', pp. 1–20.
15. Tezenlo Thong, *Progress and Its Impact on the Nagas: A Clash of Worldviews* (London; New York: Ashgate Publishing, 2014), p. 95.

16. Vinyühu Lhoungu, Anungla Aier and Moanungsang, 'The Paradox of Nagaland Total Liquor Prohibition (NLTP) Act 1989 with Special Reference to Black Economy in Dimapur', *International Journal of Research in Social Sciences* 12, no. 8 (2022), pp. 11–29.

17. Richard Kamei, 'Liquor of Rongmei Naga: Brewing Jouju in the Village against Colonial and Postcolonial State', in *Time and Alcohol: It's Five O'Clock Somewhere!* ed. Peter J. Howland, pp. 167–181 (London: Routledge, 2025), pp. 178–179.

18. Gopalkrishna Gururaj, Melur S. Gautham, and Banavaram A Arvind, 'Alcohol Consumption in India: A Rising Burden and a Fractured Response', *Drug Alcohol Review* 40, no. 3 (March 2021), pp. 368–384, DOI: 10.1111/dar.13179, epub 30 September 2020, PMID: 33000887.

19. Backed by popular support for the policy in the Muslim-majority islands, prohibition was introduced in 1979, although the sales of alcohol were allowed in the island of Bangaram only to cater to tourists. When the BJP as the central government announced its plans to lift prohibition and introduce a beef ban in Lakshadweep in 2021, a predictable pattern of protests followed. The National Congress Party and the Congress's student wing, the National Students Union of India, accused the BJP of trying to impose majoritarianism on the islands in the guise of policymaking.

20. Kalpana Sharma, *Rediscovering Dharavi: Stories from Asia's Largest Slum* (New Delhi: Penguin Books, 2000), pp. 44–45.

21. Carolyn Heitmeyer and Edward Simpson, 'The Culture of Prohibition in Gujarat, India', in *A History of Alcohol and Drugs in Modern South Asia: Intoxicating Affairs*, ed. Harland Fischer-Tine and Jana Tschurenev, pp. 203–218 (Abingdon: Routledge, 2014).

22. 'Liquor Ban Exemption Comes into Effect in Gujarat's GIFT City', *Indian Express*, 31 December 2023, https://indianexpress.com/article/cities/ahmedabad/liqour-ban-exemption-effect-gujarat-gift-city-9089334/#:~:text=The%20state%20government%20exempted%20the,provide%20a%20global%20business%20ecosystem (accessed on 3 January 2024).

23. Gururaj, Gautham and Arvind, 'Alcohol Consumption in India'.

24. Satish Jha, 'Gujarat Model: Unequal "Licence-Permit Raj" for Liquor', *Deccan Herald*, 2 September 2021, https://www.deccanherald.com/opinion/gujarat-model-unequal-licence-permit-raj-for-liquor-1026064.html (accessed on 3 January 2024).

25. Kalyani Chaudhuri, Natasha Jha, Mrithyunjayan Nilayamgode and Revathy Suryanarayana, 'Alcohol Ban and Crime: The ABCs of the Bihar

Prohibition', *Economic Development and Cultural Change* 72, no. 4 (2024), DOI: 10.1086/725452.

26. A. Joseph, 'Women against Arrack: Organizing for Change – India 1', *People Planet* 4, no. 3 (1995): 10–1, PMID: 12290000.

27. Marguerite Ross Barnett, *The Politics of Cultural Nationalism in South India* (Princeton: Princeton University Press, 1976), pp. 295–296. See also A. R. Venkatachalapathy, *Tamil Characters: Personalities, Politics, Culture* (London; New Delhi: Pan Macmillan, 2018), pp. 128–130. I refer to Venkatachalapathy's discussion of prohibition as a burning issue in the state of Tamil Nadu, revived as it has been intermittently such as following the protests ranged against the state government for its indiscriminate alcohol policy in 2015.

28. Aditi Pradhan, Ameya Bokil, Avaneendra Khare, Kanishka Singh, Nikita Sonavane, Pallavi Diwakrar, Shreya Gajbhiye, Srujana Bej and Yashaswi B. Kabde, 'Drunk on Power: Excise Policing in Madhya Pradesh', in *Criminal Justice and Police Accountability Project Report*, https://cpaproject. in/wp-content/uploads/2021/08/Drunk-on-Power-A-study-of-Excise-Policing-in-Madhya-Pradesh-CPA-Project-14-Aug-2021-1.pdf   (accessed on 11 May 2025), pp. 78–81. See also Karan Thapar, 'Adivasis, Liquor and the Politics of Law Enforcement in Conflict Zone of Chattisgarh', pts 1–2, https://lawandotherthings.com/adivasis-liquor-and-the-politics-of-law-enforcement-in-conflict-zone-of-chhattisgarh-part-i (accessed on 11 May 2025).

29. See James Manor, *Power, Poverty and Poison: Disaster and Response in an Indian City* (New Delhi: Sage Publications, 1993). See also Subir Kumar Das, V. Balakrishnan and D. M. Vasudevan, 'Alcohol: Its Health and Social Impact in India', *National Medical Journal of India* 19, no. 2 (2006), pp. 94–99, especially pp. 94–96.

30. 'Alcoholic Drinks: India, Statista Market Forecast [Internet]', cited in Gururaj, Gautham and Arvind, 'Alcohol Consumption in India'. The volume of alcohol in the Indian market increased from around 7,500 million litres in 2010 to nearly 12,400 million litres in 2019. Alcohol revenues outpaced the volume of alcohol sold as the earnings leaped from USD 16,270 million to USD 48,855 million over the same period.

31. Haq, *Drugs in South Asia*, pp. 109–111.

32. A. Mahal, 'What Works in Alcohol Policy? Evidence from Rural India', *Economic and Political Weekly* 35 (2000), pp. 3959–3968.

33. Mallya had had political ambitions too, having been elected to the Rajya Sabha for a second time in 2010 with the support of the Janata Dal and the BJP; Karnataka's former chief minister, S. M. Krishna, reportedly flew in Mallya's private jets even while on official business.

34. Larsson, *'When Women Unite!'*

35. Joop De Wit, *Poverty, Policy and Politics in Madras Slums: Dynamics of Survival, Gender and Leadership* (London: Sage Publications, 1996), p. 73–74.

36. I refer to a book written by the founder of the TNTM, C. Nallasamy, in which he questions the state's rationale for banning toddy and offers an INR 10 crore reward to anyone who can prove why it ought to be banned. See C. Nallasamy, *Kal Our Thadai Ceiyapada Vendmya Bothaiporula?* (Should Toddy be Banned?) (Arachalur: Uzhavu Achagam, 2019), pp. 2–5.

37. 'Toddy Politics Heats Up in Tamil Nadu', *New Indian Express*, 16 May 2012, https://www.newindianexpress.com/states/tamil-nadu/2011/Jan/17/toddy-politics-heats-up-in-tamil-nadu-219791.html (accessed on 24 December 2024).

Conclusion

Policies have complex lives and afterlives. They interact with contingent political and social agents and are mediated by their wider contexts, from the processes that inform their conceptualisation through their enforcement.[1] Prohibition in India originated in the context of late colonialism. It took shape as an idea, became part of a mass movement and crystallised into an ideal before emerging as a policy with the Madras Prohibition Act of 1937. The ensuing interactions are best understood as constituting the long-term process of prohibitioning, wherein each phase of the policy's development simultaneously overdetermined and constrained its subsequent iterations. As we have seen, this formative experience also enabled prohibition to migrate from the colonial context to the postcolonial era, its origins illuminating crucial parallels and precedents for developments that followed the achievement of independence. Through all this, prohibition bore – indeed, has borne – the imprint of the interactions that produced it, which are discernible in its manifestations as an idea, ideal and policy. As much a history of the policy as it is a history of the Indian state, *Sober State* has presented a history of prohibitioning that rests on three related arguments.

First, we saw that prohibition emerged as a function of the exercise of state power by the colonial and nationalist states. The colonial state engaged with alcohol policy as a means to maintain power by achieving revenue maximisation and ensuring regulatory checks and balances at a time when said power was quickly slipping out of its hands. The nationalist leadership saw the prohibition demand as a trump card that would expose the colonial state's avarice and hypocrisy, while signifying a new and superior model of governance. Even as the nationalists doubled down in pushing for prohibition, the colonial government followed suit with countermeasures to foil their plans, thus bringing forth a mutual hardening of stances. As alcohol policy was entwined with the ethos and practice of good government for both colonial and nationalist governments, it was operationalised through alternating forms of governmentality, which brings us to our next argument.

As diverse segments of Indian society interacted with prohibition in different ways, their responses left an indelible imprint on its subsequent development. By and large, the middle classes inherited and reproduced the prejudices of colonial and nationalist elites that had characterised their respective approaches to subaltern drinking. Contempt for working-class drinking intersected with and strengthened their support for Congress nationalism. At the same time, changing norms of sociability heralded a culture of imbibing imported liquor among many in the upper crust of society, who would later demand exemptions from prohibition. The responses of the Indian underclasses to liquor legislation varied considerably as well. While some communities embraced teetotalism as opening a path to self-strengthening, others devised innovative ways of sidestepping official regulations to produce and consume alcohol, particularly country liquor. As various segments of society thus interacted with the state *within* its institutions and processes – whether by generating, negotiating or withholding consent – their responses rendered prohibition a site of ongoing contestation and, hence, consensus-building.

Third, prohibition thus emerged as a bridge reflecting the search for consensus at several levels. Consensus-building processes on what prohibition should be and what it should do had – in various combinations – involved civil society, subaltern society, leaders of the Congress, Indian opposition politicians and colonial officials when it originated. Owing to its contested nature during such a formative period of its development, that too at a crucial juncture in the history of the Indian state, prohibition not only emerged as the product of a negotiated settlement in colonial India but remained one in the decades following independence as well. The state necessarily had to become sober in its approach to prohibition, with the effect that the policy bore the imprint of its pragmatism. While prohibition elicited responses that challenged the state's authority, in doing so, it also provided the impetus for the next round of negotiations on the policy. Prohibition's failures became proof precisely of the people's failures to govern themselves; simultaneously, it became justification that the state would need to be further strengthened to address the problems facing society.

The story of prohibition's origins in India is tremendously important in helping us understand the policy and the ideal behind it as they continue to interact in contemporary India. Prohibition today exists in the space opened up between idealised visions of the state's responsibility in improving the lives of its citizens, as set out in the Constitution of India, and the practical realities of its implementation. Political parties still turn to the constitution to variously either accuse incumbent governments of having failed to realise the lofty ideal of a teetotal state that accompanied the transition to independence or promise to deliver that state themselves. While prohibition remains primarily associated with the Congress, owing to the glorious memory of the freedom struggle, vote bank politics has also tempted other parties to flirt with the policy at various points in time. Yet, much as the Congress government under Rajaji's leadership realised in the Madras Presidency in 1937, prohibition tends to go south quickly. Caught between justifying the policy's introduction and addressing problems of various kinds that rapidly spiral into nothing short of a nightmare for governance, governments have had to pull back on the promised, intended scope of the policy or suspend it altogether. As a feedback mechanism between state and society, the limits of prohibition policy have been jointly determined by both.

Relatedly, prohibition's emergence as a policy of national relevance within the workings of provincial government had far-reaching repercussions for its development within the jurisdiction of the state in postcolonial India. Several compromises or adaptations – depending on how generous one is – have thus come to characterise what prohibition in India actually is. Owing to its associations with the Indian working classes, the country liquor industry has not only disproportionately fuelled demands for prohibition, it has also – by the same token – remained the most disproportionately targeted industry where the policy's implementation has been concerned. If prohibition itself exists at one level as symbolic of the state's dedication and resolve to lead society into a better future, country liquor remains the face of that symbol. As I have shown in this book, the story of the Madras Prohibition Act of 1937 and the wider history of the state that it is part of thus continue to reverberate through the policy's present lives.

So, is prohibition still relevant in India? Those who would say that it is would reiterate the position that the state owes a moral duty of care to its citizens, besides being best placed to address social problems. Those who would say that prohibition is irrelevant would argue that it does not work, pointing to its many failings over its long history as evidence that the individual should be allowed and entrusted to exercise choice in all such matters. Aside from the question that then arises as to whether any choice is actually completely free of the effects of conditioning – including, of course, by the state – this position also inadvertently upholds the individual's right to choose prohibition. As we have seen, prohibition continues to be periodically reintroduced in various parts of the country, its mandate as a policy of the people, by the people, frequently legitimised through the ballot box. Prohibition continues to work to the extent that it is allowed in India's democratic polity. Perhaps a more productive set of questions to ask then would be how state and society continue to jointly produce a policy like prohibition and, relatedly, how their interactions might help us understand what the policy is, and does, in India. As *Sober State* has shown, there is much to be said in this regard.

Note

1. See Bruno Latour, *Aramis, or the Love of Technology*, trans. Catherine Porter (Cambridge, MA: Harvard University Press, 1996), pp. 119–121; Cris Shore and Susan Wright (eds.), *Anthropology of Policy, Perspectives on Governance and Power* (London: Routledge, 1997), pp. 25–29; and Cris Shore, Susan Wright and Davide Pero, *Policy Worlds: Anthropology and the Analysis of Contemporary Power* (New York and Oxford: Bergen Books, 2011), pp. 3–5.

Glossary

abkari	From the Persian word, meaning 'strong water'. In the Indian context, the term could refer to the production or manufacture of alcoholic liquors or a tax levied on the manufacture of liquors.
arrack	From the Arabic word *araq* or *arraga*, meaning 'to sweat'. The term refers to an alcoholic spirit.
bootlegger	Someone who makes, copies or sells something illegally. The term is usually used in the context of illicit alcohol manufacture and/or sales.
chunam	Referring to slaked lime, as used in the Indian context when chewing betel leaves. It was used to delay fermentation owing to its alkaline properties.
excise	A tax levied on certain goods and commodities produced or sold within a country and on licences that were granted for certain activities.
hooch	Abbreviation of Hoochinoo, the name of a North American people of Alaska who made liquor. It refers to illicit distilled liquor that has frequently been adulterated.
neera/padhaneer	Referring to the sweet and translucent unfermented sap that is tapped from the immature 'spathe' of various palm tree varieties.
sonti soru	Referring to a liquid derived from rice or starch that has started or finished fermenting into alcohol.

toddy — Also known as *tari*. The term refers to a kind of light fermented alcohol derived from coconut and other palm tree varieties.

wash — Referring to a mixture of water and saccharine materials that has started or finished fermenting into alcohol.

Bibliography

Primary Sources

Economic and Overseas Department Records, 1937–1939.
Fortnightly Reports, 1937–1939.
Home Department, 1939.
Proceedings of the Government of Madras, Madras Record Office, Tamil Nadu
 Archives.
Public and Judicial Department Records, 1937–1943.
Revenue Department, 1886–1940.

Institutional Papers

All-India Congress Committee Papers, Nehru Memorial Library, New Delhi.
All-India Women's Conference Papers, India Office Records, London.
Tamil Nadu Congress Committee Papers, Nehru Memorial Library, New Delhi.

Private Papers

A. F. W. Dixon, Personal Diary, India Office Records, London.
C. Rajagopalachari Papers, Nehru Memorial Library, India.
Erskine Papers, Nehru Memorial Library, New Delhi, and India Office Records,
 London.
J. L. H. Williams Papers, India Office Records, London.
Jayaraman Papers, India Office Records, London.
Lord Halifax Papers, Nehru Memorial Library, New Delhi.
M. K. Gandhi Papers (Pyarelal Papers), Nehru Memorial Library, New Delhi.

S. Muthulakshmi Reddi Papers, Nehru Memorial Library, New Delhi.

T. B. Sapru Papers, Nehru Memorial Library, New Delhi.

Legislative Council Proceedings

Madras Legislative Council Proceedings, vol. 2, 1936.

Madras Legislative Council Proceedings, vol. 2, 1938.

Madras Legislative Council Proceedings, vols. 1–2, 1939.

Parliamentary Papers

East India: Accounts and Estimates 1907–1908. Parliamentary Papers, House of Commons, London, 1907.

Evidence on Drunkenness: Presented to the House of Commons by a Select Committee Appointed by the House to Inquire into this Subject and Report the Minutes of Evidence with their Opinions thereupon. London: Samuel Bagster for the British and Foreign Temperance Society, 1834.

Cabinet Papers, 'Welfare in India and Southeast Asia', vol. 5, Working Paper, 1944.

Reports

Eleventh Report of the Executive Committee of the American Temperance Union. New York: S.W. Benedict, 1841.

Memorandum on the Progress of the Madras Presidency During the Last Forty Years of British Administration. Madras: Government Press, 1893.

Mukerjie, Abhilas Chandra, *Report on the System of the Abkari Administration of the Madras Presidency, with Special Reference to Toddy*. Calcutta: Bengal Secretariat Press 1895.

———. *A Report on Toddy Taxation*. Calcutta: Bengal Secretariat Press, 1895.

Report of the All-India Temperance Conference, Allahabad, 30 December 1909. Bombay: n.p., 1909.

Report of the Excise Advisory Committee Appointed by the Government of Madras. Madras: Government Press, 1924.

Report of the Foreign Liquor Committee, 1908–09. Bombay: Government Press, 1909.

Report of the Indian Excise Committee. Bombay: Government Press, 1906.

Report of the Indian Excise Committee. Bombay: Government Press, 1919.

Report of the Prohibition Enquiry Committee, 1954–1955. Delhi: Government of India Press, 1955.

Report of the Second Decennial Missionary Conference Held at Calcutta, 1882–1983, with a Missionary Map of India. Calcutta: J. W. Thomas, Baptist Mission Press, 1883.

Report of the Study Team on Prohibition. New Delhi: Government of India Press, 1966.

Report on an Enquiry into the Family Budgets of Industrial Workers in Madras City. Madras: Government Press, 1938.

Report on the Administration of the Abkari Revenue in the Presidency of Fort St. George. Madras: Government Press, 1885–1904.

Report on the Administration of the Excise Revenue in the Province of Madras. Madras: Government Press, 1905–1937.

Report on the Administration of the Madras Presidency. Madras: Government Press, 1895–1912.

Reports on Native, Vernacular Newspapers Examined by the Translators to the Government of Madras (NNPR). Madras: Government: Superintendent of Government Press, 1868–1942.

Court Cases

Madras High Court: The Public Prosecutor v. Perianna Goundan and Another, (1938)2MLJ813, AIR 1939 MADRAS 53.

Madras High Court in Re: Vyapuri Kavandan v. Unknown, (1939) 2MLJ109.

Madras High Court in The Public Prosecutor v. Poongavana Goundan, (1942) 2MLJ37.

Madras High Court in Re: V.A. Gayasudeen v. Unknown, (1942) 2MLJ547.

Books (English)

Arthur, Rev. William. *A Mission to the Mysore: With Scenes and Facts Illustrative of India, Its People, and Its Religion.* London: Partridge & Oakey, 1847.

Burne, Peter. *The Concordance of Scripture and Science Illustrated, with Reference to the Temperance Cause, With a Prefatory Letter by Dr Lees, on the Philosophy and Philology of the Question.* London: Arthur Hall & Company, 1847.

Carpenter, William Benjamin. *The Physiology of Temperance and Total Abstinence: Being an Examination of the Effects of the Excessive, Moderate and Occasional*

Use of Alcoholic Liquors on the Healthy Human System. London: H.G. Bohn, 1858.

———. *On the Use and Abuse of Alcoholic Liquors: In Health and Disease*. London: J.B. Gilpin, 1850.

Chipperfield, W. N. *The Madras Quarterly Journal*, vol. 9. Madras: Adelphi Press; London: Robert Hardwicke, 1866.

Conder, Josiah. *The Modern Traveller*, vol. 3, *India*. London: James Duncan, 1830.

Digby, William. *The Famine Campaign in Southern India (Madras and Bombay Presidencies and Province of Mysore) 1876–1878*, vol. 1. London: Longman, Greens & Co., 1878.

E. J. M. Sastri. *The Social and Economic Effects of Prohibition in Chittoor District, Madras Presidency*. Madras: Sri Veda Vyasa Press, 1938.

Forbes, James. *Oriental Memoirs: A Narrative of Seventeen Years Residence in India*, vol. 1. London: Richard Bentley, 1834.

Fryer, John. *A New Account of East-India and Persia: In 8 Letters Being 9 Years Travels, Begun 1672 and Finished 1681*. London: n.p., 1698.

Gaekwar of Baroda (ed.). *Depressed Classes*. Bombay: n.p., 1913.

Gregson, G. H. *Drinking and the Drink Traffic in India*. London: n.p., 1887.

Grindrod, Ralph Barnes. *Bacchus: An Essay on the Nature, Causes, Effects, and Cure of Intemperance*. London: J & H.G. Langley, 1840.

Grover, Charles E. *Folk Songs of South India*. Madras: Higginbotham & Co., 1871.

Hunter, William Wilson. *Bombay, 1885 to 1890: A Study in Indian Administration*. Bombay: Government Press, 1900.

Iyer, P. Ramanatha, and P. Raghava Iyer. *The Civil Court Manual, Madras*. Madras: Modern Printing Works, 1919.

Iyer, T. Sadasiva. *Problems of Social Reform*. Madras: India Printing Works, 1919.

K. S. Venkataramani. *Kandan the Patriot*. Madras: Svetaranya Ashrama, 1932.

Landon, Ethel. *Alcohol: A Menace to India*. Madras: Christian Literature Society for India, 1918.

Love, Henry Davison. *Indian Records Series: Vestiges of Old Madras 1640–1800, Traced from the East India Company's Records Preserved at Fort St. George and the India Office and from Other Sources*, vol. 2. London: John Murray, Albemarle Street, 1913. https://archive.org/details/vestigesofoldmad00loveuoft/page/n5/mode/2up. Accessed on 12 February 2023.

Lukis, C. P. *Tropical Hygiene for Anglo-Indians and Indians*. London; Calcutta: Thacker & Co., 1911.

Maitland, Julia Charlotte. *Letters from Madras, during the Years 1836–1839.* London: Jon Murray, 1861.

Matthai, John. *Excise and Liquor Control.* Madras: Authors Press and Publishing House, 1924.

Marshall, Henry. *Contribution to a Natural and Economical History of the Coco-nut Tree.* London: John Stark, 1832.

Melchizedek, D. J. *The Temperance Mission: An Outline of the History of the 'Temperance Mission'.* Madras: n.p., 1898.

Missionary Herald. London: London Missionary Society, 1839.

Moffat, A. *The Drink Traffic in the Madras Presidency.* Madras: G.A. Natesan & Co., 1909.

Pennant, Thomas. *View of Hindoostan*, vol. 1. London: H. Hughs, 1798.

Philip, Kavita. *Civilising Natures: Race, Resources and Modernity in Colonial South India.* New Delhi: Orient Longman, 2003.

Pillai, V. Vedanayakam. *The Ancient Tamils and Total Abstinence.* Madras: n.p., 1915.

Raghavaiyangar, S. Srinivasa. *Memorandum on the Progress of the Madras Presidency During the Last Forty Years of British Administration.* Madras: Government Press, 1893.

Ranson, C. W. 'The Growth of Population of Madras'. In *The Madras Tercentenary Commemoration Volume*, pp. 317–325. Madras: G.S. Press, 1939.

Rao, B. Shiva. *The Industrial Worker in India.* London: George Allen & Unwin, 1939.

Reddi, S. Muthulakshmi. *My Experience as a Legislator.* Madras: Current Thought Press, 1930.

Sastri, Mahadeva. *The Basic Truths of Vedic Religion.* Madras: Theosophist Office, 1912.

Simple Stories Illustrating Evils from Toddy Drinking. Madras: Minerva Press, 1927.

Sinha, Tarini Prasad. *'Pussyfoot' Johnson and His Campaign in Hindustan.* Madras: Ganesh, 1922.

Slater, Gilbert. *Some South Indian Villages.* Oxford: Oxford University Press, 1918.

———. *Southern India, Its Political and Economic Problems.* London: G. Allen & Unwin, 1936.

Statham, John. *Indian Recollections.* London: Samuel Bagster, 1832.

Symson, Captain William. *A New Voyage to the East Indies.* London: H. Meere, for A. Bettesworth, and E. Curll, 1715.

Tennant, William. *Indian Recreations: Consisting Chiefly of Strictures on the Domestic and Rural Economy of the Mahomedans and Hindoos*, vol. 2. London: C. Stewart, 1804.

Thomas, P. J., *Economic Results of Prohibition in the Salem District*. Madras: Madras University, 1939.

Thurston, Edgar. *Anthropology of the Todas and Kotas of the Nilgiri Hills: And of the Brahmans, Kammalans, Pallis, and Pariahs of Madras City*. Madras: Madras Government Museum, 1896.

———. *Badagas and Irulas of the Nilgiris: Paniyans of Malabar; a Chinese-Tamil Cross; a Cheruman Skull; Kuruba or Kurumba; Summary of Results (Madras Government Museum Bulletin)*, vol. 2, no. 2 (reprint edition). New Delhi: Asian Educational Services, 2004.

———. *Ethnographic Notes in Southern India*. Madras: Government Press, 1906.

———. *The Madras Presidency with Mysore, Coorg and the Associated States*. Cambridge: Cambridge University Press, 1913.

Valle, Pietro Della. *Travels of Pietro Della Valle in India: From the Old English, Translation of 1664*. Cambridge: Cambridge University Press, 2010 (1892).

Wheeler, J. Talboys. *Madras in the Olden Time: Being a History of the Presidency from the First Foundation to the Governorship of Thomas Pitt, Grandfather of the Earl of Chatham, 1639–1702*. Madras: Higginbotham, 1861.

Wright, Arnold. *Southern India: Its History, People, Commerce, and Industrial Resources* (reprint edition). New Delhi: Asian Educational Services, 2004.

Yule, Henry, and Arthur Coke Burnell (eds.). *Hobson-Jobson: A Glossary of Colloquial Anglo-Indian Words and Phrases, and of Kindred Terms, Etymological, Historical, Geographical and Discursive*. London: J. Murray, 1903.

Books (Tamil)

Baalar Sugaathaara Vithigallum Pattugalum (Rules and Songs of Hygiene for Children). Madras: Christian Literature Society for India, 1932.

Bonnell, Y. G. *Kudumba Madhuvilakku Saastiram* (Domestic Temperance Science Manual). Madras: Minerva Press, 1916.

C. Nallasamy. *Kal Our Thadai Ceiyapada Vendmya Bothaiporula?* (Should Toddy be Banned?). Arachalur: Uzhavu Achagam, 2019.

C. Rajagopalachari. *Kal Oliga!* (May Toddy Be Destroyed!). Madras: Kamala Publishers, 1943.

'Kalki' Krishnamurthy. *Tamil Short Stories by Kalki*. Chennai: Manonmani Publishers, 2014.

Kallukkadai Ennum Kudiyar Sintu (Toddy Shop or Drinkers' Song). Madras: Sundravilasa Achu, 1901.

Kudi Arasu Tokuppu (*Kudi Arasu* Compilation). Chennai: Periyar Dravidar Kazhagam, 2008.

V. Kalyanasundaran. *Seerthirutham Allathu Ilamai Virunthu* (Reform or the Celebration of Youth). Madras: Balan Publishing House, 1930.

Bulletins, Pamphlets and Magazines

A Pamphlet Attacking the Evils of Intemperance. Madras: Christian Literature Society for India, 1923.

A. Muni. *My Open Letter to His Excellency the Governor of Madras.* Madras: n.p., 1926.

Alexander's East India and Colonial Magazine, vol. 10, July–December 1835. London: R. Alexander, 1835.

Asiatic Review. London: Swan Sonnenshein & Co., 1896.

Besant, Annie. *The Influence of Alcohol.* Madras: Theosophical Publishing House, 1892.

British and Foreign Medico-Chirurgical Review, vol. 5. London: John Churchill & Sons, 1850.

British Medical Journal, vol. 1. London: British Medical Association, 1889.

C. Jagannathachari. *A Survey of the Working of Prohibition in Salem District.* Madras: Madras University, 1939.

C. Rajagopalachari. *Prohibition: The Official Organ of the Prohibition League of India*, no. 17. Mumbai: Prohibition League of India, 1930.

———. *Indian Prohibition Manual.* Madras: Indian National Congress Prohibition Committee, 1931.

Caine, W. S. *The Indian National Congress Session at Allahabad, December 1888: Impressions of Two English Visitors.* London: n.p., 1889.

Chitambar, Satyavati S. *Systematic Scientific Teaching on Temperance and Hygiene in Indian Schools.* Lucknow: n.p., 1929.

Great Britain and the East, vol. 49. London: Great Britain and the East Limited, 1937.

Grubb, Frederick. *The Hindu and Indian Temperance News.* London, 1940.

Madras Vegetarian Society. Madras: Theosophist Office, 1914.

Markham, Cements Robert. *Travels in Peru and India: While Superintending the Collection of Chinchona Plants and Seeds in South America, and Their Introduction into India.* London: J. Murray, 1862.

Macleod, Kenneth. 'The Scope and Aim of the (Tropical Diseases) Section's Work'. *Journal of Tropical Medicine and Hygiene* 1, no. 8 (August 1898), pp. 22–31.

Sathe, G. M. *Native Newspaper Reports, Bombay.* Bombay: Government of Bombay, 1886.

Slack, Agnes E. 'The Regulation of the Liquor Traffic in England'. *Annals of the American Academy of Political and Social Science,* vol. 32 (1908), pp. 142–145.

The Biblical Repertory and Princeton Review, vol. 13. London: Peabody, 1841.

The Calcutta Review, vol. 16, July–December 1851. Calcutta: Sanders, Cones & Co., 1851.

The Congress Bulletin. New Delhi: n.p., 1930.

The Congress, Conferences and Conventions of 1909: A Collection of the Presidential and Inaugural Speeches Delivered at the Indian National Congress, the Indian Industrial Conference, the All-India Temperance Conference etc. Madras: G.A. Natesan, 1910.

The Encyclopaedia Britannica: A Dictionary of Arts, Sciences, and General Literature, vol. 15. London: n.p., 1894.

The First Year of Congress Rule in Madras, Madras: Madras Legislative Congress Party, 1938.

The Missionary Herald of the Baptist Missionary Society. London Baptist Mission House, 1893.

The Wesleyan Methodist Magazine. London: Wesleyan Conference Office, 1871.

Transactions of the Royal Botanical Society, vol. 7. London: Royal Botanical Society, 1863.

District Manuals and Gazettes

B. S. Baliga. *Madras District Gazetteers: Coimbatore.* Madras: Superintendent, Government Press, 1966.

———. *Madras District Gazetteers: Ramanathapuram.* Madras: Superintendent, Government Press, 1972.

———. *Madurai District Gazetteers.* Madras: Superintendent, Government Press, 1960.

Cox, Arthur Frederick. *A Manual of the North Arcot District in the Presidency of Madras.* Madras: Government Press, 1881.

Francis, W. *Nilgiri District Gazetteer.* Madras: Government Press, 1908.

———. *South Arcot District Gazetteer.* Madras: Government Press, 1906.

Gandhi, Gopalakrishna. *Pudukkottai District Gazetteers.* Madras: Government of Tamil Nadu, 1983.

Phillips, H. A. D. *Our Administration of India: Being a Complete Account of the Revenue and Collectorate Administration in All Departments, with Special Reference to the Work and Duties of a District Officer in Bengal.* Bombay: Thacker; Madras: Higginbotham, 1886.

R. Sinnakani. *Gazetteers of the Tamil Nadu State: Thoothukudi District.* Chennai: Government of Tamil Nadu, 2007.

Ramaswami. *Gazetteer of Salem District.* Madras: Superintendent of Government Press, 1967.

Rao, Raja Rama. *Ramnad District Manual.* Madras: Superintendent of Government Press, 1889.

Report on the Administration of the Madras Presidency, during the Year 1880–1881. Madras: Government Press, 1881.

Report on the Administration of the Madras Presidency. Madras: Superintendent of Government Press, 1880.

Report on the Mysore General Census of 1871. London: Mysore Government Press, 1874.

The Administration of Bengal Under Sir Andrew Fraser 1903–1908. Calcutta: Bengal Secretariat Book Depôt, 1908.

The Chingleput, Late Madras, District: A Manual Compiled Under the Orders of the Madras Government. Madras: Government Press, 1879.

The Madras Code. Madras: Government Press, 1888.

The Madras District Manuals, North Arcot, vol. 2. Madras: Government Press, 1894.

Newspapers, Journals and Magazines

Alexander's East India and Colonial Magazine, 1835.

Ananda Vikatan, 1926–1933.

Harijan, 1930–1937.

Indian Review, 1900–1982.

Indian Social Reformer, 1890–1952.

Journal of the American Temperance Union, 1837.

Kudi Arasu, 1925–1937.

Madras Christian College Magazine, vol. 27, 1910.

Madras Mail, 1868–1981.

Madras Missionary Register, vols. 2–4, 1836.

The Hindu, 1898–1937.
Times of India, 1910–1935.
Voice of Progress, 1900–1940.
Young India, 1920–1932.

Secondary Sources

Books (English)

A. N. Sattampillai. *A Brief Sketch of the Hindu Christian Dogma* (Palamcottah: 1890).

A. R. Venkatachalapathy. *In Those Days There was No Coffee: Writings in Cultural History*. New Delhi: Yoda Press, 2006.

———. *Tamil Characters: Personalities, Politics, Culture*. London; New Delhi: Pan Macmillan, 2018.

A. S. Mathur and J. S. Mathur. *Trade Union Movement in India*. Allahabad: Chaitanya Publishing House, 1957.

Akyeampong, Emmanuel Kwaku. *Drink, Power, and Cultural Change: A Social History of Alcohol in Ghana, c. 1800 to Recent Times*. London: Pearson, 1996.

Allen, Charles. *Plain Tales from the Raj: Images of British India in the 20th Century*. London: Hachette, 2015.

Alter, Joseph S. *Gandhi's Body: Sex, Diet, and the Politics of Nationalism*. Philadelphia: University of Pennsylvania Press, 2011.

Ambedkar, B. R. *Writings and Speeches from the Bombay Legislature, Simon Commission and Round Table Conferences*, vol. 1. New Delhi, 1979.

Amin, Shahid. *Event, Metaphor, Memory: Chauri Chaura, 1922–1992*. Berkeley; Los Angeles: University of California Press, 1995.

Appadurai, Arjun. *The Social Life of Things: Commodities in Cultural Perspective*. Cambridge: Cambridge University Press, 1986.

Arnold, David. *Science, Technology and Medicine in Colonial India*. Cambridge: Cambridge University Press, 2000.

Andersen, Lisa M. F. *The Politics of Prohibition: American Governance and the Prohibition Party, 1869–1933*. Cambridge: Cambridge University Press, 2013.

Ayrookuzhiel, A.M. Abraham. *The Sacred in Popular Hinduism: An Empirical Study in Chirakkal, North Malabar*. Charlottesville, VA: University of Virginia, 1983.

Baker, Christopher and Washbrook, David Arnold. *South India: Political Institutions and Political Change 1880–1940*. Delhi: MacMillan Co., 1975.

Baker, Christopher. *The Politics of South India, 1920–1937*. Cambridge: University Press, 1976.

Balasubramanian, Aditya. *Toward a Free Economy: Swatantra and Opposition Politics in Democratic India*. New Jersey: Princeton University Press, 2023.

Balfour, Edward. *The Cyclopædia of India and of Eastern and Southern Asia Commercial, Industrial and Scientific, Products of the Mineral, Vegetable, and Animal Kingdoms, Useful Arts and Manufactures*, vol. 2. London, 1885.

Banerjee, Nirmala. 'Working Women in Colonial Bengal: Modernisation and Marginalisation'. In *Recasting Women: Essays in Colonial History*, edited by Kumkum Sangari and Sudhesh Vaid. Calcutta: Kali for Women, 1990.

Bayly, Christopher Allan. *Empire and Information: Intelligence Gathering and Social Communication in India, 1780–1870*. Cambridge: Cambridge University Press, 1996.

Bayly, Susan. *Caste, Society and Politics in India from the Eighteenth Century to the Modern Age*. Cambridge: Cambridge University Press, 2001.

Banerjee, Prathama. 'The Abiding Binary: The Social and the Political in Modern India'. In *South Asian Governmentalities: Michel Foucault and the Question of Postcolonial Orderings*, edited by Deana Heath and Stephen Legg, pp. 81–105. Cambridge: Cambridge University Press, 2018.

Barnett, Marguerite Ross. *The Politics of Cultural Nationalism in South India*. Princeton: Princeton University Press, 1976.

Bhattacharya, Sabyasachi. *The Financial Foundations of the British Raj: Ideas and Interests in the Reconstruction of Indian Public Finance 1858–1872*. New Delhi: Orient Balckswan, 2005.

B. Kesavanarayana. *Political and Social Factors in Andhra, 1900–1956*. Hyderabad: Navodaya, 1976.

Blurton, T. Richard. *Hindu Art*. Cambridge; Massachusetts: Harvard University Press, 1993.

B. S. Baliga. *Compendium on Temperance and Prohibition in Madras*. Chennai: Government of Madras, 1960.

———. *Madras District Gazetteers: Ramanathapuram*. Chennai: Government of India, 1957.

Beyer, Mark. *Temperance and Prohibition: The Movement to Pass Anti-Liquor Laws in America*. London: Rosen, 2006.

Bhaskaran, Theodore. *The Eye of the Serpent: An Introduction to Tamil Cinema*. Chennai: East West Books, 1996.

Bhattacharya, Sanjoy, Mark Harrison and Michael Worboys. *Fractured States: Smallpox, Public Health and Vaccination Policy in British India 1800–1947*. London: Orient Blackswan, 2005.

Blackburn, Stuart. *Print, Folklore, and Nationalism in Colonial South India*. Delhi; Bangalore: Permanent Black, 2003.

Breiner, Peter. *Max Weber and Democratic Politics*. Ithaca: Cornell University Press, 1996.

Bowser, Brenda J., and Justin Jennings. *Drink, Power, and Society in the Andes*. Florida: University of Florida Press, 2009.

Bourdieu, Pierre. 'Cultural Reproduction and Social Reproduction'. In *Knowledge, Education, and Cultural Change*, edited by Richard Brown, pp. 71–84. London: Tavistock, 1973.

Brown, Judith M. *Gandhi and Civil Disobedience: The Mahatma in Indian Politics, 1928–1934*. Cambridge: Cambridge University Press, 1977.

———. *Gandhi's Rise to Power: Indian politics, 1915–1922*. Cambridge: Cambridge University Press, 1972.

Burns, Eric. *The Spirits of America: A Social History of Alcohol*. Philadelphia: Temple University Press, 2004.

Burton, Antoinette. *Dwelling in the Archive: Women Writing House, Home, and History in Late Colonial India*. New York: Oxford University Press.

Carrin, Marine, and Harald Tambs-Lyche. 'The Santals, though Unable to Plan for Tomorrow, Should be Converted by Santals'. In *Christians and Missionaries in India: Cross-Cultural Communication since 1500*, edited by Robert Eric Frykenberg, pp. 274–294. New York: Routledge, 2003.

Chakrabarty, Dipesh. 'Conditions for Knowledge of Working-Class Conditions: Employers, Government and the Jute of Calcutta, 1890–1940'. In *Subaltern Studies II: Writings on South Asian History and Society*, edited by Ranajit Guha, pp. 179–235. Delhi: Oxford University Press, 1983.

———. 'The Difference-deferral of a Colonial Modernity: Public Debates on Domesticity in British Bengal'. In *Subaltern Studies VIII: Essays in Honour of Ranajit Guha*, edited by David Arnold and David Hardiman, pp. 50–88. Delhi: Oxford University Press, 1994.

———. 'Trade Unions in a Hierarchical Culture: The Jute Workers of Calcutta, 1920–50'. In *Subaltern Studies III: Writings on South Asian History*, edited by Ranajit Guha, pp. 116–152. Delhi: Oxford University Press, 1984.

———. *Provincializing Europe: Postcolonial Thought and Historical Difference*. Princeton: Princeton University Press, 2000.

———. *Rethinking Working Class History: Bengal 1890–1940*. Princeton: Princeton University Press, 1989.

Chandavarkar, Rajnarayan. *History, Culture, and the Indian City: Essays by Rajnarayan Chandavarkar*. Cambridge: Cambridge University Press, 2009.

———. *Imperial Power and Popular Politics: Class, Resistance and the State in India, c. 1850–1950*. Cambridge: Cambridge University Press, 1998.

———. *The Origins of Industrial Capitalism in India: Business Strategies and the Working Classes in Bombay 1900–1940*. Cambridge: Cambridge University Press, 1994.

Chandra, Bipan, Mridula Mukherjee, Aditya Mukherjee, Sucheta Mahajan and K. N. Panikkar. *India's Struggle for Independence, 1857–1947*. New Delhi: Orient Longman, 1992.

Chatterjee, Partha. *Empire and Nation: Essential Writings 1985–2005*. New York: Columbia University Press, 2010.

———. 'Governmentality in the East'. In *South Asian Governmentalities: Michel Foucault and the Question of Postcolonial Orderings*, ed. Stephen Legg and Deana Heath, pp. 37–57. Cambridge: Cambridge University Press, 2018.

———. *Lineages of Political Society: Studies in Postcolonial Democracy*. New York: Columbia University Press, 2011.

———. *Nationalist Thought and the Colonial World: A Derivative Discourse*. Minnesota: University of Minnesota Press, 1986.

———. *The Nation and Its Fragments: Colonial and Postcolonial Histories*. Princeton: Princeton University Press, 1993.

———. *The Politics of the Governed: Reflections on Popular Politics in Most of the World*. New York: Columbia University Press, 2004.

C. Revri. *The Indian Trade Union Movement 1880–1947*. Delhi: n.p., 1972.

Colvard, Robert Eric. '"Drunkards Beware!": Prohibition and Nationalist Politics in the 1930s'. In *A History of Alcohol and Drugs in Modern South Asia: Intoxicating Affairs*, edited by Harald Fischer-Tiné and Jana Tschurenev, pp. 173–195. London: Routledge, 2013.

Crozier, Michel. *The Bureaucratic Phenomenon*. Chicago: University of Chicago Press, 1964.

Damodaran, K. *Indian Thought: A Critical Survey*. California: California University Press, 1967.

De, Rohit. *A People's Constitution: The Everyday Life of Law in the Indian Republic*. Princeton: Princeton University Press, 2018.

De Souza, F. *The House of Binny*. Madras: Associated Printers, 1970.

Dickey, Sarah. 'Conundrums of Caste, History, and Truth: Hindu Nadar Identities in Urban South India'. In *The Anthropology of Power, Agency, and Morality: The Enduring Legacy of F. G. Bailey*, edited by Victor C. de Munck and Elisa J. Sobo, pp. 132–148. Manchester: Manchester University Press, 2022.

Dirks, Nicholas B. *Castes of Mind: Colonialism and the Making of Modern India*. Princeton: Princeton University Press, 2001.

Dreijmanis, John (ed.). *Max Weber's Complete Writings on Academic and Political Vocations*. London: Algora Publishing, 2008.

E. M. S. Namboodiripad. *Kerala, Society and Politics: An Historical Survey*. New Delhi: National Book Centre, 1984.

Fischer-Tiné, Harald. 'Liquid Boundaries: Race, Class, and Alcohol in Colonial India'. In *A History of Alcohol and Drugs*, edited by Harald Fischer-Tiné and Jana Tschurenev, pp. 90–115. London: Routledge, 2013.

Forbes, Geraldine Hancock. *Women in Colonial India: Essays on Politics, Medicine, and Historiography*. London: Orient Blackswan, 2005.

Foucault, Michel. *Discipline and Punish: The Birth of the Prison*. Translated by Alan Sheridan.New York: Vintage Books, 1979 (1975).

———. *Discipline and Punish: The Birth of the Prison*. Translated by Alan Sheridan. New York: Vintage Books, 1995 (1975).

———. 'Governmentality'. In *The Foucault Effect: Studies in Governmentality*, edited by Graham Burchell, Colin Gordon and Peter Miller, pp. 87–104. Chicago: University of Chicago Press, 1991.

———. *Power/Knowledge: Selected Interviews and Other Writings, 1972–1977*. Edited by Colin Gordon. New York: Pantheon Books, 1980.

———. *The Birth of the Clinic: An Archeology of Medical Perception*. Translated by Alan Sheridan. London; New York: Routledge, 2012.

———. *The Hermeneutics of the Subject: Lectures at the College de France, 1981–1982*. Edited by Frédéric Gros. Translated by Graham Burchell. New York: Palgrave Macmillan, 2001.

———. *The History of Sexuality*. Translated by Robert Hurley. New York: Pantheon Books, 1978.

Fernandes, Leela. *Producing Workers: The Politics of Gender, Class and Culture in the Calcutta Jute Mills*. Philadelphia: University of Pennsylvania Press, 1997.

Freitag, Sandria. *Culture and Power in Benaras: Community, Performance, and Environment, 1800–1980*. Berkeley: University of California Press, 1989.

Fuller, C. J., and Haripriya Narasimhan. *Tamil Brahmans: The Making of a Middle-Class Caste.* Chicago: University of Chicago Press, 2014.

Gandhi, Rajmohan. *Rajaji: A Life.* Delhi: Penguin Books, 1997.

Geetha, V., and S. V. Rajadurai. *Towards a Non-Brahmin Millennium: From Iyothee Thass to Periyar.* New Delhi: Bhatkal & Sen, 1998.

Ghosh, Parimal. *Colonialism, Class, and a History of the Calcutta Jute Hands, 1880–1930.* Hyderabad: Orient Blackswan, 2000.

Gilbert, Marc Jason. 'Empire and Excise: Drugs and Drink Revenue and the Fate of States in South Asia'. In *Drugs and Empire: Essays in Modern Imperialism and Intoxication*, edited by James H. Mills and Patricia Barton, pp. 116–141. London: Palgrave Macmillan, 2007.

G. K. Sharma. *Labour Movement in India: Its Past and Present.* Jullundur: University Publishers, 1963.

Gomathinayagam, Piramanayagam. *The Role of Tamil Poets in Freedom Struggle.* Chennai: Mukil Publishers, 1989.

Gooptu, Nandini. *The Politics of the Urban Poor in Early Twentieth-Century India.* Cambridge: Cambridge University Press, 2001.

Gould, William. *Hindu Nationalism and the Language of Politics in Late Colonial India.* Cambridge: Cambridge University Press, 2004.

G. Somasekhara. *Telugu Press and Indian Freedom Movement.* Raleigh: Lulu Publication, 2018.

Guha, Ranajit (ed.). 'Discipline and Mobilize'. In *Subaltern Studies VII*, edited by Partha Chatterjee and Gyanendra Pandey, pp. 69–120. New Delhi: Oxford University Press, 1992.

———. *Dominance without Hegemony: History and Power in Colonial India.* Cambridge, MA: Harvard University Press, 1997.

———. *Subaltern Studies I: Writings on South Asian History and Society.* Delhi: Oxford University Press, 1988.

———. 'The Prose of Counter-Insurgency'. In *Culture/Power/History: A Reader in Contemporary Social Theory*, edited by Nicholas B. Dirks, Geoffrey H. Eley and Sherry B. Ortner. Princeton: Princeton University Press, 1994.

Hardgrave, Robert L. *The Nadars of Tamilnad: The Political Culture of a Community in Change.* Berkeley; Los Angeles: California University Press, 1969.

Harder, Hans and Nishat Zaidi. eds., *Language Ideologies and the Vernacular in Colonial and Postcolonial South Asia.* London: Routledge, 2023.

Hardiman, David. 'From Custom to Crime: The Politics of Drinking in South Gujarat'. In *Subaltern Studies IV*, edited by Ranajit Guha, pp. 165–228. Delhi: Oxford: Oxford University Press, 1985.

———. *The Coming of the Devi: Adivasi Assertion in Western India*. Delhi: Oxford University Press, 1987.

Harrison, Mark. *Public Health in British India: Anglo-Indian Preventive Medicine 1859–1914*. Cambridge: Cambridge University Press, 1994.

Haq, M. Emdad-ul. *Drugs in South Asia: From the Opium Trade to the Present Day*. London: Palgrave Macmillan, 2000.

Haynes, Douglas E. *Rhetoric and Ritual in Colonial India: The Shaping of a Public Culture in Surat City, 1852–1928*. Berkeley: University of California Press, 1991.

———. *The Emergence of Brand-Name Capitalism in Late Colonial India: Advertising and the Making of Modern Conjugality*. New York: Bloomsbury, 2022.

Heath, Deana. *Purifying Empire: Obscenity and the Politics of Moral Regulation in Britain, India and Australia*. Cambridge: Cambridge University Press, 2010.

Heath, Deana and Stephen Legg (eds.). *South Asian Governmentalities: Michel Foucault and the Question of Postcolonial Orderings*. Cambridge: Cambridge University Press, 2018.

Heath, Dwight B. *The International Handbook of Alcohol and Culture*. London: Bloomsbury, 1995.

Heimsath, Charles H. *Indian Nationalism and Hindu Social Reform*. Princeton: Princeton University Press, 1964.

Heitmeyer, Carolyn and Edward Simpson. 'The Culture of Prohibition in Gujarat, India'. In *A History of Alcohol and Drugs in Modern South Asia: Intoxicating Affairs*, edited by Harald Fischer-Tine and Jana Tschurenev, pp. 203–218. Abingdon: Routledge, 2014.

Hockings, Paul. *Ancient Hindu Refugees: Badaga Social History, 1550–1975* (*Studies in Anthropology*, vol. 6). The Hague: Mouton Publishers, 1980.

Hodges, Sarah. *Contraception, Colonialism and Commerce: Birth Control in South India, 1920–1940*. London: Taylor & Francis, 2017.

Hinchy, Jessica. *Governing Gender and Sexuality in Colonial India: The Hijra, C.1850–1900*. Cambridge: Cambridge University Press, 2019.

Irschick, Eugene. *Dialogue and History: Constructing South India, 1795–1895*. Berkeley: University of California Press, 1994.

Jackson, Kyle. *The Mizo Discovery of the British Raj: Empire and Religion in Northeast India, 1890–1920*. Cambridge: Cambridge University Press, 2023.

Jeffers, Honorée Fanonne and David E. Kyvig. *Repealing National Prohibition*. Chicago: Chicago University Press, 1979.

Jefferson, Ann, and Paul Lokken. *Daily Life in Colonial Latin America*. New York: Bloomsbury, 2011.

Jha, S. C. *The Indian Trade Union Movement.* Calcutta: 1970.

Jones, Kenneth W. *The New Cambridge History of India: Socio-Religious Reform Movements in British India.* Cambridge: Cambridge University Press, 2006.

Joseph, George Gheverghese. *George Joseph, the Life and Times of a Kerala Christian Nationalist.* New Delhi: Orient Longman, 2003.

Joshi, Chitra. *Lost Worlds: Labour and its Forgotten Histories.* New Delhi: Anthem Press, 2003.

Joshi, Sanjay. *Fractured Modernity: Making of a Middle Class in Colonial North India.* New Delhi: Oxford University Press, 2001.

K. Sreejith. *The Middle Class in Colonial Malabar: A Social History.* London: Routledge, 2021.

Kamei, Richard. 'Liquor of Rongmei Naga: Brewing Jouju in the Village against Colonial and Postcolonial State'. In *Time and Alcohol: It's Five O'Clock Somewhere!* edited by Peter J. Howland, pp. 167–181. London: Routledge, 2025.

Karnik, V. B. *Indian Trade Unions: A Survey.* Bombay, 1960.

Kaviraj, Sudipta. *The Imaginary Institution of India: Politics and Ideas.* New York: Columbia University Press, 2010.

Kidambi, Prashant. *The Making of an Indian Metropolis: Colonial Governance and Public Culture in Bombay, 1890–1920.* London: Routledge, 2016.

King, Anthony D. *Colonial Urban Development: Culture, Social Power and Environment.* London: Routledge, 1976.

King, Anthony D. *Colonial Urban Development: Culture, Social Power and Environment.* London: Taylor & Francis, 2012.

Kling, David H. *A History of Christian Conversion.* Oxford: Oxford University Press, 2020.

Kour, Kawal Deep. *A History of Intoxication: Opium in Assam, 1800–1959.* London: Taylor & Francis, 2019.

Kuracina, William F. *The State and Governance in India: The Congress Ideal.* London: Routledge, 2010.

Lakoff, George. *Moral Politics.* Chicago: Chicago University Press, 1996.

Larsson, Marie Louise. *'When Women Unite!' The Making of the Anti-Liquor Movement in Andhra Pradesh, India.* Stockholm: Stockholm University Press, 2006.

Latour, Bruno. *Aramis or the Love of Technology.* Translated by Catherine Porter. Cambridge, MA: Harvard University Press, 1996.

Legg, Stephen. 'Gendered Politics and Nationalised Homes: Women and the Anti-Colonial Struggle in Delhi, 1930–47'. In *Culture and Society:*

Critical Essays in Human Geography, edited by Nuala C. Johnson. London: Routledge, 2008.

Linderoth, Matthew R. *Prohibition on the North Jersey Shore: Gangsters on Vacation*. New York: Arcadia Publishing, 2010.

Ludden, David. *Reading Subaltern Studies: Critical History, Contested Meaning and the Globalisation of South Asia*. London: Anthem Press, 2002.

Mallampalli, Chandra. *Christians and Public Life in Colonial South India, 1863–1937: Contending with Marginality*. London: Taylor & Francis, 2007.

Mani, Lata. *Contentious Traditions: The Debate on Sati in Colonial India*. California: California University Press, 1998.

Manor, James. *Power, Poverty and Poison: Disaster and Response in an Indian City*. New Delhi: Sage Publications, 1993.

McGirr, Lisa. *The War on Alcohol: Prohibition and the Rise of the American State*. New York: Norton & Company, 2015.

Menon, Bindu. 'Coming into Cinema: Critical Cosmopolitanisms of Malayalam Cinema (1930–1955)'. In *A Companion to Indian Cinema*, edited by Neepa Majumdar and Ranjani Majumdar. London: Wiley Blackwell, 2022.

Menon, Dilip. *Caste, Nationalism and Communism in South India: Malabar, 1900–1948*. Cambridge: Cambridge University Press, 1994.

———. *Changing Theory: Concepts from the Global South*. London: Routledge, 2022.

Menon, P. K. K. *The History of Freedom Movement in Kerala: 1885-1938*. Government of Kerala, 1970.

Mills, James H. *Cannabis Britannica: Empire, Trade, and Prohibition, 1800–1928*. Oxford: Oxford University Press, 2003.

———. *Cannabis Nation: Control and Consumption in Britain, 1928–2008*. Oxford: Oxford University Press, 2013.

Murdock, Catherine Gilbert. *Domesticating Drink: Women, Men and Alcohol in America, 1870–1940*. Baltimore; London: Johns Hopkins University Press, 2001.

Muthiah, S. *The Spirit of Chepauk: The MCC Story, a 150 Year Sporting Tradition*. Chennai: EastWest Books, 1998.

Nair, Janaki. *Miners and Millhands: Work, Culture and Politics in Princely Mysore*. New Delhi: Sage Publications, 1998.

Natarajan, Nalini. *Atlantic Gandhi: The Mahatma Overseas*. New Delhi: Sage Publications, 2013.

Nierstrasz, Chris. *In the Shadow of the Company: The Dutch East India Company and Its Servants in the Period of Its Decline (1740–1796) (TANAP Monographs on the History of Asian- European Interaction*). Edited by Leonard Blussé. Leiden: Brill, 2012.

Nirmal, Chiranjivi J. *Madras Perspectives: Explorations in Social and Cultural History*. Madras: Institute of Indian and International Studies, 1992.

Oddie, Geoffrey A. *Social Protest in India: British Protestant Missionaries and Social Reforms, 1850–1900*. Delhi: Manohar, 1979.

Orr, Charles Andrew. *A Study of Indian Boycotts*. London: Ian Allan, 1974.

O'Hara, Matthew D., and Andrew B. Fischer. *Imperial Subjects: Race and Identity in Colonial Latin America*. Durham: Duke University Press, 2009.

Panikkar, K. N. *Colonialism, Culture, and Resistance*. Oxford: Oxford University Press, 2007.

Parel, Anthony J. *Pax Gandhiana: The Political Philosophy of Mahatma Gandhi*. Oxford: University of Oxford Press, 2018.

Pati, Biswamoy and Mark Harrison. *The Social History of Health and Medicine in Colonial India*. London: Routledge, 2009.

Peck, Garrett. *The Prohibition Hangover: Alcohol in America from Demon Rum to Cult Cabernet*. New Jersey; London, 2009.

Pierce, Gretchen, and Áurea Toxqui. *Alcohol in Latin America: A Social and Cultural History*. Arizona: University of Arizona Press, 2014.

Pillai, Mayuram Vedanayagam. *The Life and Time of Pratapa Mudaliar*. Translated by Meenakshi Tyagarajan. New Delhi: Katha, 2005.

Prakash, Gyan. 'Science between the Lines'. In *Subaltern Studies IX*, edited by Shahid Amin and Dipesh Chakrabarty, pp. 59–82. Delhi: Oxford University Press, 1996.

Ramakrishnan, S. *Bharati: Patriot, Poet, Prophet*. Madras: New Century Printers, 1982.

Ramanathan, K.V., ed. *The Satyamurti Letters: The Indian Freedom Struggle Through the Eyes of a Parliamentarian*, vol 2. New Delhi: Dorling Kingsley, 2008.

Ricci, Ronit. *Islam Translated: Literature, Conversion, and the Arabic Cosmopolis of South and Southeast Asia*. Chicago: Chicago University Press, 2011.

Rotskoff, Lori. *Love on the Rocks: Men, Women, and Alcohol in Post-World War II America*. Chapel Hill: University of North Carolina Press, 2002.

Roy, Tirthankar. *Economic History of India, 1857–1947*. Oxford: Oxford University Press, 2011.

———. *How British Rule Changed India's Economy: The Paradox of the Raj*. London: Palgrave, 2019.

Roy, Tirthankar, and Anand V. Swamy. *Law and the Economy in Colonial India*. Chicago: University of Chicago Press, 2016.

Sarkar, Sumit. 'The Conditions and Nature of Subaltern Militancy: Bengal from Swadeshi to Non-Cooperation, 1905–1922'. In *Subaltern Studies VI: Writings on South Asian History and Society*, edited by Ranajit Guha, pp. 271–320. Delhi: Oxford University Press, 1989.

Sarkar, Aditya. *Trouble at the Mill: Factory Law and the Emergence of the Labour Question in Late Nineteenth-Century Bombay.* Oxford: Oxford University Press, 2018.

Sasges, Gerard. *Imperial Intoxication: Alcohol and the Making of Colonial Indochina.* Honolulu: University of Hawaii Press, 2017.

Saxena, K. B. *Swaraj and the Reluctant State.* Delhi: Aarkar Books, 2020.

Schrad, Mark Lawrence. *Smashing the Liquor Machine: A Global History of Prohibition.* Oxford: Oxford University Press, 2021.

Schröder, Ulrike. 'No Religion, but Ritual? Robert Caldwell and the Tinnevelly Shanars'. In *Ritual, Caste, and Religion in Colonial South India*, edited by Michael Bergunder, Heiko Frese and Ulrike Schröder. Halle: Verlag der Franckeschen Stiftungen, 2010.

Schwarz, Henry. *Constructing the Criminal Tribe in Colonial India: Acting Like a Thief.* West Sussex: Wiley Blackwell, 2010.

Seal, Anil. 'Imperialism and Nationalism in India'. In *Locality, Province and Nation: Essays on Indian Politics, 1870 to 1940*, edited by John Gallagher, Gordon Johnson and Anil Seal. Cambridge: Cambridge University Press, 1973.

Sen, Samita, *Women and Labour in Late Colonial India: The Bengal Jute Industry.* Cambridge: Cambridge University Press, 1999.

Sen, Sukomal. *Working Class of India: History of Emergence and Movement, 1830–1970.* Calcutta: K.P. Bagchi & Co., 1977.

Sethi, Devika. *War over Words: Censorship in India, 1930–1960.* Cambridge: Cambridge University Press, 2019.

Shaikh, Juned. *Outcaste Bombay: City Making and the Politics of the Poor.* Washington, DC: University of Washington Press, 2021.

Sharma, Kalpana. *Rediscovering Dharavi: Stories from Asia's Largest Slum.* New Delhi: Penguin Books, 2000.

Shore, Cris, and Susan Wright, eds. *Anthropology of Policy, Perspectives on Governance and Power.* London: Routledge, 1997.

Shore, C., S. Wright and Davide Pero. *Policy Worlds: Anthropology and the Analysis of Contemporary Power.* New York; Oxford: Bergen Books, 2011.

Simeon, Dilip. *The Politics of Labour Under Late Colonialism: Workers, Trade Unions and the State in Chota Nagpur, 1928–1939.* Delhi: Manohar, 1995.

Sivunnaidu, Penta. *Proscribed Telugu Literature and National Movement in Andhra, 1920–1947.* Chennai: Reliance Publishing, 2002.

S. Jeyaseela. *Caste, Catholic Christianity and the Language of Conversion.* Delhi: Kalpaz Publications, 2008.

Skelly, Julia. *Addiction and British Visual Culture, 1751–1919: Wasted Looks.* London: Routledge, 2017.

Spivak, Gayatri Chakravorty. 'Can the Subaltern Speak?' In *Marxism and the Interpretation of Culture,* edited by Cary Nelson and Lawrence Grossberg. Illinois: University of Illinois Press, 1988.

Sreenivas, Lakshmi. *House Full: Indian Cinema and the Active Audience.* Chicago: University of Chicago Press, 2016.

Srinivas, M. N. *Caste in Modern India.* Bombay: Asia Publishing House, 1970.

———. *Religion and Society among the Coorgs of South India.* Oxford: Clarendon Press, 1952.

———. *Social Change in Modern India.* Berkeley: University of California Press, 1966.

Srinivas, S. V. *Politics as Performance: A Social History of the Telugu Cinema.* London: Permanent Black, 2013.

Srivastava, Priyanka. *The Well-Being of the Labor Force in Colonial Bombay: Discourses and Practices.* London: Palgrave Macmillan, 2017.

Sturman, Rachel. *The Government of Social Life in Colonial India: Liberalism, Religious Law, and Women's Rights.* Cambridge: Cambridge University Press, 2012.

Sundara Raj, M. *Prostitution in Madras: A Study in Historical Perspective.* Madras: Konark Publishers, 1993.

The Collected Works of Mahatma Gandhi, vol. 1. Delhi: Government of India, 1958.

Thong, Tezenlo. *Colonization, Proselytization, and Identity: The Nagas and Westernization in Northeast India.* London: Springer, 2016.

———. *Progress and Its Impact on the Nagas: A Clash of Worldviews.* London; New York: Ashgate Publishing, 2014.

Thorburn, Doug. *Drunks, Drugs and Debits: How to Recognise Addicts and Avoid Financial Abuse.* California: Galt Publishing, 2000.

Trevelyan, George Macaulay. *English Social History: A Survey of Six Centuries, Chaucer to Queen Victoria.* London: Longman, 1944.

Tyrrell, Ian. *Woman's World/Woman's Empire: The Woman's Christian Temperance Union in International Perspective, 1880–1930.* Chapel Hill; London: University of North Carolina Press, 1991.

Varma, Nitin. *Coolies of Capitalism: Assam Tea and the Making of Coolie Labour.* Berlin; Boston: De Gruyter, 2016.

Velayutham, Selvaraj. *Tamil Cinema: The Cultural Politics of India's Other Film Industry.* London: Routledge, 2008.

Valverde, Mariana. *Diseases of the Will: Alcohol and the Dilemmas of Freedom.* Cambridge: Cambridge University Press, 1998.

Viswanath, Rupa. *The Pariah Problem: Caste, Religion, and the Social in Modern India.* New York: Columbia University Press, 2014.

V. Ramakrishna. *Social Reform in Andhra, 1848–1919.* Hyderabad: Vikas, 1983.

Wald, Erica. *Vice in the Barracks: Medicine, the Military and the Making of Colonial India, 1780–1868.* Basingstoke: Palgrave Macmillan, 2014.

Washbrook, David. 'Economic Development and Social Stratification in Rural Madras: The "Dry Region" 1878–1929'. In *The Imperial Impact: Studies in the Economic History of Africa and India,* edited by Dewey Clive and A.G. Hopkins. London: The Athlone Press, 1978.

———. *The Emergence of Provincial Politics, The Madras Presidency 1870–1920.* Cambridge: University Press, 1976.

Waterson, Jan. *Women and Alcohol in Social Context: Mother's Ruin Revisited.* New York: Palgrave, 2000.

Yang, Anand A. *Crime and Criminality in British India.* Association of Asian Studies, 1985.

———. *Bazaar India: Markets, Society, and the Colonial State in Bihar.* Berkeley; Los Angeles: California University Press, 1999.

———. *The Limited Raj: Agrarian Relations in Colonial India, Saran District, 1793–1920.* California: University of California Press, 2023.

Yenadi Raju, P. *Rayalaseema During Colonial Times: A Study in Indian Nationalism.* New Delhi: Northern Book Centre, 2003.

Young, Richard Fox (ed.). *India and the Indianness of Christianity: Essays on Understanding Historical, Theological, and Bibliographical – in Honor of Robert Eric Frykenberg.* Michigan: W.M Eerdman's Publishing Co., 2009.

Books (Tamil)

Palanivelu, Kesava. *Tamizhartam Kudipazhakkam* (The Drink Habits of the Tamils). Puthucherry: Ilakkiya Publishers, 1990.

Saati Vetrumaiyum Poli Saivarum (Caste Difference and Fake Saivites). Chennai: Poompukar Publishers, 1992.

Vellaiyan, Muthiah. *Kudiyinri Amayaa Ulagu* (A World Without Liquor). Chennai: Pulam, 2009.

Journal Articles

Alagirisamy, Darinee. 'Toddy, Race and Urban Space in Colonial Singapore, 1900–1959'. *Modern Asian Studies* 53, no. 5 (September 2019), pp. 1675–1699.

———. 'The Problem with Neera: The (Un)Making of a National Drink in Late Colonial India', *The Indian Economic and Social History Review* 56, no. 1 (2019), pp. 77–97.

Ashworth, William J. 'Between the Trader and the Public: British Alcohol Standards and the Proof of Good Governance'. *Technology and Culture* 42, no. 1 (2001), pp. 27–50.

Baviskar A., and Nandini Sundar. 'Democracy versus Economic Transformation'. *Economic and Political Weekly* 43, no. 46 (2008), pp. 87–89.

Bayly, Christopher Allan. 'Returning the British to South Asian History: The Limits of Colonial Hegemony'. *South Asia: Journal of South Asian Studies* 17, no. 2 (1994), pp. 1–25.

Bhattacharya, Nandini. 'The Problem of Alcohol in Colonial India (c. 1907–1942)'. *Studies in History* 33, no. 2 (2017), pp. 187–212.

Bhattacharya, Sabyasachi. 'Laissez Faire in India'. *Indian Economic and Social History Review* 2, no. 1 (1965), pp. 1–22.

———. 'Introduction'. *International Review of Social History* 51 (supp. 14: Coolies, Capital, and Colonialism: Studies in Indian Labour History) (2006), pp. 7–19.

Chakrabarty, Dipesh. 'Of Garbage, Modernity and the Citizen's Gaze'. *Economic and Political Weekly* 27 (1992), pp. 541–547.

Carroll, Lucy. 'Origins of the Kayastha Temperance Movement'. *Indian Economic and Social History Review* 11, no. 4 (1974), pp. 432–447.

———. 'The Temperance Movement in India: Politics and Social Reform'. *Modern Asian Studies* 10, no. 3 (July 1976), pp. 417–447.

Chakraborty, Ranjita. 'Managing Public Morality: The Politics of Public Policy in India'. *The Indian Journal of Political Science* 70, no. 4 (2009), pp. 1099–1108.

Chatterjee, Partha. 'Colonialism, Nationalism, and Colonialized Women: The Contest in India'. *American Ethnologist* 16, no. 4 (1989), pp. 622–633.

———. 'Democracy and Economic Transformation in India'. *Economic and Political Weekly* 43, no. 16 (2008), pp. 53–62.

Chaudhuri, K., N. Jha, M. Nilayamgode and Revathy Suryanarayana. 'Alcohol Ban and Crime: The ABCs of the Bihar Prohibition'. *Economic Development and Cultural Change* 72, no. 4 (2024), DOI: 10.1086/725452.

Das S. K., Balakrishnan V., D.M. Vasudevan. 'Alcohol: Its Health and Social Impact in India'. *National Medical Journal of India* 19, no. 2 (2006), pp. 94–99.

Devji, Faisal. 'Morality in the Shadow of Politics'. *Modern Intellectual History* 7, no. 2 (2010), pp. 373–390.

Dickey, Sarah. 'Permeable Homes: Domestic Service, Household Space, and the Vulnerability of Class Boundaries in Urban India'. *American Ethnologist* 27, no. 2 (May 2000), pp. 462–489.

Fahey, David M., and Padma Manian. 'Poverty and Purification: The Politics of Gandhi's Campaign for Prohibition'. *The Historian* 67, no. 3 (2005), pp. 489–506.

Fischer-Tiné, Harald. 'The Drinking Habits of Our Countrymen: European Alcohol Consumption and Colonial Power in British India'. *Journal of Imperial and Commonwealth History* 40, no. 3 (2012), pp. 383–409.

Frost, Mark. '"Wider Opportunities": Religious Revival, Nationalist Awakening and the Global Dimension in Colombo, 1870–1920'. *Modern Asian Studies* 36, no. 4 (2002), pp. 937–967.

Gorringe, Hugo. 'Banal Violence? The Everyday Underpinnings of Collective Violence'. *Identities* 13, no. 2 (2004), 237–260.

———. 'Which Is Violence? Reflections on Collective Violence and Dalit Movements in South India'. *Social Movement Studies* 5, no. 2 (2006), pp. 117–136.

Guha, Sumit. 'The Politics of Enumeration and Identification in India, c. 1600–1900'. *Comparative Studies in Society and History* 45, no. 1 (2003), pp. 148–167.

Gururaj, G., M. S. Gautham and B. A. Arvind. 'Alcohol Consumption in India: A Rising Burden and a Fractured Response'. *Drug Alcohol Review* 40, no. 3 (March 2021), pp. 368–384. DOI: 10.1111/dar.13179. Epub 2020 Sep 30. PMID: 33000887.

Irschick, Eugene. 'Gandhian Non-Violent Protest: Rituals of Avoidance or Rituals of Confrontation?' *Economic and Political Weekly* 21 (1986), pp. 1276–1285.

Joseph, A. 'Women against Arrack: Organizing for Change – India 1'. *People Planet* 4, no. 3 (1995): 10–1. PMID: 12290000.

Kaicker, Nidhi. 'Alcohol Consumption During the Covid-19 Pandemic in India'. *Journal of Asian and African Studies* 0, no. 0 (2023).

Kaviraj, Sudipta. 'Filth and the Public Sphere: Concepts and Practice about Space in Calcutta'. *Public Culture* 10, no. 1 (1997), pp. 83–85.

———. 'On the Enchantment of the State: Indian Thought on the Role of the State in the Narrative of Modernity'. *European Journal of Sociology* 46, no. 2 (2005), pp. 263–296.

Lewandowski, Susan J. 'Urban Growth and Municipal Development in the Colonial City of Madras, 1860–1900'. *Journal of Asian Studies* 34, no. 2 (1975), pp. 341–360.

Lhoungu, V., A. Aier and Moanungsang. 'The Paradox of Nagaland Total Liquor Prohibition (NLTP) Act 1989 with Special Reference to Black Economy in Dimapur'. *International Journal of Research in Social Sciences* 12, no. 8 (2022), pp. 11–29.

Loomba, Ania. 'The Everyday Violence of Caste'. *College Literature* 43, no. 1 (The Banalization of War) (Winter 2016), pp. 220–225.

Mandelbaum, David G. 'Alcohol and Culture'. *Current Anthropology* 6. no. 3 (1965), pp. 281–288, 289–293.

Mahal, A. 'What Works in Alcohol Policy? Evidence from Rural India'. *Economic and Political Weekly* 35 (2000), pp. 3959–3968.

Menon, Dilip. 'From Pleasure to Taboo: Drinking and Society in Kerala'. *India International Centre Quarterly* 22, nos. 2–3 (1995), pp. 143–156.

Menon, Nikhil. 'Battling the Bottle, Experiments in Regulating Drink in Late Colonial Madras'. *Indian Economic and Social History Review* 52, no. 1 (2015), pp. 29–51.

Menon, Nivedita. 'Thinking About the Postnation'. *Economic and Political Weekly* (7–13 March 2009), pp. 70–77.

Murugiah, Karthik. 'Enforcement of Prohibition in Salem, 1937'. *Indian Streams Research Journal* 2 (2012), pp. 1–4.

Neild, Susan M. 'Colonial Urbanism: The Development of Madras City in the Eighteenth and Nineteenth Centuries'. *Modern Asian Studies* (1979), pp. 217–246.

O'Neill, John. 'The Disciplinary Society: From Weber to Foucault'. *British Journal of Sociology* 37, no. 1 (1986), pp. 42–60.

Parthasarathi, Prasannan. 'Indian Labour History'. *International Labor and Working-Class History* 82, Fortieth Anniversary Issue (Fall 2012), pp. 127–135.

Pickett, Brent L. 'Foucault and the Politics of Resistance'. *Polity* 28, no. 4 (1996). pp. 445–466.

Quintero, Gilberto. 'Making the Indian: Colonial Knowledge, Alcohol and Native Americans'. *American Indian Culture and Research Journal* 25, no. 4 (2001), pp. 57–71.

Robert, Bruce. 'Economic Change and Agrarian Organization in "Dry" South India 1890–1940: A Reinterpretation'. *Modern Asian Studies* 17, no. 1 (1983), pp. 59–78.

Rose, Nikolas, and Peter Miller. 'Political Power beyond the State: Problematics of Government'. *British Journal of Sociology* 43, no. 2 (1992), pp. 173–205.

Scott, David. 'Colonial Governmentality'. *Social Text* 43 (1995), pp. 191–220.

Singh, Radhika. 'Colonial Law and Infrastructural Power: Reconstructing Community, Locating the Female Subject'. *Studies in History* 19, no. 1 (2003), pp. 87–126.

———. 'Punished by Surveillance: Policing "Dangerousness" in Colonial India, 1872–1918'. *Modern Asian Studies* 49, no. 2(2014), pp. 241–269.

Singh, S., P. Sharma and Y. P. S. Balhara. 'The Impact of Nationwide Alcohol Ban during the COVID-19 Lockdown on Alcohol Use-Related Internet Searches and Behaviour in India: An Infodemiology Study'. *Drug and Alcohol Review* 40, no. 2 (2021), pp. 196–200.

Sinha, Mrinalini. 'Britishness, Clubbability, and the Colonial Public Sphere: The Genealogy of an Imperial Institution in Colonial India', *Journal of British Studies* 40, no. 4 (October 2001), pp. 489–521.

Srinivasan, S. 'Prohibition Policy on Liquor in Madras Presidency from 1937 to 1939'. *Golden Research Thoughts* 4 (2015), pp. 1–6.

——— 'Colonial Law and Infrastructural Power: Reconstructing Community, Locating the Female Subject'. *Studies in History* 19, no. 1 (2003), pp. 87–126.

Thapar, Suruchi. 'Women as Activists; Women as Symbols: A Study of the Indian Nationalist Movement'. *Feminist Review* 44 (1993), pp. 81–96.

Washbrook, David. 'Country Politics: Madras 1880 to 1930'. *Modern Asian Studies* 7, no. 3 (1973), pp. 475–531.

West, Michael O. 'Liquor and Libido: "Joint Drinking" and the Politics of Sexual Control in Colonial Zimbabwe, 1920s–1950s'. *Journal of Social History* 30 (1997), pp. 645–667.

Unpublished Theses and Dissertations

Anandhi, S., 'Middle Class Women in Colonial Tamil Nadu, 1920–1947: Gender Relations and the Problem of Consciousness'. Unpublished PhD thesis, Jawaharlal Nehru University, New Delhi, 1992.

Anbumozhi, M. 'Police Administration and Prohibition in Madras City (1937–1967): A Study'. Unpublished MPhil thesis, Madurai Kamaraj University, 1996.

Colvard, Robert Eric. 'A World Without Drink: Temperance in Modern India, 1880-1940'. Unpublished PhD thesis, University of Iowa, 2013.

Kumar, K. Ashok. 'Prohibition of Drinking in Salem District (1937–1943)' Unpublished MPhil thesis, University of Madras, 1992.

Lakshmi, V., 'Role of Women in Freedom Struggle with Special Reference to Tamil Nadu (1885–1947)'. Unpublished Master's thesis, Queen Mary's College, 2003.

Pasupathan, C. G., 'Madras City: Study of Evolution'. Unpublished master's thesis, University of Madras, 1967.

Perumal, S. Arunachala. 'Prohibition Policy Under C. Rajagopalachari Ministries: A Study'. Unpublished MPhil thesis, Madurai Kamaraj University, 1988.

Rajendran, K. S. 'Drama and Society: A Study of Tamil Dramatic Performances'. Unpublished research thesis, Tamil Nadu Council of Historical Research, 1989.

Sarasu, P., *Tamil Samuttayattin Villipunarciyil Pitti Tiyagarayarin Pangu* (Pitty Thiayagaraya's Role in Tamil Society's Awakening). Unpublished PhD thesis, PSG College, 1988.

Wilson, A., 'History of Missionary Work in Dindigul A.D. 1838–1938'. Unpublished master's thesis, Madurai Kamaraj University, 1991.

Magazines (English and Tamil)

Kalki: Fiftieth Anniversary Souvenir Magazine. Chennai: Kalki, 1997.

Naidu, W. V. S. Krishnaswamy. *Cosmopolitan Club Centenary Celebration Souvenir*. Madras: n.p., 1973.

Rajaji 93 Souvenir. Madras: T. Sadasivam for Rajaji Ninety-Three Souvenir Committee, 1971.

Online Sources

Jha, Satish. 'Gujarat Model: Unequal "Licence-Permit Raj" for Liquor'. *Deccan Herald*, 1 September 2021. https://www.deccanherald.com/opinion/gujarat-model-unequal-licence-permit-raj-for-liquor-1026064.html. Accessed on 3 January 2024.

'Liquor Ban Exemption Comes into Effect in Gujarat's GIFT City'. *Indian Express*, 31 December 2023. https://indianexpress.com/article/cities/ahmedabad/liqour-ban-exemption-effect-gujarat-gift-city-908#:. Accessed on 3 January 2024.

Menon, Nivedita. 'Foucault and Indian Scholarship: History, Governmentality, Modernity'. http://kafila.org/2009/06/07/and-arent-obc-women-women-loudthinking-on-the-womens-reservation-bill. Accessed on 21 May 2024.

Muthiah, S. 'Another End to Prohibition', *The Hindu*. http://www.thehindu.com/thehindu/mp/2002/04/08/stories/2002040800140300.htmI. Accessed on 12 February 2014.

Pradhan, Aditi, Ameya Bokil, Avaneendra Khare, Kanishka Singh, Nikita Sonavane,Pallavi Diwakrar, Shreya Gajbhiye, Srujana Bej and Yashaswi B. Kabde, 'Drunk on Power: Excise Policing in Madhya Pradesh'. In *Criminal Justice and Police Accountability Project Report*. https://cpaproject.in/wp-content/uploads/2021/08/Drunk-on-Power-A-study-of-Excise-Policing-in-Madhya-Pradesh-CPA-Project-14-Aug-2021-1.pdf. Accessed on 11 May 2025.

Thapar, Karan. 'Adivasis, Liquor and the Politics of Law Enforcement in Conflict Zone of Chattisgarh', pts 1–2. https://lawandotherthings.com/adivasis-liquor-and-the-politics-of-law-enforcement-in-conflict-zone-of-chhattisgarh-part-i. Accessed on 11 May 2025.

'Toddy Politics Heats Up in Tamil Nadu'. *New Indian Express*, 16 May 2012. https://www.newindianexpress.com/states/tamil-nadu/2011/Jan/17/toddy-politics-heats-up-in-tamil-nadu-219791.html. Accessed on 24 December 2024.

Index

For EU product safety concerns, contact us at Calle de José Abascal, 56–1°,
28003 Madrid, Spain or eugpsr@cambridge.org.